BULLIES,
TARGETS &
WITNESSES:

HELPING CHILDREN BREAK THE PAIN CHAIN

BULLIES, TARGETS & WITNESSES:

HELPING CHILDREN BREAK THE PAIN CHAIN

SuEllen Fried, ADTR, and Paula Fried, Ph.D.

M. Evans and Company, Inc.
New York

M. Evans and Company, Inc.
216 East 49th Street
New York, New York 10017

Library of Congress Cataloging-in-Publication Data

Fried, SuEllen.
    Bullies, targets & witnesses : helping children break the pain chain / by SuEllen Fried and Paula Fried
        p.   cm.
    Includes bibliographical references.
    ISBN 1-59077-007-2
    1. Bullying in schools—United States. 2. School violence—United States—Prevention. I. Title: Bullies, targets and witnesses. II. Fried, Paula. III. Title.
LB3013.32.F75 2003
371.5'8—dc21   2002192806

Book design and typesetting by Evan H. Johnston

Printed in the United States of America

9 8 7 6 5 4 3 2 1

CONTENTS

PREFACE

Bullies & Victims, our first book about bullying, was inspired by Kimberly Weisel, an enchanting ten-year-old girl that Paula met when she worked on the pediatric oncology unit of the Kansas University Medical Center. Kim had been diagnosed with leukemia at age four. Her cancer was in remission for many years but recurred when she was nine. She began receiving chemotherapy and radiation treatments, but by the summer of her tenth year, her condition had seriously deteriorated.

Kim's doctor recommended that Kim enter the hospital for three months of intensive chemotherapy. By the end of August, it was apparent that Kim's death was inevitable. During a poignant conversation, before Paula returned to college and Kim entered the fifth grade, Paula learned that Kim was eager to return to school to reconnect with her friends but was concerned about recess. At recess, some students thought it was fun to grab her wig and then taunt her because she was bald. That conversation burned a hole in our hearts.

Then we learned about a number of suicides and several school shootings related to bullying across the country. Though relatively few in number, they resonated strongly with our never-healed memory of Kim and the cruelty she experienced at the hands of her classmates. In the early 1990s we began collecting data and anecdotes and, in the absence of a comprehensive book on the subject of bullying, we decided to publish *Bullies & Victims*, dedicated to Kim's memory.

In 1995, as we began our literary collaboration, we agonized over whether to include reports of student shootings in our book. We were concerned that readers might think we were exaggerating the problem and discount our concern about daily abusive interactions such as those that Kim experienced. After much debate, we decided to address the issue of students killing each other, because it was true, never anticipating that a Columbine could occur.

Looking back and looking forward, we see other issues of portent that are not clear but are quite disturbing. Leonard Pitt, a nationally syndicated columnist for the *Miami Herald*, opined that Americans believe that "black shooting, it must be the culture— white shooting, mentally ill, as if the culture offers no dysfunction, no possibility of analysis that propels individual tragedies to larger questions." Pitt's comments lift the lid on the suburban, white culture, exposing all of its toxic ingredients.

In fact, the National Academies' National Research Council reports that, since 1987, the United States has experienced two epidemics of youth violence.[1] The first occurred in the nation's central cities. The second and more recent wave occurred in suburban and rural schools. The researchers wondered if suburban school rampages were caused by the same things that caused the earlier epidemic of urban violence, or if they were a separate phenomenon. They commissioned six case studies: four in suburban and rural schools in Georgia, Pennsylvania, Kentucky, and Arkansas, and two in urban schools in New York City and Chicago. These cases revealed an important difference in the social context and motivations of the offenders. In the suburban and rural incidents, the offenders felt attacked by abstract conditions that made it difficult for them to achieve the status they wanted, but they were under no real physical threat from the students that they targeted. By contrast, in the inner-city cases, the shooters were involved in specific interpersonal disputes in which the shooters believed their own lives were in danger.

There are other questions to consider. Are children killing themselves and killing each other because they believe it is the only way to make themselves heard? Are children demonstrating the natural outcome of the vengeance and violence that permeates our entertainment, sports, corporate, political, educational and religious systems? Is peer abuse an imitation of adult vindictiveness or a cry for adult attention—or both?

We see bullying as extremely relevant to the larger issues of the day. Parents have asked if it's wrong to raise their children to be nonviolent, to discourage them from playing with weaponlike toys. They wonder if they might be doing their sons a disservice when they might be drafted in a war effort someday. Children are mentioning "fight back" as a solution to bullying with greater frequency. And what about the children who suffer in silence, as in situations of abuse at home, where children are exposed to a daily assault on their sensibilities—unseen and unheard—until tragedy occurs. We are all too familiar with the sequence of pain, rage, and revenge that festers in our schools and now dominates our world. It is in this context of terrorism against children—be it in the family, the school, nationally, or internationally—that we explore the dynamics and the interpersonal power struggles that define bullying.

Our mission with our first book was to arouse an uninformed public about the dimensions, the elements, the invisible scars of children abusing children. We no longer have to plead our case. Our children, more tragically, more forcefully than we could ever have imagined, thrust the issue before our eyes. In this book, *Bullies, Targets, & Witnesses: Helping Children Break the Pain Chain*, we will integrate the myriad responses, research, analyses, strategies, models, theories, treatises, policies, and legislative initiatives that have emerged since *Bullies & Victims* was published in 1996. This book reverberates with the voices of the sixty thousand students and the thousands of educators, parents, mental health providers, law enforcement personnel, social service workers, and child advocates from whom we have learned so much.

CHAPTER ONE

BULLYING IN THE 21ST CENTURY

"In the past few years there have been many school shootings. I think this is due to them kids getting picked on and not let into groups."
—Jeremy, a student

The radio interview was about to begin. The host of the local station introduced the topical program and then announced: "Today we will be discussing bullying with a national expert. Listeners are invited to call in and ask questions or make comments. Now, to get the discussion rolling, Mrs. Fried—is bullying really that different today than it was in the past? Hasn't it been with us forever? Why are we making such a fuss about it now?"

This opening gambit, used as a lead-in on many programs, is guaranteed to bring a range of audience response that is fairly representative of current conversation on this topic. On the one hand a caller will cite childhood memories—kids ganging up on someone; boys hitting each other with fists, bats, and bicycle chains;

someone being called a sissy—and claim that bullying is a perennial rite of passage and a significant learning experience. Soon after, another caller will dial in and recount painful taunts that linger and sting though many years have passed. On many occasions, a person will reveal the debilitating consequences of early bullying that have affected lifelong choices. Other callers have spoken of thoughts of suicide, dysfunctional marriages, the inability to make a commitment to a partner, failed businesses—all directly related to the circumstances of their childhood bullying.

As we shift gears into the twenty-first century, already marked by the events of September 11, 2001, where images of outrageous acts of terrorism and suicide bombings are seared into the brains of elementary school children, can we doubt that the life experience for children is different today, excruciatingly different from the world of fifty years ago? Even before the Twin Towers crumbled, differences between the1950s and the 1990s were monumental. Half a century ago, it was unthinkable that a child would come to school with a gun and deliberately take the lives of classmates and teachers. Today's concerns about violence and peer cruelty touch private, parochial, and public schools in suburban, rural, and urban settings in all parts of the country.

Findings from three studies reported at the 107th Annual Convention of the American Psychological Association (APA) led the APA to release a statement that: "Bullying is a pervasive problem, with estimated worldwide rates of 5 to 15 percent. Bullying occurs more frequently and with greater lethality today than in the 1970s and the 1980s."[2]

According to a survey conducted by the Kaiser Family Foundation and Nickelodeon—"Talking With Kids About Tough Issues"—74 percent of eight- to eleven-year-olds said teasing and bullying occur at their school, more than the incidence of smoking, drinking, drugs, or sex. The rate increased to 86 percent among children aged twelve to fifteen years old.[3]

BULLYING IN THE 21ST CENTURY

Walter Gilliam, a child psychologist at Yale University's Child Study Center, is studying suspensions in Connecticut, where 311 kindergarteners were suspended in 1999–2000. About half involved allegations of physical violence, sexual harassment, or verbal threats.

Is bullying an inevitable part of growing up? Does it toughen kids up, teach them how to handle unexpected conflicts and make the transition from child to adult easier to negotiate? Or is it a traumatic power struggle between youthful, unequal parties—a form of unlabeled child abuse?

Joseph Epstein, a professor of literature at Northwestern University, appears to downplay the consequences of bullying today. In an article in the *Wall Street Journal,* April 30, 2001, he rebuked studies and reports that "attempt to find some solution to the sad events of recent years at Columbine and other American high schools . . . in the behavior of youthful bullies—behavior that has been around since there have been boys."

However, a study by the U.S. Secret Service in the fall of 2000 found that in two-thirds of the thirty-seven school shootings since 1974, the attackers felt "persecuted, bullied, threatened, attacked or injured."[4] *Time* magazine, in a May 28, 2001, article, "Voices From The Cell," documented the imprisonment of twelve male teens who killed teachers, students, parents, and/or wounded over 50 others. According to the article by Timothy Roche, "Almost all the shooters were expressing rage, either against a particular person for a particular affront or, more often, against a whole cohort of bullying classmates." One of the teen prisoners told a psychiatrist that he felt that going to prison would be better than continuing to endure the bullying at school.

After working with over 60,000 students; facilitating in-service training for many thousands of educators, counselors, and administrators; and presenting seminars to parents all across the country, there is no question in our minds that bullying is a form of child

3

abuse—peer abuse. If a child is hurting, it doesn't matter if the perpetrator is a parent or a peer. If a child is suffering, it doesn't matter if the source of the pain is someone who is age thirty-five or ten. No child deserves to be abused—by anyone.

Several months ago, when I was giving a professional training workshop, a counselor came to me at the end of the day to share the following thoughts: "At the beginning of this session, when you referred to bullying as a form of child abuse, I reacted negatively and thought you were exaggerating the situation. After being part of this training experience, listening to the data and hearing the feedback from other counselors across the state, I think you should stop using the term *bullying* and use the term *abuse* instead. The term *bullying* is too benign. Too many people associate it with a childhood rite of passage and dismiss the effect. I am convinced that too many children are in terrible pain and we have to use the strongest language possible to convey their trauma."

The trauma that this thoughtful counselor referred to affects many aspects of our educational system.

Truancy and Dropout Problems

According to the National Education Association, 160,000 children stay home from school every day because they fear what is going to happen to them on the bus, on the playground, in the cafeteria, in the bathroom, in the locker room, in the hallways, or in the classroom. In the September 1996 issue of *Youth and Society,* researchers studied 25,000 eighth-grade students in some 1,000 schools over time to identify reasons that students drop out of school. The dropout rates were tracked from eighth grade onward. Students were given a list of twenty-one factors that contribute to dropping out and were asked to check each answer that applied to them. Some factors were categorized as "push"—situations from within the school that pushed them out, such as feeling unsafe, feeling like they didn't belong, difficulties with other students, being expelled—while others fell into the "pull" category, external factors that pulled them away from their educational path, such as marriage, pregnancy, having a job, caring for a family member. The push factors appeared to be most significant for predicting students' decisions to leave school. As a result, one of the suggestions for encouraging students to remain in school was to create a more positive and caring human climate.

Suicide

Former U.S. Surgeon General David Satcher claimed that more than 30,000 Americans take their lives annually. There are three suicides for every two murders. Among young people, the rate has tripled since 1952, making it the third-leading killer of those ages ten to twenty-four. One of every five high school students has thought seriously about attempting suicide, and one in fourteen has made an attempt, according to federal estimates.[5] Several studies have shown that gay, lesbian, and bisexual youths face an increased suicide risk. A Massachusetts survey published in the *American Journal of Public Health* found that gay high school students were about four times more likely to have attempted suicide than heterosexual students. According to the March 21, 2001, issue of *Education Week,* in the 1998–1999 school year, 2,700 young people, ages ten to nineteen, took their own lives.

Statistics from the Centers for Disease Control and Prevention clearly indicate that our youth are at greater risk than ever. Between 1980 and 1997, the rate of suicide increased 109 percent for ten- to fourteen-year-olds and 11 percent for fifteen- to nineteen-year-olds. A recent study by the CDC indicates that adolescents show up at hospital emergency rooms with self-inflicted injuries—usually suicide attempts—more often than people of any other age group. Although more females attempt suicide than males, males are much more likely to die from suicide. Among fifteen- to nineteen-year-olds, boys were five times as likely as girls to commit suicide.[6]

The suicide rate among young people is highest for white males. However, from 1980 to 1996, the suicide rate increased most rapidly among black males ages fifteen to nineteen, more than doubling from 3.6 to 8.1 per 100,000. A 1997 survey of high school students found that Hispanic students (11 percent) were significantly more likely than white students (6 percent) to have reported a suicide attempt.[7]

Kids' increased access to firearms has had lethal consequences. Among fifteen- to nineteen-year-olds, 62 percent of the increase in the total number of suicides from 1980 to 1997 was due to the increase in firearm-related suicides.[8]

Some suicides are not reported. Medical examiners cannot always determine whether a person's death was deliberate. Even if suicide is suspected (for example, in the case of a self-inflicted gunshot wound or a one-car crash) the official cause of death may be listed as unintentional. Although such reporting may spare the family some emotional distress (or ensure that beneficiaries receive proceeds from life insurance), it results in the underreporting of suicides in the United States.

A number of parents have gone public and disclosed the devastating events of bullying that led to their children's suicides. In a number of cases, boys who were overweight were taunted, ostracized, and ridiculed beyond endurance. One father, on national television, spoke of what it was like to cut his firstborn son down from the limb of a tree where he had hanged himself in their backyard. The boy killed himself because, after a summer of dieting, he looked in the mirror and decided he wasn't thin enough to please his taunting classmates.

A high school student in the Midwest left school one afternoon, slid into the seat of his pickup truck, put a gun to his head, and fired a deadly bullet. Before killing himself, he left a note addressed to the three boys who had bullied him relentlessly. He wrote: "I feel sorry for you because you are going to have to remember what I did for the rest of your lives."

Madison Shockley, a board member of the Southern Christian Leadership Conference/Los Angeles, believes that many of the school shootings were attempts at suicide. Most of the boys who killed and/or injured their classmates made no effort to escape. He calls it the "Samson syndrome"—related to the biblical story of Samson, who after relentless humiliation at the hands of the Philistines, in one final heroic act destroyed the pillars of the temple, killing three thousand of his enemies as well as himself. Shockley continues: "For the boys in today's school shootings, the bullies, the athletes, the homecoming queen, the BMOC—all are pillars of the school temple that they must destroy. So in one final desperate act, they are destroying as many Philistines as they can." Eric Harris and Dylan Klebold, the infamous shooters at Columbine High School, fully intended to take their own lives along with the lives of many students.

When Elizabeth Bush, a fourteen-year-old student from Williamsport, Pennsylvania, was interviewed following the shooting incident at her parochial school, she claimed that she didn't want to harm Kimberly Marchese as much as she wanted Kim to be a witness to her (Elizabeth's) suicide. Elizabeth wanted Kimberly to know the pain that she felt because of her friend's betrayal. Elizabeth had tried self-mutilation, but her deep depression was not assuaged. She brought the gun to school and shot Kimberly in the shoulder. Kimberly, the cheerleading captain, a basketball and soccer player, does not know when she will have full use of her arm again, and Elizabeth, an introverted, deeply religious girl who thought of being a nun, is serving a sentence in a juvenile psychiatric facility and could remain there until she is twenty-one.

Then there is the case of Andy Williams, the fifteen-year-old student at Santana High School in California, who killed two students and wounded thirteen other people. His classmates had taunted him because of his small size, pale complexion, and high voice. Students would regularly beat him up and call him a pussy. Following his arrest, Andy told investigators that he planned to run away and kill himself after the shooting. Instead, he will spend fifty years in prison—three years in a juvenile prison and forty-seven years in a maximum-security facility.

A comprehensive study looking at the correlation between bullying and youth suicide was conducted in Finland in 1997.[9] The researchers analyzed responses from 16,410 eighth- and ninth-grade students in two Finnish regions. Depression was most common among those who were both bullied by others and were also bullies themselves. Among girls, severe suicidal ideation was associated with frequently being bullied or being a bully, and for boys it was associated with being a bully. The researchers noted that the link between depression, severe suicidal ideation, and being a bully was correlated to family issues. Emotional distance between family members, a lack of warmth, and inconsistent discipline for children are reported more frequently in families of students who bully and experience suicidal thoughts.

The link between suicidal ideas and violent behavior is even more evident in a report released by the CDC and the U.S. Department of Education, December 4, 2001. Their data indicate that students who committed acts of violence were nearly seven times more likely than their nonviolent peers to have expressed suicidal thoughts or to have plans or actually attempted suicide.

Crime

More than thirty years ago, Leonard Eron, Ph.D., and his colleagues were one of the first groups of researchers in the country to look at the issue of bullying.[10] Working with a school district in rural upper

New York, they invited 875 third-grade students to indicate those classmates they considered to be bullies by putting a check mark beside their name. After collecting the bully nomination forms from the third graders, Eron and his team did extensive interviewing with family members, students, and teachers. They waited ten years until the third graders had become seniors in high school, then repeated the process. Not surprisingly, they learned that most of the seniors who were named as bullies by their peers were the same students identified as bullies when they were in the third grade. When the original group of students was tracked, twenty years later, the research team discovered that one out of four of the bullies recognized at the age of eight or nine had a criminal record by the age of twenty-eight to thirty. The male bullies were at much greater risk of becoming abusive husbands, and the female bullies were more likely than their counterparts to have become abusive mothers. Other children have about a one-in-twenty chance of becoming adult criminals. Research indicates that, in addition to criminal behavior, bullies are more likely to become involved in gangs and/or have employment difficulties, mental health problems, struggles with alcohol and substance abuse, and higher rates of divorce. The children identified as bullies in the third grade were more likely to become parents of children who were identified as bullies by their peers when they were in the third grade. Eron's study was the first to illustrate both the enduring nature of bullying behavior and the apparent intergenerational transmission of bullying behavior.

Support for these findings was demonstrated by Dan Olweus in a Norwegian study.[11] He found that 60 percent of children identified as bullies between grades six and ten were cited for criminal behavior as adults, and 40 percent had three or more convictions. Moreover, a study published in *Learning 94*, concluded that bullies whose behavior is allowed to continue are five times more likely than their classmates to wind up in juvenile court, to be convicted of crimes, and to have children with aggression problems.

Though highly visible reports of student shootings have created the perception that schools are dangerous environments, the 2000 Annual Report on School Safety—jointly authored by the U.S. Department of Education and the U.S. Department of Justice—confirms that 90 percent of the nation's schools reported no serious violent crime during the previous school year. Forty-three percent experienced no crime at all. A companion document to the report reveals a significant decline in the number of students in grades nine though twelve who reported carrying a weapon to school one or more days during the previous month—from 12 percent in 1993 to 7 percent in 1999.

> To put the probelm of targeted school-based attacks in context, from 1993 to 1997 the odds that a child in grades 9 to 12 would be threatened or injured with a weapon in school were 7 to 8 percent, or 1 in 13 or 14; the odds of getting into a physical fight at school were 15 percent, or 1 in 7. In contrast, the odds that a child would die in school—by homicine or suicide—are, fortunately, no greater than 1 in 1 million. . . . The findings of the Safe School Initiative's extensive search for recorded incidents of targeted school-based attacks underscore the rarity of lethal attacks in school settings. The Department of Education reports that nearly 60 million children attend the nation's 119,000–plus schools. The combined efforts of the Secret Service and the Department of Education identified 37 incidents of targeted school-based attacks, committed by 41 individuals over a 25-year period.[12]

In "Violence in American Schools," the authors report that in 1999, the odds of dying a violent death in school were 1 in 2 million.

Yet, for the school year 1996–1997, the U.S. Department of Education reported 188,000 fights or physical attacks not involving weapons in schools, 11,000 fights involving weapons, and 4,000 incidents of sexual assault. In addition, a Department of Education report covering the school year 1997–1998, states that 1.3 percent of 2,752 murders of youths aged five through nineteen took place in schools. Schools were the setting for 31 percent of 802,900 serious violent crimes against students, aged twelve to eighteen. Violent crimes are defined as rape, sexual assault, robbery, and aggravated assault.

Our traditional child protection systems are not set up to protect children from abuse by peers. Adults are protected from assault and harassment and can more readily use the judicial system to charge an attacker. Children, victims of the same assault by a peer, are left to the mercy of intervening or nonintervening adults. Child abuse statutes in our fifty states specify the definition of child abuse as maltreatment perpetrated by an adult. Reports of children abused by other children are not investigated by social service departments. Acts of bullying break the law when they become extortion, theft, assault, battery, weapons possession, murder, arson, hate crime, hazing, sexual abuse, sexual harassment, rape, or a violation of civil rights. Those reports are handled by the juvenile justice system. Even though this process is quite intimidating, more parents are choosing to use the courts as a solution and are engaging lawyers to serve as legal advocates for their children's protection when schools are indifferent. In one case, the school district was mandated to pay for the educational and counseling services for two children who had been forced to leave school because of harassment. A school district in Pennsylvania will pay $312,000 to settle a lawsuit filed by a gay teenager who alleged that officials did nothing to stop other students from tormenting him. He claimed he was pushed down stairs and subjected to other physical assaults as well as name-calling and obscene jokes.

Teacher Shortages

According to a study conducted by the National Education Association, 6,250 teachers are threatened with bodily injury on a daily basis, and 260 are physically attacked. In an average month in public secondary schools, 5,000 teachers are actually harmed.

In one week in 1995, three teachers died as a result of bullying. Two were killed outright by students, and the third teacher died of a heart attack while being assaulted. Several teachers have lost their lives in the multiple school shootings that have occurred. Richard M. Ingersoll, a researcher at the University of Pennsylvania, analyzed the federal schools and staffing survey data from more than 50,000 teachers nationwide. Ingersoll reports that 29 percent of teachers leave the field after three years on the job and 39 percent leave within five years. In addition to the teacher-exodus rates, there is concern about unusually high turnover rates. While the average annual turnover rate in most other professions is 11 percent, teachers leave theirs at a rate of 13.2 percent a year. Suggestions for stemming the tide include increasing support for teachers, raising salaries, reducing student misbehavior, and giving faculty members more say in school decision making. Teachers also expressed concerns about school safety, student motivation, and discipline.[13] The average teacher's salary is $42,000, and according to Quality Education Data, a division of Scholastic, U.S. elementary school teachers spend more than a $1 billion a year of their own money on supplies for their classrooms, a $521 annual personal contribution. Teachers today are expected to be educators, social workers, parent substitutes, and law enforcement officers. Their dreams of educating young people about history, science, math, literature, language, and social studies are often shattered by the reality of the disruptive classroom. When I ask students how many of them want to be teachers as an occupation when they reach adulthood, I am saddened by how few middle and senior high school students want to be teachers.

Learning Issues

Clearly, students who fear going to the bathroom and freeze at the thought of recess are going to have difficulty focusing on subject matter. A mind that is swirling with memories of past physical, verbal, emotional, and/or sexual jibes and terrified at the prospect of the next assault is not free to absorb complicated information. An example of this situation came to our attention at a private elementary school in Maryland. A parent made a special point to relate the circumstances of her son's sudden drop in grades. He had always been an A student and was suddenly making C's and D's. It took quite a while to unravel the mystery, but what emerged was that the classroom teacher had established a rule that students who had not completed their homework assignments would not be permitted to participate in recess. Bingo! For the boy who dreaded recess because of the bullying activity directed at him, this rule was his saving grace. He did as much homework as he could during the recess period, but it was never enough to keep him at his previous grade level. Avoiding recess became much more important to him than making A's.

W. Thomas Boyce, a professor of epidemiology, and other researchers contend that there is a biological aspect to bullying. They claim that over time, exposure to threats and acts of violence interfere with how the brain functions. The premise is that a student's emotions will overtake the cognitive process when faced with fear of abuse.

I have heard many personal stories from students who are isolated because of their academic success. They feel that they have to make a choice between excelling in school and doing poorly to please their peers. This anecdotal information comes from children who couldn't handle the harassment, reports from counselors and teachers, and the expressions of gratitude of parents who saw their children's grades improve when bullying prevention and intervention programs were initiated. These voices are sounding a call for further research to confirm the strong connection between bullying and learning problems.

Witnesses to Violence

What about those children who witness cruelty and feel impotent to alter the situation? If you can't protect others, can you ensure safety for yourself? What are the lifelong effects of guilt brought about by not speaking up? Again, there are many areas of this issue that have not been fully explored. We suspect that studies of peer witnesses to bullying would show evidence of gnawing shame in later years and that the reluctance to take action can affect self-esteem over the long term. Many parents have described childhood situations in which they were acutely aware of a classmate's raw wounds and did nothing to intervene. Some have even shared poignant stories of having joined the group assault for self-protection. As they watch their children endure the indignities of others, they are racked by painful memories of their own cruel behavior. One woman told the story of attending a rural school where most of the children rode the bus. One little girl became the scapegoat for all the other bus riders, who refused to have any contact with her. This woman reported that the only sin she could remember this girl committing was to have lived the farthest away. For that reason the other children decided to ostracize her. After a while it became habitual, and no one wanted to be the first to contradict the school-bus culture. Years later, the woman who related the story became a psychiatric nurse. On her first assignment, she walked onto the ward of a psychiatric hospital and a patient approached her. The patient stared at her and said, "Do you remember me?" The nurse immediately recognized the distraught woman as the girl who had been ignored all those early years. The nurse replied, "Yes, I do." The patient looked her directly in the eye and said, "I just want you to see where you are and where I am."

These memories haunt the souls of men and women who participated, sometimes unwittingly, in childhood acts of cruelty. They agonize as they try to reconcile the person they are now with the wounds they caused others in the past. We heard the story of a man who chose not to attend his high school reunion but sent a videotape instead. In the tape he expressed shame and remorse for the hurtful way he had treated his classmates when he was young. There is a good chance, however, that the people he hurt so badly did not attend the reunion, either. Adults who live with unresolved pain from their childhood frequently avoid any reconnection to reminders of their hurtful past.

Sometimes you can make amends. Singer, songwriter, and minister Lee Domann composed a poignant song called "Howard Gray" about his role in taunting a seventh-grade classmate whose real name was Howard Ray, Jr. A Kansas native who now resides in Nashville, Tennessee, Domann turned the song into an educational video and is committed to its distribution as an instrument to promote tolerance and acceptance, especially between children. Ray and Domann reconnected many years later, after Ray had heard the song and decided to forgive his former tormentor.

Sometimes you cannot make amends, but you can atone. Brandi Guardino, a woman who has become a dedicated advocate of bullying prevention, related the following story on a radio interview. When she was in sixth grade, a girl in her class who was large for her age started developing more quickly than the other girls. A popular saying at that time was "Where's the beef?" so the kids started calling her "Beefer." One day a substitute teacher was calling the roll and when she came to the name of the taunted girl, the students told the teacher that her name was Beefer, so for the next three days the substitute teacher called the girl Beefer. The target was too embarrassed to ask the teacher to call her by her real name. To add to her humiliation, every day in gym class a group of girls would grab their classmate's towel from her when she stepped out of the shower, and she would cower in the corner to hide her body. She cried as she pulled on her wet clothes, only to be ridiculed because of the way her clothing clung to her skin.

Years later, Brandi was working for a psychiatrist and was asked to file the chart of a deceased female patient who had committed suicide. Because they were the same age, the doctor asked if she knew the former client. She did not recognize the client's name, but when she reviewed the client's history, she realized that the young woman was Beefer. Brandi is now determined to do whatever she can to prevent this situation from being repeated with another child. While she did not participate in the excruciating actions, she feels deep remorse for not making some effort to protect the reviled young girl. One result is that, as president of the Catawba County Medical Society Alliance in North Carolina, she made bullying prevention a priority for her group.

I was asked to conduct our BullySafeUSA Training Institute in her community for twenty-two school counselors who will now present our program to thousands of students in their local schools.

Sometimes there is nothing you can do to erase the sins of the past, but you can work to affect the future.

Isn't it time for us to accept the fact that bullying is a form of child abuse?

CHAPTER TWO

BULLIES, TARGETS, AND WITNESSES

"The angel on one shoulder is telling me to do what is right and just. The devil on the other says just go with the flow or you might be next."
—Lindsay, a student

The multiple shooting of twelve students and a teacher at Columbine High School by Eric Harris and Dylan Klebold in Littleton, Colorado, was the Berlin Wall of the bullying issue in the United States. Prior to that tragedy, there were relatively few people who were researching, thinking, and concerned about bullying. Now, just say the word *Columbine* and it conjures up a profusion of visual images: students running and crying, armed police officers, sirens, ambulances, stunned adults. The fact that the Columbine tragedy occurred in an affluent, mostly white suburban school shattered the illusion of immunity from school violence that many students and parents had previously held. Our world will never be the same.

In the face of horrific, shocking death, we onlookers often ache for some sense of meaning, some context to rearrange our chaotic

17

thoughts, some direction to return to emotional stability. How we wish those students and that teacher had not lost their lives, how we wish the injured students were not forever burdened with physical and emotional flashbacks, how we wish the parents—every parent of a Columbine student—were not forever scarred by the events of April 20, 1999. But if we are to find some transcending hope out of that unacceptable horror, some way to bring purpose to those students' sacrifice, perhaps it will be the end of our naivete about children's cruelty and the beginning of our enlightenment about the abuse of bullying.

There are some who have suggested that we should not label children as bullies, that we should talk about children who engage in bullying behaviors lest we stereotype a child who is struggling to find a sense of personal power in a powerless arena. There are some who say that almost every child has been a bully and/or been bullied and the roles are quite interchangeable. To that point, Dorothy Espelage, Ph.D., of the University of Illinois at Urbana-Champaign says that nearly 80 to 90 percent of adolescents report some form of victimization from a bully at school, and kids who bully a lot also say they've been victimized, too.[14] Dr. Espelage believes that we should describe bullying as a continuum of behaviors rather than label any kid a bully, a nonbully, or a victim.

All of those statements have merit. We have decided to use the term *bully* with some misgivings about the labeling issue, recognizing that many bullies were once or still are targets, and that they deserve to be seen as a whole child who behaves in a defensive or strategic way toward some end. We are using this terminology as a kind of communication shorthand, and it is very important to us that our readers know our concern is for all children.

We believe that bullying is a learned behavior, acquired primarily from family members and/or friends. However, there are children who are more likely to become bullies because of inborn traits, such as those who were crack babies, who suffered from fetal alcohol syndrome, and some children with attention deficit disorder (ADD) or attention deficit hyperactivity disorder (ADHD) whose disruptive behavior patterns may have a biological basis. They often become targets, as well. Ritalin makes it possible for some of these children to accommodate to the classroom environment, control their actions and interactions, and contain bullying behavior. Two widely used drugs, Concerta and Adderall XR, last twelve to fourteen hours and spare children the embarrassment of leaving the classroom to receive a dose of Ritalin, which lasts only four or five hours. While concern has been expressed about medicating some children unnecessarily, and while these drugs may cause side effects, the majority of families with children who are diagnosed with ADD or ADHD are grateful for the benefits of medication.

Some parents of children with ADD or ADHD are finding a therapeutic element in karate and other forms of martial arts. Many doctors support thist idea, as do several national nonprofit resource groups for people with the disorder, including the National Attention Deficit Disorder Association and Children and Adults with Attention-Deficit/Hyperactivity Disorder. They say that such courses help ease the symptoms of the disorder: impulsiveness, inability to concentrate, and, in some cases, hyperactivity. Other experts who say that it is nothing more than wishful thinking, however, dismiss this theory. They point to a lack of medical evidence to back up the theory.

In the past several years, a mounting number of children who have been diagnosed with Asperger's syndrome, a mild form of autism, are entering the school system. Psychiatrist Leo Kanner was the first person to apply the term *autism* to children who were socially withdrawn, preoccupied with routine, and had difficulty with language yet often possessed a level of intelligence that ruled out mental retardation. The following year, in 1944, Hans Asperger applied the term to children who were socially awkward and consumed with bizarre obsessions, yet highly verbal and very bright.

These children have shown up as targets and occasionally bullies because of social-skill issues.

Most everyone agrees, however, that bullies generally become bullies through their life experiences. Bullies are more likely to have been abused themselves. Nathaniel Floyd, Ph.D., says that seeing other children who appear vulnerable is uncomfortable for the bully.[15] "When these bullies see kids they perceive as vulnerable, they are threatened because it reminds them of the shame and humiliation of their own victimization." Bullies are more likely to have witnessed their fathers physically abusing their mothers or have seen other forms of violence in their homes. The link between viewing TV violence and aggressive behavior has been clearly established. Recently researchers have explored the relationship between playing violent computer games and aggressive behavior, and the effects appear to be even stronger.[16] In one recent study, subjects were asked to play one of two video games: an analytic virtual computer game, Myst, or Wolfenstein, a violent video game where the object is to track down and brutally kill their enemies. After playing the video games, subjects were observed in a laboratory with a peer. Subjects who had played Wolfenstein were consistently more aggressive toward the peer in the laboratory situation than subjects who had played Myst, and the effect was even greater in subjects who identified themselves as having a bad temper. The researchers speculate that the active rehearsal aspect of video games creates an even stronger effect then the well-established effect of the passive viewing of television violence.

This is an appropriate time to point out the value of analytic video games that promote complex thinking and thoughtful responses to solve problems. There are many such games that motivate the player to explore optional solutions to complicated problems that require work and patience to gather information, that stimulate the imagination and improve abilities and skills to create inventive solutions.

Then there are violent video games whose purpose is to develop sharp-shooting skills. One story that has been widely circulated concerns the two boys in the Jonesboro, Arkansas, tragedy. The boys pulled a fire alarm and watched from a distant grove of trees as students and teachers poured out onto the school playground. Using rifles they had stolen that morning, they targeted, shot, and killed four students and a teacher and wounded eleven others. The male shooters were extremely accurate. One boy had accompanied his father on hunting trips, but the extraordinary accuracy they displayed has been attributed to the hours they spent practicing their skills on video games in arcades. The combination of media influence and access to weapons endangers our children.

Several researchers have investigated the cognitive processes or thinking patterns of bullies. Psychologists Kenneth Dodge, Ph.D., and John Coie, Ph.D., have described two different styles of aggression in their research with children: reactive and proactive.[17] The reactive aggressive child is emotional, has poor impulse control, and reacts to an accidental bump as an act of provocation. These children see the world though a paranoid lens, feel constantly threatened, and thus believe that their aggressive response is justified. An accidental brush against such a child's arm can be interpreted as a direct assault. These children do not see themselves as bullies but as protectors of their space. In their minds it is the other child who is the troublemaker. These thinking patterns are well in place by the age of seven or eight.

Proactive bullies, on the other hand, are more calculating about initiating hurtful acts. They behave in a nonemotional, controlled, deliberate manner. They are selective about their targets and look for satisfaction and rewards in their choosing. The aggression is delivered with the hope of achieving some goal that comes from within the aggressive child, like coercion or domination, rather than in response to some external threat.

Robert Selman, Ph.D., has examined another aspect of the thinking patterns of bullies.[18] He focuses on the immaturity of bullies' cognitive style, describing it as unilateral in nature. These children think in terms of simple one-way directives and commands to others—for example, "Give that to me." They lack the more mature form of thinking that allows for a reciprocal exchange of ideas and collaboration that enable people to effectively resolve differences with each other. Selman and his colleagues suggest that this type of bully has limited skills to manage relationship conflicts, and this, in turn, leads to anger and aggression.

A third kind of bully that we have observed is the elitist bully. This is the bully who is very attractive, or is an outstanding athlete, or has acquired social status because of his or her parents' financial, corporate, or political position. Not all children become corrupted by their elitism but a significant number succumb to the power given them and use it to torment those they feel are inferior. We have heard countless stories of "jocks," athletes who took advantage of their fame to ridicule and humiliate other students. Often they were even bold enough to do it in the presence of coaches and other faculty members, knowing they would never be admonished. School rules, which all other students are expected to follow, are not applied to them.

A particular case in point is a young female student at a private school who was extremely malicious and verbally hurtful to other students, especially to girls. A fellow classmate commented, "She lives in a palace, she's treated like a princess, and she thinks she is more important than other people." One of the mothers consistently complained to the principal, who appeared to be sympathetic to the specific incidents that were described. As time went on, and the bully's behavior never changed, the mother sought out other parents to see if they were mindful of the problem. They added anecdotes of abuse regarding their targeted daughters, but all concluded that because the bully's family had made considerable contributions to the building fund, the offender would never be reprimanded.

It is important to include in these observations that many children of high-profile, extremely successful parents are class leaders, are models of considerate behavior, and have learned at an early age the responsibility of concern for others and commitment to a greater good.

We frequently hear students speak negatively about the "popular" students. We have come to understand that *popular* is not a synonym for *well liked*, but instead describes someone with high status. Kids, like adults, tend to assign status based on appearance, athletic ability, affluence, and, more rarely, academic ability. Patricia and Peter Adler studied peer groups among a community of third to sixth graders for a period of eight years.[19] They identified four groups:

The popular clique. This group functions under an influential leader or the best friend of the leader. The leader's status is unchallenged, but the status of the rest of the group can fluctuate. Membership is closed, and the leader determines who is inside and outside of the group. Members work hard at maintaining their position in the group.

Friendship circles. These are smaller groups of five to fifteen friends. They function in a more democratic manner, with more fluid boundaries. Less effort is required to stay in these groups.

The Wannabes. These kids hang out near the popular clique, adopting their clothing styles and taste in music. They may be granted membership on a temporary basis, depending on the circumstances, but they know, as does everyone else, that they are not official members.

The Loners. These are the isolated outsiders who don't fit in anywhere. They are the ones who eat alone in the lunchroom and stand alone before and after school.

The Adlers report that popularity usually involves different traits for boys and girls. The main requirement for status among boys is athletic ability, often paired with a cool toughness. For girls, status comes with appearance, manner of dress, and degree of wealth.

There is an interesting debate going on now about the relationship between aggression and self-esteem. The traditional view has been that low self-esteem gives rise to aggression. Recently this view has been challenged. Dan Olweus, one of the leading experts in the field, found that bullies do not have low self-esteem.[20] John Coie and Kenneth Dodge, two researchers who have studied aggression in children for years, have reported that aggressive boys do not have low self-concepts.[21] Martin Seligman,[22] past president of the APA, has questioned the value of programs that promote high self-esteem in children as a result of these more recent research findings.

This discussion is complicated by the fact that many overlapping concepts fall into the murky category of self-esteem. Self-importance or even smugness, for example, concepts that suggest a sense of superiority or entitlement, could result in high scores on many self-esteem scales. Although we think of these traits as negative, in fact some research suggests that these characteristics are associated with popularity. One study of 452 fourth- through sixth-grade boys found that tough, antisocial boys were viewed as popular (and antisocial) by their peers, their teachers, and themselves.[23] Thus, in this study, argumentative, disruptive boys were esteemed by themselves and their peers. We believe that there are bullies who appear to have self-esteem but in truth are self-centered, narcissistic, and impressed with the power showered upon them. In our work with students, who spend more time with children who bully than anyone else, we found that they consistently describe bullies as insecure, needy, and socially unskilled. Ervin Staub, Ph.D., professor of psychology at the University of Massachusetts, says that "the self-esteem of aggressive boys appears to be very vulnerable, very fragile. Its maintenance requires specific circumstances and behaviors on their part. This raises the question whether we can consider it a genuinely positive self-esteem."[24] Perhaps, as psychologist Lauren Slater suggests, we should focus not on how the self *feels*, but how well it *does* in life and work.[25] Or, as psychologists/authors Gershen Kaufman, Ph.D.; Lev Raphael, Ph.D.; and Pamela Espeland suggest in their book *Sticking Up for Yourself*, "self-esteem means being proud of yourself because you've done things you're proud of." We believe the lack of clarity about how self-esteem is defined and measured makes it difficult to draw any firm conclusions in this area.

In the information available in the field now, there seems to be consensus on a general definition of bullying behavior as one or more individuals inflicting physical, verbal, or emotional abuse on another. However, based on conversations with tens of thousands of students, we believe that sexual bullying should be added as a separate category to physical, verbal, and emotional peer abuse. It is a major cause of concern to students, even at the elementary school level between fourth, fifth, and sixth graders. Definitions that specify sexual harassment as a form of physical bullying ignore the verbal sexual bullying that is very damaging to many students. Another form of sexual bullying operates in the psychological or emotional realm, as when someone is pressured or manipulated to engage in behaviors that aren't comfortable. In fact, sexual name-calling was one of the triggers that set off Eric Harris and Dylan Klebold, the two students responsible for the killings at Columbine High School. Therefore, we believe that sexual bullying—including physical, verbal, and emotional aspects— should be included as a distinct definition. Bullying can also include:

- any written, verbal, or physical act that would harm a student or student's property
- repeated and systemic harassment and attacks on others
- repeated, unprovoked behavior intended to cause harm or distress to a victim who is vulnerable due to a real or perceived imbalance of power.

BULLIES, TARGETS, & WITNESSES

The National School Safety Center states that bullying is any hurtful or aggressive act toward an individual or group that is intentional and repeated.

While these definitions may serve quite well for adults dealing with policies and/or legislation, when working with children, we find that it is not only helpful, but also necessary, to be as specific and concrete as possible.

Bullying takes many forms, can include many different behaviors, and can be perpetrated by individuals or groups. Bullying involves both males and females and begins at a very early age. Preschool teachers and day-care providers share harrowing stories and examples of bullying that takes place between three- and four-year-olds. A Montessori teacher spoke of four- and five-year-olds who had learned to use temper tantrums as a way to get power. When they lash out at other children, they discover that they benefit from a lot of attention. In addition, when unwarranted concessions are made to them, it teaches them to value bullying. Behavior patterns that are tolerated at an early age do not fall away. They tend to escalate rather than recede.

A major topic of discussion with both students and adults is the issue of teasing and/or bullying. Some believe the terms are synonymous, but most students are of the opinion that all teasing is not bullying. Teasing is a kind of give-and-take situation—sometimes affectionate, sometimes humorous, a bantering style of communication that makes it possible for children to affirm their fondness for each other without broaching on uncomfortable, tender expressions. At the same time, it can be the modus operandi of the student culture where children chide and corral each other to stay attuned to the social expectations of the tribe. A study released by the University of California at Berkley in the summer of 2002 comes to the conclusion that teasing can be helpful and lead to more intimacy.

Bullying, on the other hand, can be described as a situation where one person does all the giving and the other does all the taking. There is no fun for the person on the receiving end, or as one bright student from Clay Center, Kansas, suggested, "Teasing is when two people are laughing; bullying is when only one person is laughing!"

A guidance counselor, Mary Beth Peterson, at Tomahawk and John Diemer Schools in Olathe, Kansas, extends the continuum even further and talks to students about the difference between

Joking:
- Both students are on the same level.
- Both are comfortable.
- Often there is laughing or giggling.

Teasing:
- One student is higher and treating the second like they are not on the same level.
- One student is becoming uncomfortable and wishes the teasing would stop.
- One student is laughing, but the other's laughter may be forced or sound different.

Bullying:
- One student is definitely the "King Kong" while the other is receiving the "King Kong" behavior.
- One student is definitely very uncomfortable and desperately wishes the bullying would stop.
- One student has power and the second has none. Laughter and name-calling is directed toward the victim or the target. Physical behavior such as shoving or pushing may be a part. Rude language is present.

One thing is certain. When bullying occurs, no bully should be released from responsibility by saying, "I was only joking." It is not up to the bully to determine the nature or the extent of the offense.

Based on a survey that we conducted among members of the American Dance Therapy Association, published in our first book, *Bullies & Victims* (M. Evans, 1996), we believe that behavior is clearly bullying when:

1. **There is intent to harm**—the perpetrator finds pleasure in the taunting and continues even when the target's distress is obvious.
2. **There is intensity and duration**—the taunting continues over a long period of time, and the degree of taunting is damaging to the self-esteem of the target.
3. **There is abuse of power**—the abuser maintains power because of age, strength, size, and/or gender.
4. **The target is vulnerable**—the target is more sensitive to teasing, cannot adequately defend him- or herself, and has physical or psychological qualities that make him or her more prone to vulnerability.
5. **The target is unsupported**—the target feels isolated and exposed. Often the target is afraid to report the abuse for fear of retaliation.
6. **The target experiences significant consequences**—the damage to self-concept is long lasting, and the target responds to the abuse with either withdrawal or aggression.

The first three elements focus on the status of the bully. The last three elements focus on the status of the target. Because so much peer interaction is unobserved by adults, we believe that changes in the behavior of the target might be noticed before indications are detected in the behavior of the bully.

An article on bullying behavior among U.S. youth appeared in the *Journal of the American Medical Association*.[26] A representative sample of 15,686 students in grades six through ten in public and private schools throughout the United States completed a self-reporting survey sponsored by the World Health Organization during the spring of 1998. According to the report, a total of 29.9 percent of the sample reported moderate or frequent involvement in bullying: as a bully (13.0 percent), one who was bullied (10.6 percent), or both (6.3 percent).

Males were more likely than females to be both perpetrators and targets of bullying. The frequency of bullying was higher among sixth- through eighth-grade students than among ninth- and tenth-grade students. The study found that both bullies and those bullied demonstrate poorer psychosocial functioning than their noninvolved peers. As to the prevalence of bullying, the report estimated that 5,736,417 youth reported some type of involvement in moderate or frequent bullying. Poorer relationships with classmates and increased loneliness were associated with both being bullied and coincident bullying/being bullied. The report concludes that "The prevalence of bullying among US youth is substantial" and ". . . the issue of bullying merits serious attention, both for future research and preventive intervention." The report did not include data from elementary school students. We strongly believe that prevention strategies should begin in the primary grades.

One of the most significant aspects of the study just described was retrieving information from students who defined themselves as both bullies and being bullied. Frans de Waal, a primatologist at Emory University, thinks we should study the characteristics of the bully and the scapegoat/target simultaneously. In primate groups, he has observed a pattern of interaction whereby those at the top of the hierarchy harass subordinates simply because they can. At the same time, low-ranking members of the hierarchy are selected by the group to become the resident scapegoat. This seemingly innate dance serves a useful purpose for the group. It unites them against a common enemy and serves as a bonding experience. Researchers who have studied family systems have come to similar conclusions about the scapegoating syndrome in families. The most powerful person in the system will begin to target a weaker member and the other family members will join in the game. This gives other weak members a way to solidify their own uncertain position within the family system.

I learned more information about the link between bullying and being bullied from a powerful discussion with prison inmates. STOP Violence! an organization I founded in Kansas City in 1982, sponsors self-help programs for inmates in six correctional facilities in Kansas. I met with members of one of the groups to discuss the topic of bullying and its connection to criminal activity. Following a brief overview of the definition and factors that impact bullying, I opened the meeting for discussion.

DANNY: "When I was young I was picked on all the time by kids at school. I was fat, I wore glasses, and I lacked social skills. I was an obvious target and got no sympathy at home. My father told me to beat the guys up, but I didn't want to fight. My father finally threatened to give me a whipping if didn't stand up for myself. I began by calling them names but that just made them nastier and it wasn't long before I started swinging and became a full-fledged bully myself. Did that have anything to do with why I'm in prison? I'm serving time for aggravated battery."

ROCKY: "I was a target, but not from the kids at school. I was bullied by my six brothers. To look at me, you wouldn't think anyone could beat me up. Being a target isn't always about size. There's always somebody bigger than you. As big as I am, I was the smallest one in my family—the runt of the litter. They all ganged up on me. My Dad abused me the worst. I stored up all of my anger until I was seventeen and then I fought each and every one of them. I came very close to killing my father. They never bothered me again."

BULLIES, TARGETS, & WITNESSES

BEN: "I was bullied a lot. I worked really hard to stay cool and I never fought back. Finally, I reached a boiling point, I was ready to explode but our family moved to California before anything happened. In California, I got beaten up by a big bully and that was a turning point for me. When we moved back to Kansas City I started beating up on the bullies who had picked on me. I took up boxing to gain respect as a fighter and pretty soon the whole thing spiraled out of control. In my neighborhood, you had to be a fighter to be a part of the group and pretty soon it just became a way of life. I've been in prison for fifteen years."

TERRY: "My situation was kind of unusual. I was very competitive with a boy in my class. One day it came to a head and we got into a big fight. The strange thing is that after we fought, he became my best friend."

JIM: "I'm sitting here listening to this conversation and I have something to tell about bullying but it didn't happen when I was young. It's happening now. When I was young I never was a bully and never was a target. I've always been large so kids left me alone. There is an inmate in here that screams at me and talks to me disrespectfully. I've never done anything to him. I have no idea why he wants to bully me. I am a very religious person and I've talked to the Lord about this and his message to me is to ignore it and that's what I've been doing but it hasn't stopped this guy from giving me trouble. Do you have any advice for me?"

I have learned from my contact with hundreds of inmates in this program to trust the wisdom of the group. (The same is true for students!) The following suggestions came forth from the men who had gathered for their weekly meeting:

"Whatever you do, don't ever hit him because you know the price you'll have to pay for that. Just walk away from him whenever he comes up to you."

"It takes a lot more strength to walk away from a fight."

"Don't let him push your buttons. You're a mature man and he's acting like a kid in junior high school. Don't let him get to you."

"Can you ask to be changed to another unit so you don't have to ever be with him?"

"I don't think the answer is to get away from him. I think this is an opportunity for you to figure out how to deal with him. That's what we're supposed to be learning in here—how to build character and handle situations that we might have to face somewhere else."

"You're a religious man. Have you thought of reciting proverbs to him?"

"He's obviously trying to get your attention. Do you think he wants to make a connection with you?"

"That's not as strange as it sounds. He seems to have picked you out for some reason. Maybe he's jealous of you. Maybe he envies the faith you have. Maybe he's trying to put you to the test to see if your religion really works for you."

"You've been ignoring him but you can't ignore what's going on inside of you. If you let it build up, the stress can get the best of you. You're going to have to deal with the feelings that he's bringing up for you."

"If you let him push your button, he gets the victory. You have to believe that how you handle this situation is *your* choice, not his."

"We are witnesses! You've got a group here that can give you some support. Now that we know what's going on, we can work together."

As the discussion came to a close, Jim expressed appreciation for all of the ideas they had generated. He promised to let their suggestions "stew" inside of him and thanked them again. He thanked me for initiating the topic, but it must be obvious that I am grateful to have been present at their meeting and deeply inspired by their thoughtful words.

Bullies

Remember, psychologists Kenneth Dodge, Ph.D., and John Coie, Ph.D.,[27] have described two different styles of aggression in their research with children—reactive and proactive.

The reactive aggressive child is emotional, has poor impulse control, and reacts to an accidental bump as an act of provocation. This child feels constantly threatened and thus believes that his aggressive response is justified. Some researchers suggest that this form of aggression is the most violent.

Proactive aggressive children differ in that they behave in a nonemotional, controlled, deliberate manner. The aggression is delivered with the hope of achieving some goal that comes from within the aggressive child, like coercion or domination, rather than in response to some external threat.

The elitist bully that we describe behaves in a manner more like the proactive aggressive child, but his or her dominating motivation does not stem from internal, sociopathic roots, but rather from the external status bestowed on them.

Most researchers agree that bullies generally become bullies through their life experience, as opposed to being born bullies. Leonard Eron, Ph.D., and Rowell Huesmann, Ph.D.,[28] have been following a large group of students for over thirty years. They say that there are three ideal conditions for learning aggressive behavior: watching others act aggressively, including viewing aggression on television; being rewarded for acting aggressively; and being treated aggressively. These researchers say the patterns for aggressive behavior are already well established by the age of eight.

For many years, the word *bully* conjured up a tough boy beating up smaller kids on the playground. Today, thanks to a number of books about the cruelty of girls, our society is more acutely aware that bullies come in all shapes, sizes, and genders. The viciousness of girls has been exposed, and in another chapter, we will discuss bullying in the context of gender issues more thoroughly.

When I ask students why some kids become bullies, their answers are very astute. Even third- and fourth-grade students have amazing insight into the reasons for bullying behavior. The most frequent observations are:

- They have problems in their family
- They're being abused at home
- Their older brother or sister is picking on them
- They want revenge
- They need attention—maybe their parents are ignoring them
- They want to be noticed
- They want to be popular
- They're bored
- They're mean
- They've been bullied by someone else and now they're going to be the bully

- They've seen something on TV or the movies and they're copying it
- They can get away with it
- If they want to be accepted by a certain group, they have to behave like them
- Peer pressure
- They're really scared inside and they don't want anyone to know that, so they act real tough
- They don't know how to handle their anger
- Maybe one of their parents has died or is sick and they are very sad and they can't handle the pain
- Maybe they just want to be loved but they don't know how to get it
- Maybe they're lonely
- They don't feel good about themselves so they just want everybody else to suffer, too
- They have no self-esteem
- They think it's fun
- They think it's cool
- They're jealous
- They don't know how to get along with people
- Their parents never taught them what was right and what was wrong
- They feel like they can't do anything right so they try to put everybody else down so they can be on the same plane
- They're involved with drugs or alcohol
- They want power
- Bullies want to control everybody else because they can't control themselves

Day after day, session after session, those of us who go into classrooms and do the BullySafeUSA program with students are astounded at the profound understanding that young people have about the dynamics of bullying.

Researchers are more inclined to talk about children who bully using terms such as *aggressive, temperamental, hyperactive, lacking impulse control, loners, having academic problems, disrespectful, behavior disordered, antisocial,* and others that stress their social skill deficits. We are impressed with the students who also pick up on the sorrow, the neediness, the stress, and the pain associated with bullies and speak of them with a sense of compassion as well as fear. The student descriptions help us to see the commonalities that are shared by bullies and targets.

There is one other student observation that deserves notice. Many students have commented that one purpose of bullying, by both sexes, is to attract the attention of the person they are picking on. Students who have a "crush" on someone do not always have the confidence or the language to establish the kind of relationship they would like to have, and in the absence of a tender tactic, they will resort to taunting.

Targets

The title of our first book was *Bullies & Victims*. From our interactions with students and educators, we learned that the word *victim* implies helplessness and powerlessness and excludes the power of hopefulness. Thus, we have chosen to use the term *target* because it implies that you may be the object of an attack, but the assault may not be successful. The arrow, so to speak, may completely miss the intended target or, even if it manages to arrive as intended, it can be deflected. Students definitely prefer the word *target*, although one earnest student suggested that we should have called our book *Bullies & Ducks*. When I reacted with a puzzled look, she went on to explain that she had a teacher who said, "If you walk like a duck, and you talk like a duck, and you act like a duck, you're going to be a duck!" The student said she had observed students who "walk like targets, talk like targets, act like targets, and they are going to be targets!"

The wisdom of that observation is that some students do seem to send a message that attracts bullies. It can be in their body language, their obvious distress or vulnerability—the ways in which they send some kind of a signal to bullies on alert. Gary Ladd, Ph.D., a psychologist in Illinois, conducted a study and discovered that bullies engage in a "shopping" process to find students that will become their preferred targets.[29] Ladd suggests that bullies do not pick on others at random, but use a calculating strategy to narrow their selection. While over half of the students in his study reported being victimized at least once a year, and about 22 percent of the students reported being victimized frequently at the beginning of the school year, by the end of the year only 8 percent of students reported being regularly subjected to a bully's attacks.

There are things that targets can focus on to deny bullies' satisfaction. A study by David Perry, Ph.D., and his colleagues, who have studied victims extensively, say that other, nonvictimized children describe victims as consistently having three qualities that may make them vulnerable to bullies:[30]

1. They are more likely to "reward" their bullies with tangible resources, like giving over lunch money when it is demanded, or giving up the ball they are playing with at recess.

2. They are more likely to show distress, to let the bully know that he or she is getting to the victim. Some children see this as the intangible "reward," which is different from a child's depriving the bully of the gratification of understanding how powerful he or she is by acting indifferent.

3. They are less likely to punish the bully by retaliation.

We have added a fourth quality: They are more likely to explode on cue. In our workshops, when we integrate these findings, we refer to this as the Cry, Comply, Deny, Fly Off the Handle syndrome.

1. **Cry**—It is very important for students to know that bullies thrive on tears. The obvious distress—when they can make someone cry—makes bullies feel very powerful. While crying may be a most legitimate response, postponing tears if at all possible is a strategy to be desired.

2. **Comply**—Targets who willingly relinquish their homework, their lunch money, their lunch, or the ball they are playing with will find the bully coming back to them over and over again because they offer no resistance.

3. **Deny**—Targets who are easily intimidated and pose no threat of identifying their tormentor are more likely to be selected because the bully faces no consequences for his or her behavior. Even when asked, some targets will firmly deny that they have been abused, out of fear of retaliation.

4. **Fly off the handle**—We are grateful to the student who described the following scenario. A bully will turn on the fire under a selected target who, though upset, will keep his/her feelings under control. The bully will back off and come back at a later time and turn the flame up a little higher. At that point, the target begins to unravel but musters every ounce of energy to behave appropriately. The bully will back off and then wait until an adult arrives on the scene. At that moment the bully will turn the flame on full force—causing the target to explode—and succeed in getting the target in trouble for acting out.

Our first task is to raise the child's awareness of when he or she is being bullied. Often, children view bullying as an inescapable hazard of their environment, especially when it is not identified by adults as a problem. Even when their suffering increases, children do not always perceive their abuse as significant. As a behavior, it can be likened to that of a frog that jumps into a pot of boiling water and jumps right out when it becomes aware of its predicament. Another frog, placed in a pot of cold water, senses no danger as the temperature gradually increases. By the time the water comes to a boil, the poor frog is cooked. Likewise, children who are being bullied may not sense when the level of cruelty is being turned up and can find themselves in hot water before they realize their plight.

Researchers have identified two types of targets. Olweus describes them as passive (anxious and insecure) and provocative (hot-tempered and restless). The passive targets appear to do nothing to invite the bully's aggression, and also do not attempt to defend themselves when attacked. The provocative targets create tension by irritating and annoying others and are more likely to fight back when attacked. Provocative targets may have ADHD, Asperger's syndrome, or learning disabilities that prevent them from picking up on social cues other children intuitively understand. These children can irritate others without even realizing it.

One group of researchers took the exploration of the dynamics between rejected targets and other peers one step further. These researchers had students identify other students in their class with whom they enjoyed playing. The students who were *not* listed—the rejected targets—were brought into a new group of students whom they had never met before. The group was given a task to complete together. The rejected students interacted in the new group in two ways that appeared to annoy the other group members: They were more likely to give up or act helpless from the start, and they were more likely to distract the group from the task by drawing attention to themselves. We don't know how the dynamic gets started—whether some kids act like nails, so they get hammered, or if after being hammered long enough some kids begin to look like nails—

but it seems clear that some targets interact with their peers in ways that create difficulties for themselves.

There are even some targets reluctant to relinquish the role of target, when given the opportunity, because they prefer negative attention to no attention at all. They are so starved for recognition, so unwilling to be a cipher, that they tolerate abuse as an affirmation of their existence.

This came to our attention following a student-empowerment session when several fourth-grade boys made a commitment not to pick on a particular target. Instead of being elated, he fretted that no one would talk to him anymore. He could always count on someone to say, "It's math time, now, dummy" or "We're on page twenty-five, stupid." He dreaded the loneliness the new behaviors promised.

We believe, however, that most targets would choose not to be taunted or excluded.

Most students who dread peer rejection would happily trade places with classmates who manage to escape the anxiety and embarrassment that plague their lives.

Of particular concern is the correlation between the boys who participated in multiple school shootings and their experiences as targets. They were not students who had been identified as bullies. Many had suffered in silence until they reached a breaking point. Others gave some warning signs that were noticed only in retrospect. The lesson to be learned from those tragedies is that we need to be vigilant in identifying and supporting children who are being abused by their classmates.

Many therapists have spoken to us about an increase in student clients who are seeking help for depression, sleep disorders, headaches, stomachaches, intestinal problems, personality development, and problems with schoolwork related to bullying. In the first chapter, we reported alarming findings on youth suicide from the Centers for Disease Control and Prevention in Atlanta, Georgia, and the large number who find excuses to stay home from school.

BULLIES, TARGETS, & WITNESSES

When we ask students why some kids become targets, they usually respond, "Because they're different." In response, we have collected a list of "differences." You can become a target if you are too tall or too short, too heavy or too thin, too smart or too slow, too rich or too poor; if you have different color hair, different color skin, if you have a different religion or culture, come from a different country, if you wear glasses, have braces, have freckles, if you stutter or lisp, if you have a physical or mental disability, if someone in your family has a physical or mental disability, if your parents are divorced, if one of your parents has died, if you're adopted, if you're gay or lesbian, if you've just moved to the school, if you've been advanced, if you've been held back a year, if someone in your family is in prison, if your ears or your nose are too big, if you wear clothing that is not fashionable, if you like different kinds of music or have different hobbies than most children, if you have different goals or dreams than others, if you don't know how to get along with people, if you buy your athletic shoes at a discount store, if you have a name that people like to make fun of, and the list goes on and on and on.

Though it is not possible to name every difference between people, the obvious conclusion from this list is that *everyone* is different. Every student in the classroom fits into at least one of those categories, so being different cannot be the sole explanation for bullying. The urge for power can supersede any sense of humanity. If a student thinks that it's cool to be cruel, he or she will always be able to find something about a person to use as an excuse to be cruel to him or her.

Targets need to realize that their "flaw" is not the cause of their torment. We need to help them understand that the problem lies with the bully, not with them. At the same time, we want to assist them to understand how their behavior unwittingly contributes to their vulnerability to bullying.

Witnesses

If studies indicate that 29.9 percent of students are engaged in bullying either as bullies or targets, then potentially 70 percent of students are witnesses. We use the term *witness* to mean anyone who
has ever observed a bullying interaction. One student would not
settle for a mathematical description, however. He said: "Everybody
is a witness at some time." And he is right. But for discussion purposes, let us consider the statistical aspect. Seventy percent is a siz-
able majority. Seventy percent of individuals in any group wields an
enormous amount of influence. We believe that witnesses are the
key to eradicating bullying. They are the group that has the most
information, the most power, and the most opportunities to effect
a solution to the problem.

Not all witnesses who observe an incident react in the same way.
We describe six different kinds of witnesses: Inactive, Angry,
Fearful, Voyeur, Accomplice, and Helpful.

Inactive witnesses are somewhat aware of bullying situations but
they try to avoid them and build a wall around their feelings to
obstruct the pain.

Angry witnesses become annoyed with the targets for not acting
to deflect their bullying. They express contempt for and become
impatient with students who, through inaction, force them to
become an audience to the persistent abuse.

Fearful witnesses confess that it hurts to watch their classmates
being picked on day after day. Many of them have given serious
thought to intervening and confronting the bully, but they fear the
bully will turn on them, so they focus on self-protection. They have
considered reporting the problem to an adult, but they are loath to
be called a snitch or, even worse, to become the object of retaliation.

Voyeur witnesses get some sadistic pleasure out of observing the taunting that occurs. Perhaps they reap some benefit from the realization that they have escaped the cruelty, if only temporarily.

Accomplice witnesses cause the most harm because of their collusion. In order to ingratiate themselves with the bully and avoid being a target, they laugh at the bully's put-downs and become an apt audience. When the bully decides to ostracize a fellow student, they join forces with the bully, giving him or her greater power than he or she could ever obtain on his or her own. Accomplice witnesses give bullies power, status, and popularity they don't deserve. If mature adults can be corrupted by power, imagine the corruption that can occur when twelve-year-olds have more power than they can manage.

Helpful witnesses are the real heroes in this heartbreaking dynamic. Some of them challenge the bully and the taunting ceases. A Canadian researcher, Wendy Craig, believes that the average bullying situation lasts thirty-eight seconds and can best be stopped within ten seconds of the incident.[31] Witnesses can be extremely helpful by supporting a target on the spot or by reaching out to someone who feels helpless and isolated, even if their intervention doesn't make it stop. Helpful witnesses understand the difference between tattling and reporting. As many bright students have said: "Tattling is when you're trying to get someone *in* trouble. Reporting is when you're trying to get someone *out* of trouble." Reporting the situation to an adult may be the most helpful thing a witness can do.

Students are profoundly aware of the fact that most bullying occurs when adults are not around. Bullies can be very clever about choosing the time, place, and person that will produce the greatest reward and least risk. Since students are frequently the only witnesses to the daily horrors, it is essential to help them understand the power they have and to persuade them to take on a major role. There are witnesses who are willing, often eager, to become involved, but they need some reassurance, support, and skill training before they feel comfortable tackling such an awesome task.

Administrators are pointing out that students are much more likely to report rumors or threats of violence than they were in years past. In fact, a survey released in the publication *Save Our Kids* indicates that 81 percent of teens state they are more willing, in the aftermath of Columbine, to report students who threaten their safety. A number of tragedies have been averted. A group of students at Silver Lakes Middle School in North Lauderdale, Florida, alerted administrators about an arsenal of weapons that had been stored underneath the stairs of a portable classroom by two girls, ages twelve and thirteen. According to a report in the Broward County, Florida, newspaper, the two were planning to lure three of their classmates behind the portable classroom to slash their throats with knives. Their motive was revenge. A pager had been taken from one of the girls, passed around the playground, and never returned.

Students at Sickles High School in Tampa, Florida, held a rally in response to a series of bomb threats at their school. They pledged to report any student who placed such a call and the threats stopped. Florida is taking the lead in a national program called Silence Hurts. It came about following the shooting of a middle school teacher by a thirteen-year-old student. A classmate knew that the young murderer had a gun but kept silent. An association of school public relations officials is launching a national campaign with a video documentary featuring interviews with students who have been victims and students who have been motivated to participate in antiviolence programs. In the same Broward County, Florida, newspaper article, it was reported that during the 1998–1999 school year, Broward schools identified 210 cases of weapons possession, the largest number since 1994–1995.

A three-year partnership between the U.S. Department of Education and the U.S. Secret Service resulted in a joint report, the Safe School Initiative.[32] One of the most critical findings was that before more than 75 percent of the incidents, at least one person knew about the attacker's idea or plan to attack. Most attackers also engaged in some behavior that caused others concern or indicated a need for help. In virtually all the cases where someone knew of the plan, the person with advance notice was a peer—a friend, schoolmate, or sibling. In only two cases did an adult know of the idea or plan.

Summary

Students don't clearly fall into separate categories as bullies, targets, and witnesses. We need to view students on a continuum of behavior that often reflects their desire for self-protection. Targets can become bullies, bullies can become targets, and practically every student is a witness to some bullying situation.

Despite the labeling and overlapping, researchers have identified profiles of bullies and targets that can be helpful to us as we reach out to work with students. Language allows us to make a connection with healing possibilities. Bullies are described by researchers as reactive or proactive, and we have added an elitist category. Students describe bullies as lonely, scared, unsure of themselves, vengeful, or dealing with their own abuse. Targets are described by researchers as passive or provocative. Targets are described by students as different, weird, weak, or scared. Bullies cover up their anxiety with a tough exterior, while the targets' apprehension is more exposed. Discussions about these characteristics can deflate bullies and give targets a new perspective, but until we deal with issues of prejudice, diversity, and intolerance, targets will be vulnerable to classroom terrorism. All the more reason to help them understand the signals they send that attract bullying.

We place great emphasis on the role of the witness. We categorize witnesses as inactive, angry, fearful, voyeur, accomplice, and helpful. Because the witnesses have leverage, information, and greater access to occurring situations, we see the potential to coach and mobilize witness power as a key factor in bullying prevention and intervention.

Though student discussions reveal amazing insight into the causes of bullying situations, they can benefit greatly from guided conversation about the differences between joking, teasing, and bullying; the different forms of bullying; the difference between tattling and reporting; and the dimensions and consequences of peer abuse.

With the exception of some physiological or psychological problems that can be helped with medication, counseling, and/or therapeutic activities, bullying is a learned behavior that can be changed, or at least modified. Targets need to feel supported and comfortable with taking more control of peer interactions. Most importantly, witnesses can and are reporting valuable information. They are learning that silence hurts, and they can save lives when they speak up.

CHAPTER THREE

PHYSICAL, VERBAL, EMOTIONAL, AND SEXUAL BULLYING

"When I see bullying I feel really bad for the person that is being picked on and harassed, but then again, I feel good because it is not me being bullied."

—Mandy, a student

Bullying, in reality, is more complex, more lethal, and quite different from the concept of bullying that we are familiar with. Bullying has typically been synonymous with physical abuse. Enlarging adults' and children's understanding of the definition of bullying to include verbal, emotional, and sexual offenses is an ongoing process. But even our concept of physical bullying requires expansion. Added to yesterday's choking, kicking, and fisticuffs, which produced bruises, welts, and broken limbs, are today's stabbings and shootings, which produce gaping wounds, paralysis, lifelong injuries, and death. According to a nationwide survey of high school students in 1999 conducted by the Centers for Disease Control, 9 percent of male students reported carrying a gun to school at least once in the thirty days preceding the survey. The threat of pipe bombs adds to the paranoia that is very real for children. Metal detectors in our schools would have been unthinkable a few decades ago.

Defining verbal abuse also obliges us to broaden our predetermined ideas. Today's children are exposed to a constant lack of civility. Curse words that were culturally verboten yesterday are in common usage today. A survey conducted by a nonprofit research group, Public Agenda, reported that 79 percent of the adults surveyed said a lack of respect and courtesy in American society is a serious problem and more than a third admitted that they use foul language in public.

Lilia Cortina and Vicki Magley, reporting the results of research at a meeting of the APA, found that "in your face" rudeness is rampant in the U.S. workplace.[33] Their study indicated that 71 percent of 1,100 workers surveyed said they'd experienced put-downs or condescending and outright rude behavior on the job. As encounters with uncivil behavior rose, so did symptoms of anxiety and depression. Those who said or did nothing about maltreatment had the worst mental health. These findings are relevant to childhood.

"Trash talk" is accepted as the norm. Models for young people in sports, entertainment, and politics have broken all the boundaries of refined behavior. People who engage in questionable ethics are rewarded with fame, power, and money. No wonder, then, that children imitate our current icons and bring to the playground a kind of social warfare that would have been unthinkable forty or fifty years ago. They also bring to the playground weapons that we could not have imagined in the hands of preteens and adolescents twenty years ago. Young people who haven't developed the maturity to sort out fantasy and reality, short-term and long-term consequences, power and control, are parading in the outer accoutrements of an adult world without the inner character to make good choices.

Paula and I and our colleagues Vicki Price, Sue Farrar, Trish Hardin, Mara Weyforth, Su Randall, and Mary Fischer have devoted numerous years and countless hours to bringing the discussion of bullying into the classroom. I developed BullySafeUSA, a format that stimulates animated conversation, brings clarity and focus to the session, and collects an amazing amount of information in a short period of time. Our mantra is "empower children to break the pain chain." We recognize the crucial role that adults play in bullying prevention and intervention, and part of the task of empowering children is to persuade them to report important information that they alone have, to parents, educators, and trusted adults.

One of the most helpful ways to begin a dialogue with students is to ask students to give examples of physical, verbal, emotional, and sexual bullying. We have conducted these discussions with children as young as first graders, through senior high school. (We do not use the term *sexual bullying* with the younger grades.) Most of our sessions have been with fourth- through eighth-grade students. The data that we will share comes from conversations with over 60,000 students in public, private, parochial, urban, rural, and suburban schools. We have worked in the North, South, East, West, and Midwest, in twenty-nine states and more than sixty-five cities.

Physical Bullying

Students define physical bullying as: punching, shoving, choking, tripping, poking, stabbing, spitting, beating up someone, kicking, throwing an object at someone, pushing someone into a locker, taking someone's lunch money or someone's lunch, giving someone a black eye, tearing someone's clothes, head butting, shooting, swirlies, indian rubs, noogies, nipple twisting, jabbing, throwing someone into a trash can, stepping on someone's toes, urinating on someone, and imitating wrestling holds. One student even reported being held down while cigarette smoke was blown in her mouth until she vomited.

Girls are more likely to slap, pull hair, scratch, pinch, dig their fingernails into someone, or bite. Boys are more likely to punch, choke, kick, throw objects, and use weapons. Boys have mentioned that girls take advantage of their gender, knowing that they can slap, scratch, or pinch with impunity, as it is considered ungentlemanly for the males to retaliate against a female peer. Physical contact of any kind that is hurtful or harmful is a form of physical abuse. Students find it quite easy to give examples. Some of the specifics that students have reported are:

"Some bigger boys made me eat mud. I had to do it and it was disgusting."

"When I was in elementary school, this bully kept sticking me with lead pencils and he would break the pencil off and leave the lead inside my skin."

"These kids would shove me into my locker and then lock the door so I couldn't get out. I would have to pound and scream for someone to rescue me. I was scared and it was so embarrassing."

"A girl got mad at another girl and she took a knife from the science lab and cut her throat while they were in the cafeteria line."

"An older boy would take my lunch money from me every day, so I stopped bringing it to school. Sometimes students would feel sorry for me and give me some of their lunch. A lot of times I just went hungry."

"I read in the paper about this boy that practiced a wrestling hold that he had seen on TV on this younger boy. He snapped the younger boy's spine and now he's paralyzed."

"These girls kept pinching me and I had bruises all over my arms. I was afraid to tell my mother, so I kept wearing long-sleeved blouses and sweaters even when it was hot."

"I was walking up the steps when this boy started pulling on my backpack. I tried to keep my balance but I couldn't. I fell and hit my head on the concrete steps."

"I'm afraid to go to the bathroom at school because once when I walked in, there were three other boys and they decided to push my head in the toilet and then they flushed it. I thought I was going to drown and when I went back into the classroom my hair was all wet but the teacher didn't ask me about it and I was afraid to tell her what happened."

"When I was walking home from school, some boys were throwing rocks at this girl. She was screaming and crying. I wanted to help her but I was scared so I just ran away."

"There was this boy at my school who was in a wheelchair and when he walked, he walked on the sides of his feet. The boys never wanted to play with him because he had a disability. Once he wanted to play kickball with the other guys. They wouldn't let him. They said he was no good because of his legs. One of the boys got so mad he pushed the boy out of his chair and onto the grass and cement."

"I don't know what kind of bullying you call this, but there was this kid, and these other guys would pour Coke over his clothes all the time. It became a game to see who could be the first one to pour Coke on his head. Everyone stayed away from him because they didn't want to get 'Coked.' It was really sad. He committed suicide."

These are just a small sample of the physical bullying stories we've heard. We've heard countless stories about bloody beatings, including fistfights between girls, and tragically, the shootings that are now legend.

Though school violence is decreasing, some new trends are emerging, including the younger age of offending students, the increased use of weapons, and the greater availability of guns. In April 2002, in Chicago, nearly two dozen children ages ten to fourteen were arrested on charges of mob action against students from a nearby school. Their weapons were baseball bats and planks of wood. Their victims were eighteen students who were treated for cuts and bruises at hospitals. The assault occurred on the school playground before school began. While these students used baseball bats and wood planks, a growing number have used guns. According to the Brady Center to Prevent Gun Violence, "In one year, firearms killed zero children in Japan, 19 in Great Britain, 57 in Germany, 109 in France, 153 in Canada and 5,285 in the United States."

Whenever we work with police officers, or peace officers as they are called in some places, they remind us that laws designed to protect adults from the onslaught of physical abuse are invisible where children are concerned. Officer Craig Hermann, a school resource officer at Hocker Grove Middle School in Shawnee Mission, Kansas, was quoted as saying, "Fighting used to be viewed as just part of school. Now we're saying it's serious—that you can't hit people. When you get older and out there in the world, there are serious consequences. We're trying to apply the consequences earlier and head some of them off."

How can we watch all the footage of playground battles aired on national TV shows—children ganging up and kicking a contorted classmate, videotapes of youngsters pummeling a helpless student that make us wince in horror—and not make the connection that this is criminal behavior? How can we go to such lengths to ensure that no adult can be victimized in this way and then dismiss it as a "rite of passage" when the victim is a student?

Verbal Bullying

Verbal bullying can be name-calling, put-downs, threatening, cursing, swearing, yelling, making up stories, gossiping, spreading rumors, talking about someone's mother or another family member, telling "mama" jokes, making fun of someone's physical characteristics, imitating a lisp or a stutter, screaming, being sarcastic, ridiculing, making up a derogatory song, daring someone, whispering about someone as they approach. Any use of language or words to hurt someone would qualify as verbal bullying. We always ask students to finish this sentence: "Sticks and stones can break your bones, but . . ." Every child can complete the phrase with "words can never hurt you." This sentence has been handed down for four or five generations and it isn't true. In our first book, we asked students to change the phrase to "Sticks and stones can break your bones but words can break your heart." Most broken bones will heal in a few weeks, but as the students tell us, a broken heart may never heal. It is very gratifying to go into schools and have students complete the sentence with "words can break your heart" because their teachers or counselors have read our book and have taught them the new ending. A poignant moment occurred when a fourth-grade boy suggested that the saying should be: "Sticks and stones can break your bones, but words can shatter your soul."

We have heard some very touching stories. This is a small sampling:

"I have muscular dystrophy and the kids at school started calling me 'rabie boy.' They said I had rabies and a lot of other things. I cried and cried. It was so depressing. I just wanted to crawl into a ball and die."

"I've been called 'shorty' since I was in the first grade. I'm in the fifth grade now, and I'm still being called shorty, and even some of my best friends do it, too. Some people like to do it because they want me to feel bad all my life, and I guess they got what they wanted."

"I'm a little bit overweight and the kids call me all kinds of names. They call me 'gas bomb,' 'bubba,' and 'fat freak.'"

"When I first came to this country, the Oklahoma bombing had just occurred. In the beginning, people thought that the bombing was caused by Arab terrorists. I am a Muslim and I wear a hajib, the traditional head-covering for Muslim women. When I went to school, students called me a terrorist. I am also thin, and they called me anorexic. I learned how to deal with it but now the same thing is happening to my little sister. She cries every night and I try to comfort her, but I cannot stop the verbal bullying that is happening to her. It hurts me to see her suffer so much and I am reliving my own pain."

"On the bus this group of girls would make fun of me every day because my hair is curly. They called me 'afrohair' and I didn't even know what that meant. But I knew they were trying to hurt my feelings and I hated getting on the bus."

"I always made good grades and that caused a problem for me. Other students would call me names and make fun of me. They called me 'teacher's pet' so I stopped raising my hand when the teacher asked a question."

"I like to wear makeup. Some of the kids spread a rumor that I had AIDS and I was wearing makeup to cover up the sores. I denied it, but nobody believed me. They chose to believe the rumor no matter what I said and everyone avoided me."

"As soon as I would get on the bus, these kids would start swearing and cursing at me. They would yell these words in my ears and all the other kids would laugh. I would hold my hand over my ears but it didn't make any difference. I could still hear what they were saying and I could hear the other kids laughing, too."

"One day when we were on the playground, I said a bad word. This boy overheard me and he threatened to tell the principal if I didn't give him my toys. This went on for weeks. Every day I brought him another one of my toys until I had none left." (This is also an example of exploitation.)

"My father died and I was really depressed. My classmates would tell me to stop feeling sorry for myself and it made me feel even worse."

"When someone calls me 'retard,' they hurt me, but they're also being hurtful to children who are retarded because they can't help it."

Many students have shared their pain about being called names because of their size, their race, their height, a perceived shortcoming of some kind. Frequently, students will talk about how much it hurts to have someone say something about their mother. There is a collection of "mama" jokes that has traveled all across the country. These are some samples: "Your mother is so fat she has to use the highway for a sidewalk." "Your mother is so ugly that when she looked out of the window, she got arrested for mooning." Some students say it doesn't bother them because they know kids are just repeating jokes, but other students reveal that it really gets to them to have someone say something mean about their mother, regardless of the origin.

During a discussion with a very bright fifth-grade class, a girl brought up the subject of daring someone to do something that can be dangerous. When asked if she had a particular situation in mind, she shared a family story. When her father and his brother were in their teens, her uncle dared her father to jump in a river that was swollen with rushing water. Intent to prove that he was not a coward, he jumped in and immediately found himself unable to swim against the water's force. As he was dragged downstream, his brother became terrified and ran for help. Her father survived two miles in treacherous waters before he was rescued. He recounted the story to impress upon his children how important it is not to feel challenged by a dare that puts you at risk. In our community there had been several fatal automobile accidents related to "hill jumping," and there was speculation that some of those fatalities had resulted from dares.

On the subject of rumors, a middle school girl raised her hand one time to ask about "spreading the truth." When asked to elaborate, she said: "What if you confide a secret to a friend and ask her not to tell anyone and then she betrays you and tells everyone in the class what you told her? Does that count as verbal bullying?" Students, when asked, will almost always confirm that they consider betrayal of a secret a form of verbal bullying. One student raised the question, if the secret is a confession of being abused, shouldn't you tell someone? That was an important difference to make, but everyone agreed that the best procedure might be to tell a counselor or the principal, but certainly not other classmates.

An adult who was present during a discussion of "spreading the truth" related a personal story and asked that we share it with future classes. She said that when she was in the third grade, a friend invited her to her very first sleepover. She had never slept at someone else's home, and she was quite excited about the prospect. She recalled the thrill of packing her suitcase and putting in her pajamas, toothbrush, and clean clothing. She said she knew she was excited— what she didn't realize was that she was nervous. That night, for the first time, she wet the bed. She was so embarrassed. But the worst was yet to come. When she and her hostess returned to school, the hostess told everyone about her accident. As she said: "My friend didn't make up a story about me, she didn't spread a rumor about me, all she did was tell the truth—but no one ever invited me to spend the night with them during all my years of school."

The following story was shared by an anguished mother of a target who is still reeling from the events. Because of the bullying her daughter had experienced, she attempted suicide with over-the-counter-drugs. Her bullies spread a rumor that the target was in the hospital because she had overdosed on crack and proceeded to sneak into the hospital to further their verbal attacks on her.

The Internet enables us to find new ways to taunt—techno-bullying. Students are reporting a variety of ways in which access to the Internet has produced appalling acts of cruelty. For example, one student found a way to gain another student's password and proceeded to send a series of hateful letters to classmates from the unknowing student. She had no idea why her peers suddenly turned on her with tremendous anger. In another incident, a boy posted a horrific essay about a girl on a Web site that invited visitors to express hatred about anyone or anything. Word spread about this essay and soon it was the talk of the school. Although the posting had not occurred at school, a school administrator checked out the site after a number of students brought it to his attention. The essay was so cruel and damaging that school officials felt some responsibility to intervene. They met with the girl involved, and then the boy, and both sets of parents. The boy felt deep remorse when he realized that what had seemed an impulsive and insignificant act had had such a profound effect on the girl. He contacted the Web site manager and asked to have the essay removed, but the Web site manager refused, saying that to do so would be a violation of free speech and would constitute censorship.

And then there are Web pages on the Internet where students can make stinging, anonymous comments for all the viewers to read. Several students have expressed special disdain for the cowardice of those who would capitalize on computer anonymity to be hurtful.

Emotional Bullying

We define emotional bullying as a type of abuse in which there is no physical contact and no words are exchanged. There are two categories of emotional bullying: nonverbal and psychological. Nonverbal emotional bullying is pointing, staring, mugging, laughing, rolling your eyes, making faces, sticking out your tongue, writing notes, drawing pictures, flicking people off, using the third finger or a number of other hand signs that imply "loser," "crazy," or irreverent and sexual innuendos.

Psychological emotional bullying comes in the form of indirect abuse such as exclusion, isolation, rejection, turning your back on someone when they try to talk with you, shunning, ostracizing, and ignoring. It may be subtle, or it may be overt. Sometimes these natural schisms form between girls who are becoming more interested in boys and girls who still want to spend most of their time with other girls. Frequently, however, this heartbreaking form of abuse is intentional and without apparent reason. While not exclusive to girls, this type of bullying is inflicted more habitually by female students.

I often tell children that when someone commits a crime in our society, we send them to prison. Prison officials had to come up with something worse than incarceration for those who break a law while they are jailed, so they created solitary confinement. One of the cruelest forms of punishment that humans can inflict on one another is total isolation. Prisoners of war who have been physically tortured and isolated state that the isolation is at least as bad, if not worse, than the physical torture. John McCain, a U.S. senator from Arizona and a former prisoner of war, recounts that he and his fellow prisoners devised an elaborate communication system so they would not feel so alone during their internment. It appears that the places in our society where isolation is most likely to happen are prisons and playgrounds!

Some examples from students of nonverbal emotional bullying are:

"When I would walk into class, these girls would start whispering to each other and looking right at me. I had no idea what they were saying but I knew it wasn't nice and it would freak me out."

"If the teacher calls on me to read, I get real nervous. I start to stutter and the kids giggle and roll their eyes. I always pray she won't call on me."

"Last year, whenever these kids saw me they would make a sign with their fingers that stood for 'Loser.' Pretty soon, other kids started doing it, too. I was so miserable. I tried to ignore them but they would just make the sign more obvious. It was a horrible year for me."

"This boy would come up to me and make a fist in my face like he was going to hit me. He didn't ever hit me but I knew he could punch me out if he wanted to. I was scared but I couldn't tell anyone because he never hit me."

"Mugging is the worst! It's when somebody stares at you but they start at the top of your head and go all the way down and back up again. You feel like they're undressing you with their eyes."

Some student examples of psychological aspects of emotional bullying are:

"I always wanted to belong to this one group. It was the most popular clique at school and I would have given anything to be

part of it. One day the leader asked me to become a member. I was absolutely thrilled. The next day, the girls in the group started asking me all kinds of personal questions about myself. I thought that this was how you got to be their friend, by telling them whatever information they wanted to know. After they 'sucked me dry' of everything they wanted to know, they dropped me, blabbed about me to everyone, and completely rejected me."

"It was my birthday and my mother and I talked it over and we decided to invite the whole class so no one's feelings would be hurt. We went to the store and got favors and cupcakes for everyone. We blew up a lot of balloons, and the day of the party, I waited and waited and nobody came."

"I saw this crumpled note on the floor, so I picked it up to throw it away and I saw that it was about me! My closest friend had written it. She wrote that I talked about my mother dying of cancer because I just wanted attention. How could anyone think that I shared something about my mother's illness because I wanted attention! It hurt even more because I thought that she was my friend."

"This girl in my class passed out invitations at school to come to her roller-skating party. There was just one other girl besides me who didn't get an invitation. At recess and lunch everybody talked about going roller skating, and I just wanted to die but I had to pretend like it wasn't bothering me."

"One day I went through the cafeteria line and put my tray down at a table where a group of boys was sitting. As soon as I sat down, they all got up and took their trays to another table. I'll never forget the humiliation."

"The gym teacher always lets the best athletes be the team captains. Then each captain picks the players. I'm not good at sports and nobody ever wants me on their team, so I always get picked last. This happens every gym period, year after year. I wish the gym teacher would select teams a different way."

"There was this group of kids standing together in the hall. I called out to them 'cause I wanted to join up with them and they just turned their backs on me—in front of everyone."

The concept of emotional bullying is the most challenging of the four types to transmit. It is hard for the students to grasp and understand in a few sentences because it is a new idea for many of them. As one child advocate, Dorothy Dean, stated, "Emotional abuse is the most difficult type of abuse to define and diagnose. Physical abuse, and some sexual abuse, involves tangible or observable evidence, which can be documented and verified. The victim, if old enough, can describe what occurred. Emotional abuse, however, is intangible. The wounds are internal but they may be more devastating and crippling than any other form of abuse."

Sexual Bullying

Examples of physical sexual bullying that students have described include touching someone in an inappropriate place, lifting up a girl's skirt or pulling down a boy's pants, pushing a boy and a girl together so their bodies touch, brushing against a person on purpose, grabbing a girl's breasts, pinching someone's butt, pulling a girl's bra strap, kicking a boy in his private parts, hugging or kissing someone when they don't wish to be hugged or kissed, and rape. Students frequently use the term *harassment*, without knowing what the term means, but one student gave a very professional answer: Sexual harassment is unwelcome sexual behavior that makes you feel uncomfortable or unsafe. One boy wanted to distinguish touching *with* consent from touching *without* consent. Concerns of mine would be interpretation of consent ("She said 'no' but she didn't really mean it") and reluctant consent to gain popularity.

One example that came to my attention was the case of a boy who was stripped down to his underwear in the locker room and then thrown out into the hall as students were going from one class to the next. This was described during a discussion with a large group of middle school students. When it was mentioned, all the students howled with laughter except for one boy whose face was contorted in pain. It was obvious who had been "pantsed."

When elementary school students offered "rape" as an answer, I would remind them that I had asked for examples of sexual bullying at their age level and therefore rape was not appropriate for our discussion. On one occasion when I gave this little speech, the teacher followed me out into the hall when the session was over and told me that one of the girls in the fifth grade had been raped.

Students have spoken of sexual bullying that is also emotional. This can come in the form of pressuring someone to engage in sexual activity that makes him or her feel uncomfortable. It can be certain hand and finger gestures, or licking lips in a suggestive way. One young girl reported that someone kept thrusting pictures of naked people in her face. It can be whistles or rude noises. Girls have also spoken about being manipulated or "used" so the male can brag about his sexual conquests to peers. Boys can be pressured by their peers to earn "stud" status. They feel they have to insist on having sex with a girl or pretend that they have, to escape being branded as gay. One boy arranged to have a videotape made of himself and his girlfriend having sex, unbeknownst to her, to show to his friends.

Sexual emotional bullying can also be a form of gender discrimination—not allowing someone to do something because they are male or female, such as team sports. Children mention this with great frequency.

Some girls become very competitive about boys in middle school and high school. A lot of bullying between girls at that age revolves around boys. Girls who have a conversation with another girl's boyfriend risk getting threatened or screamed at. Girls have been known to try to break up relationships because of jealousy or revenge. This territorial aspect of bullying appears to be more common among teenage girls than boys.

Most sexual bullying is male to female or male to male but it can also be female to female. A principal told me of a situation where she called thirty-five girls into her office to resolve a sexual bullying problem. The girls were ridiculing a girl whose breasts jiggled when she ran. The principal dealt with the incident by confronting the entire gym class and letting them know that such taunting would not be tolerated.

Many people who work with teenagers are concerned about the widespread practice of oral sex among teenagers. Even teenagers as young as twelve and thirteen are experimenting with this activity. Many teenagers engaging in oral sex do not really consider this sex at all, or consider it a form of safe sex. On the *Oprah Winfrey Show* in May 2002, several teenagers, male and female, appeared on the program with Oprah and Dr. Phil McGraw and openly discussed their participation in oral sex. One girl explained that kissing a boy on a date was a bigger deal than giving oral sex to boys in the bathroom or on the school bus.

What most commentators on this subject fail to mention is that in the vast majority of oral sex encounters, it is the girl who performs oral sex on the boy. So, while many adults are describing this as a new phenomenon, a new form of teenage sexual exploration, it appears to be just another variation on a familiar theme, where girls try to please boys with sexual activity. The same double standard continues to exist, as well. Later, on the same episode of the *Oprah Winfrey Show*, the young woman who had been so nonchalant about oral sex was clearly distressed to hear several male teenagers say they would never ask a girl to the prom or introduce a girl to their parents who had performed oral sex on multiple partners. Obviously, many girls are performing oral sex voluntarily, but the asymmetry of boys' and girls' experience, and the significantly different consequences for each gender in terms of reputation, suggests an imbalance of power in these relationships. We think this warrants inclusion in our discussion of sexual bullying. Some might question whether oral sex is sexual bullying if it is voluntary and noncoercive, but if young girls are unaware of the possible consequences of herpes, sexually transmitted diseases, and AIDS, or if they are willing to forfeit their health for the sake of popularity, we see this as sexual exploitation.

Then there is the category of sexual bullying that is verbal. In third or fourth grade, if boys and girls even have a conversation with someone of the opposite sex, kids will sing songs like: "Keith and Kayla sitting in a tree, k-i-s-s-i-n-g." By sixth grade it's dirty jokes and obscene phone calls. One boy spoke about some awful graffiti in the boys' bathroom. Guys would write on the walls that some girl was a "slut" and then other boys would add really nasty comments about things she supposedly did. He said, "These girls would die if they knew what was being written about them."

Sexual bullying can be calling someone the name of a body part or ridiculing someone because they have developed more quickly or more slowly than his or her peers. This has been mentioned by girls on many occasions. They have spoken of being called "cows" or "pancakes." As young people approach puberty and hormonal changes take over, they become extremely sensitive about their bodies. It is a time of confusion, stress, and anxiety. Sexual bullying can be spreading sexual rumors about someone that are untrue but wholly believed because of the salacious interest. Another facet of

64

verbal sexual bullying is the use of words like *gay, queer, faggot, homo, pussy, wuss, pervert, punk, lesbo, tramp, slut, whore, ho, trick, hoochie mama, dyke,* and *bitch.* A word like *sissy,* common a generation ago, has been replaced with *buttf---er.* This kind of language is rampant and pervasive, beginning in elementary schools.

I used to be tentative about mentioning some of these words if they were not forthcoming from the students, but circumstances have changed that reluctance. In many cases of multiple school shootings, the particular form of taunting that pushed boys over the edge was the relentless tagging of being a "homo," a "fag," a "pussy," or some other sexually pejorative term. Sometimes students will try to deny the meanness of the word *gay* by claiming that they were just referring to the person as "happy." My response to that disclaimer is to suggest that if you are wishing to offer a compliment for their cheerfulness, be sure to use words that can't be interpreted any other way. Dodging the slur is *not* acceptable.

In a discussion with seventh graders one morning, one boy asked if it was bullying to call someone gay who is gay. This led to a conversation about the climate in the school. Are students who are gay accepted by their peers? Do gay students feel comfortable acknowledging their sexual preference? Would a gay student hear the comment as one of respected recognition or intended humiliation? Our ongoing pitch to children is to inform them of the possible consequences of intentional hurtfulness. They need to know that if they inflict pain on someone, it does not evaporate; it does not disappear—most likely it collects. When enough pain has collected in a person's soul, it can turn to rage. As Dr. Karl Menninger stated at a Kansas Mental Health Association conference many years ago, "Some people turn the rage inward and commit suicide, other people turn the rage outward and commit homicide." Our task is to stop the pain!

At a workshop conducted for professionals, a therapist who works with sex offenders reported to me that 75 percent of the sex offenders that she had worked with disclosed that they had been bullied about their sexuality when they were in school and felt they had to prove their sexuality to themselves and others.

These are challenging issues to address with students, and we know of teachers and administrators who would prefer to avoid them altogether. The fact that students consistently raise these issues with me, often taking great risks in front of their peers to do so, compels me to match their courage with my own. Too many innocent children pay a price for our unwillingness to confront the sexual behavior that happens in our schools.

At the end of every discussion on the four types of bullying—physical, verbal, emotional, and sexual—we ask the students to vote for the type of bullying that is most common at their school. Physical bullying hardly ever gets any votes. When a fight does break out, it is obvious and intervention occurs almost immediately. Not so with verbal bullying. The majority of students vote for verbal bullying as the most pervasive form of abuse.

A nationally representative group of 1,001 young people in the fifth through twelfth grades was asked this question: "If you could make ONE change that would help stop the violence that young people experience today, what would that change be?" Their responses were published in *Youth and Violence: Students Speak out for a More Civil Society.* The largest proportion of young people talk about teasing that goes beyond playful, cruel put-downs and gossip, and rejections as very real violence to them. In the words of one young person, "The one thing I would change is gossiping/talking behind people's back in a negative way. That tends to start 90 percent of the violence at school."

A second issue that emerged was: "A seemingly inescapable culture that celebrates sameness." One student urged: "Help students understand that we are all different and should be treated equally."

The third major finding was that young people with better relationships with mothers, with fathers, with teachers, and with friends are much less likely to experience violence, either as victims or as aggressors. Positive support from important people in kids' lives is a defining quality of civil society.

In addition, many students call for measures to keep them safe, such as gun control, better security, and stricter punishments.

Teachers as a group tend to vote for emotional bullying as the most pervasive form. Fewer students vote for emotional bullying. I am not sure how to interpret that, as it definitely ranks as a serious problem. It could be that the verbal bullying is prevalent to such an extreme, or it could be that they have not fully integrated a rather new, more complex definition of bullying into their choices.

When I ask for a vote on which of the four kinds of bullying causes the most stress or concern, there has been a consistent vote all across the country by students for sexual bullying. Middle school students have always identified sexual bullying as a major issue, but in the last two years or so, even fourth, fifth, and sixth graders are casting their votes for sexual bullying.

At one school, a counselor was so shocked with the response of sexual bullying by the fourth-grade classes that she suggested that I call for the vote in reverse order to see if changing the order would change the vote. I changed the order with the next fourth-grade class. The vote remained the same.

Summary

We've explored various ways in which children cause each other pain. Physical bullying, the most obvious form of cruelty, is the easiest to confront. It is more challenging to prevent and intervene in verbal, emotional, and sexual peer abuse. Here again categories overlap. Verbal abuse can provoke physical bullying. Verbal cruelty can cause psychological consequences. Sexual bullying can be physical, verbal, and/or emotional. Verbal bullying is the most common form of peer abuse, by far. Sexual bullying causes the most stress and has proven to be lethal in some cases.

Bringing children and adults to a more sophisticated understanding of the definitions and dimensions of bullying is an essential step in any long-range plan to reduce and/or eliminate peer abuse.

CHAPTER FOUR

BULLYING IN A SOCIAL CONTEXT

"Now I think of things differently. You never know how long someone may live. If you bully someone, the next day they may be gone. A person only lives on Earth a short time, so why make it miserable?

—Emily, a student

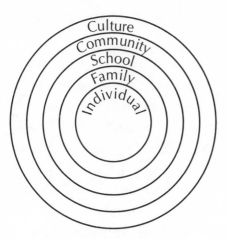

The Complex Factors Affecting Bullying

Children who are engaged in bullying are affected by a number of factors, best pictured as five concentric circles. Each circle represents a significant element, beginning with the individual child viewed in the context of family, school, community, and culture.

69

Individual

Research on brain development in the past fifteen years has given us astounding information about the profound influence of early experiences on newborn babies.[34] The brain is the only organ in the body that is not fully developed at birth and changes dramatically as the baby interacts with its environment. Babies are born with approximately 100 billion brain cells, or neurons, more than they will ever use. Those cells that are not stimulated or used in the first years of life will disappear, which is why so much emphasis is being placed on these precious early years. Scientists have shown that there are sensitive periods, "windows of opportunity," of brain development for certain abilities such as vision, speech, language, and movement. Once those windows of opportunity close, learning can take longer and be more difficult. Some abilities can be permanently lost.

While some brain researchers search for biological roots of violence, others believe that the nature versus nurture theory is not either/or, but both/and. In addition to the brain research, the innermost circle also looks at genetic factors, specific personality traits, physical characteristics, risk factors, and behaviors of the individual child. Personality traits include shyness, outgoingness, contentedness, irritability, patience, resourcefulness, and determination. Even identical twins have distinct personalities. Risk factors could include fetal alcohol syndrome, HIV, or retardation. Physical characteristics have to do with size, attractiveness, and whether a child is healthy, colicky, or has a disability of some kind. Behaviors can include passivity, aggression, and responsiveness. Each of these qualities, alone and in combination with others, influences a child's interactions with others. Some children have attributes that will be helpful in their relationships, while other children have traits and behaviors that make forming relationships more difficult. Nature and nurture combine to have long-lasting effects.

Family

Important studies have shown that secure attachment is essential for the healthy development of a child. Attachment between the infant and the primary caregiver is so crucial that when severe deprivation and neglect occur within the first two or three years of life, there are serious consequences for brain and psychosocial development. These consequences include the development of empathy, trust, and reciprocity. A baby is so completely dependent on the parent or caregiver that when those responsible adults are not capable of meeting their child's needs because of immaturity, limited mental ability or mental illness, alcoholism, drug addiction, domestic violence, and/or overwhelming grief, the child faces a grim future unless care is assumed by someone more capable.

Because we have become such a transient society, the extended family support network is often not available the way it once was when families congregated together in neighborhoods and communities. Too often, new mothers feel isolated, overwhelmed, and unprepared to deal with the responsibility and the exhaustion that go hand-in-hand with early motherhood. In response to this void, a number of important home visiting programs have been developed to support new parents. Two effective programs are Parents as Teachers and Healthy Families America.

Parents as Teachers (PAT) was created under the direction of Mildred Winter in 1981 for the Missouri Department of Education. She realized that by the time some children arrived at school at the age of five or six, they had deficits in cognitive, social, and health development that required a significant response from the school system.

Winter wanted to focus on prevention. She believed that parents want to be good parents and would be receptive to valuable support that would assist them to become their children's best first teachers. The idea is to train parent educators to serve as coaches, resources, and trusted family friends who could serve a family from birth to three years, after which time less extensive services would be offered for an additional two years. The program offers personal visits, group meetings, developmental screenings, and resource referrals. The program is voluntary, free, and usually offered through the school system. Parents register to receive the service at the PAT site in their school district. In a number of states it is funded by the state Department of Education through the legislature. Unfortunately, access to the program is limited by available funding. Because of budget constraints, some communities who provide the program often have waiting lists.

A similar program provided to families who are identified as high risk, is Healthy Families America. Healthy Families America trains home visitors to work with parents whose backgrounds and circumstances might put them at risk for abusive behavior. The home visitors work more intensely with their assigned families, but this program is also voluntary and free. The Healthy Families program was developed in Hawaii by a pediatrician, Calvin Sia, M.D., in 1975 and is usually connected to public health systems and hospitals where a risk assessment screening takes place. Prevent Child Abuse America has mobilized to make this a national program. Both programs have strong research components and have proven to be well worth the investment in early parenting.

Head Start, a nationally recognized program, credited to child expert Ed Ziegler, M.D., has been funded for many years by the federal government as an important primary prevention program for low-income families.

Family systems vary. One parent, two parents, divorced parents, no parents, stepparents, multiple foster parents, adoptive families, traditional families, nontraditional families, homeless families, families dealing with illness, families dealing with absent parents, families dealing with loss, the number of siblings, absence of siblings, and sibling issues are all variables that affect children's functioning.

Similarly, discipline practices run the gamut in homes. Parents use varying discipline styles, including authoritarian, flexible, rigid, abusive, and/or negligent. Marked parental inconsistency, when a parent overlooks misbehavior one day and then exacts an unjust punishment for the very same behavior the next day, appears to create significant difficulties for children. All of these variables can profoundly influence children's interactions with others.

Some families falter under the pressure of unemployment, chronic illness, or abuse, while other families are relatively free of such burdens. Families can rise to challenges presented or they can be defeated. Families can tap inner and external resources, find strengths in each other, muster the energy the moment requires, or become exhausted and debilitated. Families can deepen bonds, develop fierce loyalty, become advocates for their children, or they can buckle under the strain, causing relationships to become permanently severed. Parents can boost their children's confidence and esteem, develop reasonable objectivity about their offspring, or deny any negative qualities and become defensive when confronted.

By the time children reach school age, they have accumulated years of painful or wonderful experiences in their families—experiences that will play havoc or serve them well in this completely new culture.

School

The school culture is composed of varying elements—the physical environment; the quality and morale of the faculty; the teacher-to-student ratio; the presence and role of ancillary staff such as counselors, psychologists, social workers, school nurses, and art, dance, music, and physical education instructors; financial resources; textbook and technology resources; and the administrative style and personality of the principal. But the school culture is also inextricably tied to the particular families and their children who attend classes.

Some schools address safety concerns with external emphases on fences, identification badges, metal detectors, drug-sniffing dogs, surveillance cameras, security officers on campus, and emergency plans, for example. Other schools emphasize a more internal focus, including awareness of students' distress, disciplinary philosophy of the school staff, willingness of the staff to intervene in student conflicts, staff members' ability to handle their aggressive feelings, and tolerance or intolerance of abusive behavior.

Schools can extend safety concerns by developing policies about bullying, establishing clear rules and consequences, introducing programs and curriculum to modify school culture, making school counselors and nurses a personnel priority, and providing support for teachers who take a strong position against bullying.

Schools are sandwiched between the influences of the individual and family characteristics on one side and the community and cultural characteristics on the other. They are bombarded from both sides by ever-changing personalities, policies, and political winds. We expect them to be a stable foundation, a bulwark of our learning tradition. But legislators, superintendents, school boards, and constituents all claim authority for the educational cornerstone of our society. Such awesome responsibility and such diffused accountability!

In these hallowed halls our children count on their teachers, counselors, and principals to provide the security and support they deserve, to anchor them as they explore a universe of subject matter just beyond their reach. Their peers have enormous influence. All the factors of an ideal school setting can be in place, but the presence of classmates who terrify or abandon one another can turn school into a nightmare experience, leaving a lifetime of scars.

Community

Community can refer to a borough, a neighborhood, a parish, a political or geographic boundary. It can encompass the presence of Boys and Girls Clubs; Scout troops; athletic leagues; churches, synagogues, temples, and/or mosques; the quality of the medical, psychological, educational, and social service delivery systems; diversity of age, ethnicity, and economics; rural, urban, or suburban features; the abundance or lack of athletic, artistic, and cultural experiences. These elements and many more shape the social environment in which young people develop their interactive styles.

Each community has its own distinct personality and unique set of demographics. For instance, in the California wine country, community schools are populated by the children of wealthy vineyard owners on one end of the economic spectrum and children of migrant workers on the other. Economic, language, and cultural factors create a very special mix of students and families, which requires schools to address this special agenda.

Communities where layoffs abound during times of recession, where homeless youth face unconscionable burdens, where crime and drugs terrorize and seduce innocent children, where despair shrouds daily functioning, where immigrant families have migrated, where limited resources and overwhelmed parents are the norm must be taken into account by the educators and administrators who are determined to instill enthusiasm for learning in the boys and girls who struggle to survive.

Private schools that benefit from exceptional facilities, highly motivated students, engaged parents, and extraordinary resources are often faced with special situations that accompany affluence. Parents can put undue pressure on their children to be accepted into the most prestigious colleges and universities. Competition anxiety can have a deleterious effect on self-esteem and peer relationships. The social strata of the parents can spill over into the power issues of students struggling to find their niche, including tensions that arise when the children of generous patrons are treated deferentially.

Community attitudes can have great bearing and influence on what kinds of interpersonal relationships, styles and behaviors are considered acceptable or normal.

Culture

Cultural influences envelop the child, the family, and the community. Bruce Perry, Ph.D., believes that "the biological unit of survival for human beings is the clan."[35] The clan, or the family, is in great distress these days. The family anchor that society counted on to instill the necessary values and skills in its own children, and our collective children is not as imbedded as it once was. Parents spend 40 percent less time with their children than they did thirty years ago. Many conflicting values are bobbing around in the atmosphere, creating mixed messages for young people, especially when it comes to violence.

Other important factors include the cultural attitudes toward racism, sexism, gender identity, and poverty; cynicism or hopefulness about our ability to solve problems; consumerism; the role of the media in shaping the values of our society; and access to weapons.

Consumerism is a subtle but prickly element in the social context of bullying. The November/December 2000 issue of Sierra magazine reports that the average American child watches more than 20,000 TV ads a year. From infancy, children are exposed to seductive ads that urge them to eat brand-name cereals and play with specific toys. In 1999, the U.S. toy industry spent more than $840 million to advertise its products to parents and children, about $3 for every man, woman, and child in this country. Teens and preteens are also encouraged to wear faddish clothing, buy certain athletic shoes, and flaunt the status symbols of their peer group. Jealousy is mentioned invariably as a motivation of bullies. The power of advertising combined with the driving need to "fit in" cannot be ignored.

According to a news report from Knight Ridder newspapers, a large body of research data has confirmed the correlation between TV watching and aggressive behavior. A study followed 707 children in upstate New York for seventeen years. The researchers documented the viewing habits of the students beginning in 1983 when they were fourteen years old, and again eight years later, when they were well into adulthood. Teens who watched three or more hours of TV a day were five times more likely to commit aggressive acts in the next several years as those who watched less than one hour a day. Among those who watched TV less than one hour a day in 1983, fewer than 6 percent were found to have committed an aggressive act in the next eight years, compared with 22.5 percent of those who watched one to three hours, and 28.8 percent of those who watched more than three hours daily. Acts considered aggressive were assaults resulting in injury, threats of violence, robberies, and use of a weapon in a crime. The research was distinct from other studies because it linked TV viewing in general—not just viewing of violent programs—to later aggression. "Our study suggests that kids would be better off if they watched less than one hour a day, on average," said the lead author, Jeffrey G. Johnson of Columbia University. "And this is not just for little kids, but through adolescence."[36]

The American Medical Association contends that media violence:

- causes an increase in mean-spirited, aggressive behavior
- causes increased levels of fearfulness, mistrust, and self-protective behavior toward others
- contributes to desensitization and callousness to the effects of violence and the suffering of others

- provides violent heroes whom children seek to emulate
- provides justification for resorting to violence when children think they are right
- creates an increasing appetite for viewing more violence and more extreme violence
- fosters a culture in which disrespectful behavior becomes a legitimate way for people to treat each other

One-third of young male felons imprisoned for homicide, rape, and assault report that they consciously imitated techniques learned from TV programs. Since 1982, TV violence has increased 780 percent. During the same time, aggressive acts on the playground increased by 800 percent.

David Walsh, coauthor of a new study, observed: "Whoever tells the stories defines the culture. This study shows that the class bullies may be getting their lessons from the screen. If we think Sesame Street taught our 4-year-olds something, we better believe WWE Smack Down is teaching our 11-year-olds something."[37] When students tell me that they rush home from school to watch *Jerry Springer,* I wonder what they are learning from *that* program.

When I was traveling with some bright high school students on their way to a national academic competition, I couldn't resist inquiring about their bullying experiences. They began by describing student groupings in their school. They told me that students fell into the following categories:

1ST GROUP—Athletes/student government
2ND GROUP—Academic/band
3RD GROUP—Theater/arts (most of the gay and lesbian students were in this group)
4TH GROUP—Outcasts

Our conversation turned to the influence of the media on youth behavior. They vehemently denied that television, movies, music, and video games affect the way teenagers behave. As one student said: "No matter what I watch, I would never kill someone." They assured me that media provides them with entertainment but wields no influence on their values. Assuming that their moral principles came from their parents, I asked them if they had any concerns about students viewing violent images who hadn't received a strong value system from their parents. Keith, a thoughtful junior, replied that his ethical foundation didn't come from his parents. When I asked where indeed his values came from, he pondered for a long time and replied: "Captain Picard—*Star Trek: The Next Generation*." So much for no influence.

It is not only television that has the power to transform children's behavior. There are movies, video games, music, and the Internet. Most parents would be horrified at the language and the urging to rape and kill that are wrapped into the music of some of the most popular rap artists. Video arcades provide unlimited hours of target practice for children who acquire deadly accuracy with virtual guns that can be easily transferred to genuine shotguns, rifles, and handguns. The average child has witnessed 8,000 murders—through television, video games, and the Internet—by the time he or she finishes elementary school, according to Jerome Freiberg of the University of Houston.

According to the American Academy of Pediatrics, one child is killed with a loaded gun every ninety minutes. The *Child Protection Leader*, a publication of the American Humane Association, reports that an average of twelve children are killed each day by guns in the United States. In 1997, 4,223 children and teenagers were killed by guns. This figure from the National Center for Health Statistics does not even include the number of children injured or permanently maimed by firearms. An estimated 22 million children in the United States live in homes where there are firearms, and it is estimated that guns are not kept locked up or fitted with trigger locks in 43 percent of those homes. Guns are available to children in the communities they reside in as well as their homes. This ease of accessibility in our country contributes to the rate of child homicides involving a firearm being *sixteen times greater* than in twenty-six other industrialized countries combined. For suicides of children under age fifteen involving firearms, the U.S. rate was almost eleven times the rate of the other countries combined.

Children's Voice, published by the Child Welfare League of America, has amassed important data on the subject of children and guns. Since 1979, more than 80,000 American children and adolescents have been killed by guns, according to the National Center for Health Statistics—far more than the number of Americans who died in the Vietnam or Korean wars.[38] Homes with guns can be dangerous for children. According to the National Safe Kids Campaign, 306 young people were killed accidentally with guns in 1997—nearly all in or around the home. A 1996 survey by the Office of Juvenile Delinquency found that 29 percent of males in the tenth and eleventh grades possessed a gun.

In a Centers for Disease Control and Prevention survey of 1,000 inner-city middle and high school students in Chicago, 23 percent reported having seen someone murdered; 40 percent of the victims were people they knew.

A survey released by the Louis Harris Research firm in 1993 says that 59 percent of school children in sixth through twelfth grade say they "could get a handgun if they wanted one." More than a third say they could get one "within an hour." Is it any wonder that our children can put their hands on a gun so readily when Americans privately own an estimated 200 million firearms—revolvers, pistols, rifles, shotguns, and assault weapons, and BB, dart, and pellet guns? Some 25 million households have handguns.

At an international conference on violence in Paris in March 2001, Eric Debarieux, founder of the European Observatory of School Violence and one of the conference organizers, said the bottom line on violence in American schools is the availability of guns. "It is a problem of the commerce of arms. As long as the United States hasn't regulated the sale of arms, we will have this type of thing." Experts hold that a national culture of violence as well as large schools that breed alienation are among the culprits behind school shootings in the United States.

As long as violence is honored for its entertainment value, as long as our appetite for gratuitous acts of cruelty against each other compels us to support commercial products and ventures that glorify violence, as long as violence is encouraged by witnesses who are excited and stimulated by fighting, bleeding, and mauling, we have every reason to be fearful about the fallout of such horror. And these attitudes are formed very early. An illustrative incident occurred on an elementary school playground. Two young boys traded a couple of punches, which might have concluded immediately except that a group of children formed a circle around the fighters and became an encouraging audience. The two boys responded to the shouts of the crowd—"Hit him harder," "Kick him in the stomach," "Make him bleed"—and a recess scrap turned into a full-blown boxing match without benefit of gloves or referees. One of the boys became seriously injured.

Another form of crowd psychology is the isolation of someone who is different. Once a small group (even two or three) decides not to associate with another child, others who might defend the child will not act for fear of being left out themselves. Their silence seals the fate of the target.

Jerome Freiberg says that culture, the school climate, and violence are related. Large schools that fail to create interpersonal bonds with the students are to blame. Like tourists, students pass through but leave nothing of themselves behind. The solution, he believes, is in creating small unit organizations within the school, and teachers and adults serving as mentors and role models.

A Case Study

The names of the family members have been changed, but this case study is an accurate account of their experience.

Ellen and Ted Thomas enrolled their son, Josh, in kindergarten at a small Catholic school in the Midwest. When Josh was a year old he had developed asthma, accompanied by coughing and sneezing spells. On occasion he would vomit from the accumulation of mucus in his respiratory passages. When he was in third grade, Josh's asthma became more severe, and it was then that the taunting began. Several boys in his class started calling him names like "phlegm wad." Once started, the name-calling quickly gathered momentum. Ellen finally contacted her son's teacher to see if she could quell the embarrassment that her son was experiencing. The teacher spoke with the offending students several times, but the bullying continued. Ellen's next approach was to contact the parents of the bullies. She spoke with several of them about the difficulties Josh was having and was deeply disappointed in their disinterest, denial, and unwillingness to get involved.

Having failed in her effort to engage the teacher or parents in a solution, Ellen determined that Josh was going to have to help himself. She encouraged him to imagine wearing a suit of armor and watch the names and the words bounce off of it. She even went to a local toy store and purchased a suit of armor for him to wear around the house to help him gain a sense of invincibility and power.

To further empower their son, his parents spent many hours role-playing as a family. Ellen and Ted would take the part of the bully, repeating the verbal attacks Josh had received. They advised him not to show a reaction and gave him some verbal responses to practice, such as "Whatever" and "That's real mature!" Some helpful witnesses in his class even joined in on the "That's real mature!" comeback and the strategy began to work.

But more challenges lay ahead. During the summer between his third- and fourth-grade years, Josh exhibited symptoms found in obsessive compulsive disorder (OCD), ADHD, and possibly Tourette's syndrome. When he had problems with eye blinking, Ellen thought it might be due to allergies. When his neck seemed stiff and he repeatedly turned his head, she recalled reading an article about James Eisenreich, a major league baseball player, who had similar symptoms. James Eisenreich had Tourette's. Her deepest fears became reality.

His OCD became more invasive, however, than his tics. It took hours for him to do his homework because each letter had to be perfect. When his letters weren't perfect, he would erase his work repeatedly, which would make holes in the paper, and he would have to start all over again. One of his teachers in elementary school requested an Individualized Education Plan (IEP) for Josh, but the principal denied the request because Josh was such a quick learner and his grades were "too good."

With the additional and more obvious symptoms, the bullying increased. In the spring of his fourth-grade year, Josh and his mother asked for an opportunity to address his classmates. Coincidentally, a schoolwide theme was focusing on the Gifts of the Holy Spirit, such as courage, kindness, and other valued qualities. Ellen chose to capitalize on the gift of courage and related a story about Josh when he was two years old. He had been rushed to the emergency room and informed by the nurse that he was going to receive a shot. Josh looked at the nurse and said: "That's okay, I won't cry." "That," his mother explained, "showed a lot of courage for a two-year-old and it takes a lot of courage for him to stand before you today and talk about his diagnosis." She expressed hope that students in his class would have the courage not to join in if other kids made fun of Josh because of his tics. Josh gave an explanation of his condition and invited conversation. The students had lots of questions and paid close attention to the answers. The strategy was very successful. When a new student moved into the school district and started making fun of Josh, his classmates immediately came to Josh's defense and put a stop to the bullying. He had an understanding teacher who required that he do only five math problems for homework instead of ten. She arranged for Josh to sit in the first row so that when students passed their completed papers to the front, no one would see that Josh's assignments were different than theirs. Things were going quite well.

Unfortunately, Josh had to transfer to a public school in his fifth-grade year. It was a dreadful experience—new school, new students, and new forms of bullying. His teacher immediately recognized the plethora of issues Josh was dealing with, and requested an IEP. This time the individualized plan was approved. All of his instructors were made aware of his special needs, and they responded accordingly. There was one student, however, who tormented Josh and made his life miserable. A principal pointed out that this school bully had a pattern of selecting one student each year to be his victim. Though the administrator confirmed Josh's predicament, the school seemed helpless to stop it. Ellen and Ted sought private counseling for Josh and reiterated the "suit of armor" concept. They inquired about suitable medication, but it took many attempts before they found a doctor familiar enough with Tourette's syndrome to prescribe helpful medications. Meanwhile, Josh drew enough strength from his religious faith to help him survive the daily badgering.

At the conclusion of a year of relentless, consummate cruelty, Josh grabbed his bully, put him in a headlock, and yelled at him to back off. For this reaction, he received an in-school suspension. On only one other occasion during all of his school years did Josh defend himself physically—quite harmlessly and then only as a last resort. When the principal contacted his parents about the incident, Ellen made it clear to the principal that Josh wouldn't be punished at home. Josh was an expert in karate and had a repertoire of martial arts techniques he could easily have used. If anything, Ellen and Ted were in awe of the restraint he had shown for so long, knowing school personnel were unable to protect him.

Middle school was the worst period for Josh. The bullying at this level took another form, the cruelest of all—total isolation. The loneliness was heartbreaking for Josh and heartbreaking for his parents to witness. Josh had not a single friend his age. All of his support came from godparents and family members. His parents were his companions. They would take him to movies but were careful to go to a movie theater across town, where none of his peers could possibly catch him in the embarrassing presence of his parents.

In seventh grade Josh dreaded going to school. He began having panic attacks. The principal was incredibly sensitive to Josh's situation. He made it possible for Josh to attend school for only half a day so he could take his core subjects and leave without being exposed to the humiliations in physical education and other elective subjects. Even with that allowance, Josh dreaded his daily foray onto the school campus. The principal set up a signal system with his secretary. When Josh objected to going to school, Ellen would call the secretary. She, in turn, would alert the principal, who would stand outside to greet the morning students. When Josh would pull up to the curb, the principal would very casually walk with him into the building and take him to his office. A calming conversation prepared Josh for the day and enabled him to complete his part-time schedule. Some days, even after the soothing preparation, Josh could not face the ostracization and his mother would come back to school and take him home.

Eighth grade was better. Some new students entered school in the middle of the term. They, too, found it difficult to be accepted, and Josh made a connection with the other "outsiders." Josh maintained very high grades and his academic path was going extremely well, but the emotional bullying remained a constant. However, by the end of the year, he got along with many people and engaged in conversation with students from the popular crowd. His yearbook contained both degrading and encouraging messages from classmates.

His parents were unwaveringly supportive. His dad was put in charge of supervising Josh's homework. They would work for fifteen minutes, then stop and play a game. They would work another fifteen minutes, then shoot baskets, and so forth. There were so many factors to deal with simultaneously—the compulsive element, the distractions caused by ADHD, and the tics. They eventually found a support group for families dealing with Tourette's, a therapist who had an understanding of the neurological disorder, and a medication protocol that worked.

They never gave up their quest for every available resource to enable Josh to thrive.

Of all the challenges, bullying proved to be the most formidable. His parents felt that the burden of bullying always fell on the target. When targets would finally react, out of desperate frustration, they would end up paying the consequence. The bullies had the upper hand.

Today Josh is a junior in high school. He is making straight A's, he has a girlfriend, he volunteers his time to work with students who have come into the juvenile justice system, and he talks with parents whose children have Tourette's. He has many career choices to choose from as he looks ahead to college. Josh's case is useful for us to analyze because of the many levels involved.

Let us go back to the concentric circles and look at the role of the individual, his family, his schools, his community, and the culture.

The Individual

- Josh had physical, neurological, and psychological issues.
- Josh had no learning difficulties, in fact he was a very strong student.
- Josh was persistent in reaching his academic goals in spite of obstacles.

- Josh capitalized on his personality traits and developed qualities that would enable him to cope with the peer abuse, such as courage, kindness, patience, etc.
- Josh acquired verbal and physical skills to stand up for himself.
- Josh was resourceful and drew on a spiritual dimension to sustain him through his difficulties.
- Josh uses his experience to benefit others.

Family Role

- Josh's parents took an active and responsible role in parenting from the time he was born.
- Josh's parents picked up on their son's cues and sought appropriate treatment.
- When Josh's mother realized that she could not count on the school or on other parents to protect her son from the assaults of his classmates, she focused on empowering him to withstand the attacks and found a creative way to build his confidence.
- Josh's mother reached out to teachers, principals, and administrators to obtain their assistance whenever possible and to gain access to all available resources.
- Josh's father took on the significant task of being his homework coach in a way that accommodated his needs.
- Josh's mother addressed his classmates, tapped into their compassion, and challenged the witnesses to use their collective power instead of supporting the bullies.
- Godparents and other family members were available.
- The parents sought support for themselves from other families with similar disorders.
- The parents pursued medical information and interventions.
- The parents supported their son when school officials punished him for dealing with the bully situation that the school had ignored.

- The parents have found a philosophical construct to bring meaning into their experience and volunteer for a local agency that provides resources and information to families that are newly diagnosed.

School Role

- A parochial school had limited resources for students with special needs.
- An elementary school was easier for Josh to handle than middle school.
- Some schools confirmed bullying but were ineffective to prevent it.
- Some teachers did not protect Josh from bullying.
- There were no school policies or programs that addressed bullying problems.
- Consequences were invoked against inappropriate behavior of targets but not bullies.
- A sensitive principal took extra steps to accommodate Josh's difficulties.
- Empathetic teachers found numerous ways to work with Josh's issues, for example, adjusting his homework assignments and seating arrangements to protect him from the scrutiny of other students.
- Josh and his mother were permitted to speak to his class about his diagnosis.
- Teachers were consistent in following the IEP.
- A secretary, a learning resource counselor, a teacher, and a principal acted on his behalf.
- Empowered elementary school students defended Josh against a new bully.

Community Role

- A knowledgeable therapist who understood Tourette's syndrome was available.
- Informed medical support was accessible to families.
- Support groups existed to offer experience and caring.
- Karate classes were available.

Culture

- Discrimination against anyone who is different abounds.
- Libraries, media, and the Internet provided important information to the family.
- Bullying wasn't taken seriously when Josh was in primary grades.
- Tendency in society to deny/ignore problems.
- Sensitivity to the seriousness of bullying was heightened because of the multiple school shootings that received ubiquitous coverage.

The following addendum comes from Ellen, in her own words:

"When Josh was first diagnosed with Tourette's syndrome I was mad at God for two weeks. Josh had been so sick with asthma when he was little and hospitalized several times, I felt as if he had stood in the suffering line twice. I told God some other child that had not already suffered so much (or better yet make it disappear) should have Josh's Tourette's. I cried throughout those two weeks and let God know how angry I was and how unfair this was. Josh had been such a trooper about the asthma and all the times it had caused him to miss out. Many times we canceled plans. When he was three years old he had an asthma attack on Halloween morning and had to stay home wearing the costume he had been so excited about. He had to drop out of

preschool that year and avoid going to the pool where he might catch something. Josh was so accepting of these things that it made me wonder how God could possibly let Josh now have Tourette's syndrome. Yet, after those two weeks, I realized we were really stuck with this mysterious disorder. I then began accepting and saying to God that I would need his help in giving our family strength and guidance in finding the right doctors to help Josh. I knew we would have to learn all we could about Tourette's syndrome."

Summary

When I think about the significance of the concentric circles, I am reminded of Deborah Prothrow-Stith's Slot Machine theory. In a speech she delivered, I heard her say that dealing with youth violence requires many simultaneous strategies. Hoping to solve the problem on the back of one solution will never work. It's like a slot machine—all the cherries have to come up at the same time or you don't win!

And so it is with our concentric circles. All the school policies, teacher interventions, consequences invoked, and student empowerment sessions won't put bullying fractures back together again unless we address the larger social issues that impinge on the problem. Family systems will always have more influence (with the possible exception of television, as we are learning). Community attitudes undeniably shape the conduct of kids in their 'hood, for better or worse, and the culture is a force to be reckoned with. Even the Amish, with their incredible determination to avoid encroaching social pollution, find it more and more difficult to prevent intrusion into their protective isolation.

There are no simplistic solutions to this problem, but as this case study has shown, there are solutions. Positives and negatives abound in every circle. Josh and his family inspire us to meet each difficulty, each setback, each dilemma with resolve. Their passionate effort to seek out people and resources and connect every possible link to support Josh's grit is a wonderful example of commitment to a solution.

CHAPTER FIVE

GENDER ISSUES

"We were all being nice to her and pretending we were her best friends. After we got what we wanted, we started being mean to her again."
—Francine, a student

For years the term *bully* conjured a masculine image. Comic books never pictured girls kicking sand in someone's face or facing off with someone in an alley. Have there always been girl bullies? If so, why didn't we notice them? What is the current understanding about the differences in the ways that boys and girls express their aggression?

Several books on the topic of female cruelty were published in 2002. Rosalind Wiseman's *Queen Bees and Wannabes: Helping Your Daughter Survive Cliques, Gossip, Boyfriends and other Realities of Adolescence*, Rachel Simmons's *Odd Girl Out: The Hidden culture of Aggression in Girls*, Emily White's *Fast Girls: Teenage Tribes and the Myth of the Slut*, and Phyllis Chesler's *Woman's Inhumanity to Woman* are a few. The terrors of girlhood ostracism and aggression are finally being examined. Male bullying, especially those cases involving multiple shootings, has garnered all the newsprint.

In conversations with thousands of students, we have heard four differences between the ways girls and boys bully:

1. Boys are more likely to bully physically and sexually, while girls are more likely to bully verbally and emotionally. Included in boys' sexual bullying is the use of language like *gay, queer, fag, homo, pussy,* etc.
2. Boys are more likely to bully each other directly, "in your face," while girls are more apt to be indirect and talk behind each other's backs.
3. When boys get into conflicts with each other, they are more likely to make up quickly and move on. With girls, however, the conflicts are more likely to continue indefinitely.
4. Boys are more likely to bully one-on-one, while girls are more likely to form cliques to exclude another.

In this chapter we will explore these gender differences in detail, looking at why such differences exist. Why are girls so indirect in their expression of aggression? Why do boys focus on sexual verbal bullying so frequently? We will also look at the exceptions to these "rules" and try to understand their meaning.

Girl Bullying

In 1982, Harvard psychologist Carol Gilligan published her groundbreaking book *In a Different Voice.*[39] Gilligan showed us that widely accepted theories of human development were, in fact, not one size fits all. The universal idea that development is a steady journey toward separation and independence was developed, not coincidentally it turns out, by the male scholars and researchers of the early 1900s. These ideas were confirmed in observation, not coincidentally it turns out, of boys in a variety of settings over the next seventy years.

Gilligan proposed that these ideas were, in fact, right on target—for half of the people in Western culture, the males. The other half, the females, she argued, grow side by side, raised in the same families by the same parents, but on a different path, moving toward connection and interdependence. In short, Gilligan argued, in our culture boys are socialized to value achievement as their most important goal, and girls are socialized to value affiliation as their most important goal. Gilligan's arguments were compelling and offered a fresh perspective that helped make sense of some significant differences between boys and girls. Over the past twenty years, many other researchers and scholars have amplified Gilligan's ideas, focusing on the "relational" nature of female development.

So how do we make sense of the emotional and verbal bullying that is so widespread among girls? Every girl and woman can readily recall stories of girls' cruelty to each other that they either experienced or witnessed. In addition to the books, there have been a spate of articles in newspapers and magazines concerned with girls' agonizing experiences inside and outside of cliques. Some might argue that since relationships are so important to girls, they would be more kind and less cruel to each other.

Rachel Simmons weaves these seemingly contradictory ideas together in her book *Odd Girl Out: The Hidden Culture of Aggression in Girls.*[40] The central role that relationships play in girls' development "all but guarantees a different landscape of aggression and bullying," creating the backdrop for a specific kind of abuse. This focus on relationships combines with another powerful force in girls' development—the cultural prohibition against feelings of anger and aggression. Simmons argues that mainstream culture, and girls by extension, sees anger and aggression as unacceptable for girls. Despite significant changes in women's roles in society, some traditional ideas about how females should act remain unchanged.

Early on "good girls" learn that they are to be "nice," which really means *not aggressive, not angry, not in conflict.*

Simmons cites research that confirms that girls are discouraged early on from expressing aggression directly or physically, while the same behaviors are either ignored or encouraged in boys. In one 1999 study, girls were told to use a "nicer" voice, to be quiet, or to speak softly about three times more often than boys, even though the boys in the study setting were louder.

Girls grow up uncomfortable acknowledging their own feelings of anger and aggression and having very little opportunity to learn how to manage those feelings. The girls in Simmons's interviews repeatedly expressed great concern that any kind of direct conflict, no matter how small, could bring an end to a relationship. The fear of being alone, of being isolated or ostracized, was repeatedly identified as the greatest hardship one could endure.

These twin forces—the fear of being alone and the prohibition against aggression—combine to create a particular way of managing anger. Some researchers describe this as "relational aggression," where the relationship itself is used as a weapon (e.g., "I won't be your friend if you spend time with her"), or where relationships serve as the vehicle for expressing aggression (e.g., the usual lunch group can't make room at the table for the targeted girl one day). Because anger isn't expressed directly, often the targeted girl has no idea why she is being excluded. Her efforts to find out are usually futile. Most often the girls who are excluding her won't respond, or may even deny that anything is wrong.

Sarah's case is an example of peer isolation. In third grade she moved to a new school and began to establish herself with her classmates. During the next two years she threatened the social power of two girls who had been unchallenged since kindergarten. Teachers favored Sarah, she excelled in her schoolwork, and, most threatening of all, she was attracting attention from the popular boys. By fifth grade the two girls decided to teach Sarah a lesson and devised a sinister plan. They organized their classmates, girls and boys, to isolate her from all interaction. No one was to speak to her, choose her to be on a team, call on her to read, or walk in the halls with her. She was to be ostracized from all contact. The mass psychology was very seductive and everyone supported the conspiracy—except for one girl, Cindy. At the age of eleven, Cindy was well on her way to becoming an artist and had developed the ability to think for herself and stand apart from the crowd.

Cindy was not very athletic and consequently team captains did not fight over her. She and Sarah would huddle together for the "picking" session and were consistently passed over, finally requiring the gym teacher to assign them to a team. Reading period was another crisis. Every afternoon, the teacher would call on a student to begin the oral reading. Boys and girls alternated, so that a boy chose a girl to read next and a girl chose a boy to read next. Each day, the torturous process would conclude with the teacher asking: "Is there anyone who hasn't been called on?" At first, Sarah would raise her hand and acknowledge that she hadn't had a turn, but as the weeks went by, she pretended that she hadn't heard the question. Cindy couldn't rescue Sarah from the alternate gender reading ritual and there was always someone in the class who was gleeful to point out that Sarah hadn't been chosen.

Every recess, every gym class, every reading session was a painful, humiliating reminder of her excommunication from her former friends. Cindy remained loyal, in spite of her parents' counsel that Sarah wouldn't be her best friend anymore if the "in crowd" changed its mind and welcomed her back. Sarah's mother was sympathetic but unsure of what she could do to intervene in the follies of fifth-grade perils, so she counted on Cindy to be her daughter's buffer against the isolation. It is hard to imagine that the teacher never caught on to the mass abandonment of Sarah, but she never interfered.

At the beginning of sixth grade, the bullies decided that Sarah had been punished enough. Her year-long embargo was lifted, and she was allowed to resume her role with the popular crowd. Cindy's parents were right. Sarah no longer had time for Cindy.

Girls have their own way of explaining relational aggression. An interesting discussion occurred at a middle school in Napa, California. The students affirmed the "four differences" mentioned earlier and when asked why girls are so much more verbally and emotionally hurtful to each other, a perceptive reply came from an eighth-grade female student. She observed: "When boys get together they talk about sports. When girls get together they talk about feelings, so if you want to hurt someone, you have a lot more ammunition to use against them." This statement is also a commentary on the different way that boys and girls approach relationships. Girls are encouraged to identify and share feelings—except feelings of anger—with each other. These exchanges become fertile soil for the roots of relationship. Sometimes the connection that blooms is thorny and dangerous, while at other times it can spread its boughs to offer shade and a place to rest. Girls and women alike often report that friends, or just one really good friend, have been one of life's greatest gifts. Girls who have been through a terrible time with their peers frequently say that it was the friendship of another girl that kept them going.

Competition creates challenges for girls. There is greater competition in all aspects of children's lives today: academic competition—it is more difficult to make it into the top colleges and universities, even with excellent test scores; athletic competition—there are scholarships and high status in the school hierarchy at stake; social competition—there is undue pressure to imitate the fashions, jewelry, and hair styles that are currently deemed "in." Boys are weaned on competition. When faced with competition, girls are challenged to win and avoid conflict at the same time. For boys there is no dilemma, no expectation to be pleasant. The phrase "winning is everything" came from the football field, not the home economics class.

While girls and experts alike agree that girls are much more likely to bully with emotional and verbal means, there is growing evidence that some girls are becoming more physically aggressive. Students tell of fistfights and shoving matches between girls in many of the schools we visit. Research bears this out, too. One study reported that violent crime among male youths has fallen since 1995, while violent crime among female youths has increased during the same period.[41] Adolescent males still commit more violent crimes than adolescent females, but the accelerated rate among females is noteworthy. More research is needed in this area, too.

Boy Bullying

In the last several years a number of books have been published expressing concern about how boys are faring in contemporary culture. The school shootings, where all the perpetrators but one have been male, sharpened this concern. Dan Kindlon, a child-development researcher at Harvard and coauthor of *Raising Cain: Protecting the Emotional Life of Boys,* points to the "emotional miseducation" of boys, where boys are taught to shut down feelings of empathy and sympathy.[42] Ron Levant, Ed.D., says that boys learn to convert more vulnerable feelings like sadness into anger in order to conform to expectations of masculine behavior, so that "when a boy is pushed down on the ground . . . he knows that his job is to come back with a fistful of gravel, rather than a faceful of tears."[43] Levant describes research that shows how this process occurs. Mothers expose baby girls to a wider range of emotions than baby boys are exposed to, and work harder to control their sons' emotional volatility. Fathers begin to interact with boy and girl children differently when they reach about three months of age, verbally roughhousing their sons and talking in more emotional terms with their daughters. As kids get older, both parents discourage sons from expressing vulnerable emotions, while encouraging daughters to express such emotions.[44]

These processes that occur within families are set against a backdrop of exposure to increasingly violent television shows, movies, song lyrics, and video games. Media heroes have also become more violent and have replaced strong yet milder models like Roy Rogers and Superman. *Leave It to Beaver,* so ardently followed a generation ago, would, alas, be comedy material today.

Then, Levant says, at school and with friends, peer-group interactions cement boys'emotional disconnection from their feelings by promoting structured group activities that foster toughness, teamwork, stoicism, and competition. Boys who don't play by these rules suffer, as "boy culture is notoriously cruel to boys who violate male norms."[45] When some boys have reached their boiling point, the combination of all of these forces has been lethal. William Pollack, author of *Real Boys: Rescuing Our Sons from the Myths of Boyhood,* says, "When we don't let boys cry tears, some will cry bullets."[46] James Garbarino explores these pressures in detail in his book *Lost Boys: Why Our Sons Turn Violent and How We Can Save Them.*

Rachel Simmons makes the point in *Odd Girl Out* that girls' relationships suffer because girls aren't allowed to express anger and aggression. Levant, Pollack, and others are making the point that boys' relationships suffer because they are allowed to express only anger and aggression. And most often, in middle and high schools across the country, the anger and aggression are expressed through sexual bullying in the form of name-calling, like *fag, queer,* and so on. The incidence of physical bullying appears to be dramatically lower than the sexual name-calling, and students consistently report that the verbal and sexual bullying are much more troubling to them than the physical bullying.

Jordan volunteered to be on a panel at a community program about bullying that we moderated. Jordan was a tall, muscular, handsome young man who began by recounting his great life at a rural, midwestern school when his father was appointed to be the principal of an elementary school in a larger community. Jordan was reluctant to move but was pleased about his father's promotion. Nothing could have prepared him for his reception at the new school. Because of his physical stature, his classmates expected him to go out for football, but he loved music, so he tried out for the chorale group instead. Several of his new classmates questioned this decision, but he knew he was making the right choice for himself and didn't give it much further thought. As he walked down the hall the next day, he saw a crowd gathered around his locker. When Jordan approached, they moved aside, revealing a poster with the words "God hates fags" taped to the locker door. The harassment that followed was relentless. Every day was worse than the last. His only respite was at home, where his parents ached with him and understood his misery. His father was filled with guilt for having transplanted him to such despair. His father contacted the principal of his son's school, hoping to effect a breakthrough, to no avail. No solace, no attempt at intervention brought relief.

By this time, Jordan's thoughts turned to suicide. His parents arranged for him to transfer to another school. The first week that he arrived at the new school, auditions were held for a talent show, and Jordan signed up to sing a solo. He was quite nervous and deeply concerned that the student reaction to his interest in music rather than sports would be repeated. The night of the talent show, he approached the microphone, stood before hundreds of strange faces, and sang his song. He was overwhelmed by the response, a standing ovation, which is most unusual for a high school program.

As he shared his story, a hushed and empathetic audience, tears welled up in his eyes. Despite the warm acceptance of the kids at his new school, the memory of his humiliation ran deep. So deep, in fact, that he disclosed that he was in therapy and working very hard to overcome his lingering depression.

Why is sexual name-calling so widespread among teenage boys? Sexuality and sexual identity are major concerns for this age group. A poignant example came when we were conducting a workshop for educators in Hutchinson, Kansas. As usual, we requested a panel of students to strengthen our message. When the issue of sexual bullying became the topic, Tony, an eighth-grade student, shared his anxiety: "When someone calls you 'gay' or 'faggot' day after day, you begin to wonder if they know something about you that you don't know yourself." For males, then, this is the "ammunition" that creates the most destruction.

The hypermasculine models of Arnold Schwarzenegger's Terminator character and "bad boy" millionaire athletes and rap artists make most boys feel inadequate by comparison. At the same time, sex roles in daily life have become more androgynous and less proscribed. Men are more involved in parenting, sharing household chores, assuming more nurturing responsibilities. It is a struggle for young men to balance these competing pressures, especially with the limited experience of a teenager. To make matters worse, boys are expected to go it alone, to figure out these complex and subtle issues for themselves without consulting or commiserating with friends. Perhaps this confusion and uncertainty are expressed in the only emotional form—anger or disdain—that is socially endorsed for boys. And perhaps putting someone else down is a way of reassuring yourself that you are measuring up.

Maybe boys show aggression through sexual name-calling because physical fighting is no longer tolerated. When male bullying becomes physical, it is noticed immediately and stopped. A male teacher in California posed this idea: "When we clamped the lid on boys fighting with each other, we eliminated a solution to a lot of problems! That is just the way males deal with things. They punch and kick and wrestle until the battle is over—a winner is declared and life goes on. In denying their nature to work these conflicts out in a physical way, we have forced them to simmer with anger and it's detrimental to them and to society!"

Girls have always aimed for the psychological jugular. They use rumors, shunning, gossiping, and exclusion. Girls have used the same arsenal of verbal and emotional weapons for decades. There is not much new in girl bullying, it's just that we're finally recognizing it for what it is. There is something new in boy bullying. It's the homophobic language and access to weapons.

At the beginning of this chapter we described four "rules" about how boys bully. It is important to note that while these general trends seem consistent across the country, we regularly hear of exceptions. In particular, we often hear of a group of boys picking on another boy, an exception to the one-on-one rule offered earlier. And while we hear about boys fighting one minute and skateboarding together the next, we also hear of situations that continue for long periods of time. Eric Harris and Dylan Klebold, the infamous Columbine shooters, appear to have been targets of sexual name-calling by a number of students for an extended period of time, as was Jordan in the story we told earlier in this chapter.

Researchers are beginning to note this kind of ostracizing, referred to as relational aggression among girls, as a phenomenon among boys, as well. Nicki Crick and Maureen Bigbee looked at both relational and overt physical aggression among 383 fourth and fifth graders.[47] They found that girls were significantly more likely to be targets of relational aggression and boys to be targets of overt aggression, but that relational aggression did occur among boys just as overt physical aggression did occur among girls. Crick and Bigbee noted that targets of relational aggression, be they male or female, experienced significant adjustment problems. They reported more self-restraint problems, more difficulty inhibiting anger, and greater impulsivity than their peers.

Summary

In this chapter we have looked at some of the differences in the ways boys and girls bully. Girls focus on relationships, and their difficulty dealing with anger and aggression make them more likely to bully in a particular way. Isolating, ostracizing, and gossiping are common kinds of bullying practiced by girls. Boys are often more comfortable expressing anger than other, more vulnerable emotions like sadness or distress. They are more likely to bully physically and sexually, especially with sexual name-calling. Boys and girls both report that conflicts between girls are more likely to occur in groups, and to last for indefinite periods of time, while boys are more likely to deal with each other one-on-one and then put it behind them. There are, however, exceptions.

CHAPTER SIX

SKILLS CHILDREN NEED FROM ADULTS

"The way to keep children from doing the wrong thing is to teach them to love doing the right thing."
—Sue N. Teel, *The Essential Curriculum*

In the next several chapters, we will go into detail about strategies that can be used by schools, educators, parents, and students themselves. In this chapter, we present a list of valuable skills that children need and parents can teach. Parents can provide all of these skills for their children before they leave the protection of their family to make their debut into the school social scene. Too often, however, children arrive at the learning maze without the benefit of essential skills, at which point our schools struggle to take up the slack. Having a repertoire of appropriate behaviors that have become second nature and can be drawn upon during ordinary interactions as well as unexpected encounters will serve a child well from kindergarten through the elementary and secondary levels.

Some schools are formalizing the teaching of these skills as reinforcement of parental instruction or as an alternative to bad habits that have been formed. We offer the acronym SCRAPES to help the reader remember skills prevalent throughout the bullying intervention and prevention literature, whether at home, school, or structured youth activities. In our chapter on Resources, we offer reference sources that are available for adults who wish to pursue the SCRAPES recommendations.

Social skills and self-esteem
Conflict resolution and character education
Respect for differences
Assertiveness and anger management
Power and problem solving
Empathy
Sexuality

Social Skills

Time and time again, the lack of basic social skills has caused problems for children. Educators are appalled at the manners that are missing from their classrooms and the need to compensate for this deficiency.

Many elementary schools are offering courses on learning how to share, initiating friendships, accepting responsibility for your mistakes, cooperating with a group, waiting your turn, eating in a mannerly way, understanding the importance of saying "please," "thank you," "excuse me," "I'm sorry," and "can I help?" Children bereft of such instruction often irritate their peers with annoying behaviors and become targets and/or bullies in the primary grades. Their habits become ingrained, and, by the time they reach the fourth and fifth grades, they can become isolates or full-fledged meanies.

A wonderful little book has come to my attention—*365 Manners Kids Should Know,* by Sheryl Eberly. The subtitle is *Games, Activities, and Other Fun Ways to Help Children Learn Etiquette.* Brief but potent introductions to manners can be easily introduced on a daily basis.

According to the May 2002 issue of the National School Safety Center newsletter: "The teaching and use of manners in our school communities might possibly deliver more powerful and longer lasting results for school safety than some of today's popular prevention and intervention programs."

A social skills program developed at the Oregon Social Learning Center in Eugene, Oregon, called Linking the Interests of Families and Teachers (LIFT), targets all children, not just those who are aggressive, and is unique in that it also involves both parents and teachers. The program was tested in twelve Oregon elementary schools on small groups of first and fifth graders. The findings, published in the *Journal of Consulting and Clinical Psychology,* showed a significant improvement in aggressive children's behavior.

Once, when I was working in an elementary school with several fourth-grade classes, one student was obviously rejected by others. As they gathered to sit on the floor, everyone left big gaps of space between themselves and Monty. If he tried to move closer to anyone, that child scooted away. He would blurt out inappropriate answers for almost every question I asked. He was rude and constantly drawing attention to himself. Even I, with all of my empathic feelings on full alert, found his behavior to be obnoxious. Toward the end of a very poignant but structured discussion about pain and anger, the class focused on Monty and confronted him with some reasons for their rejection. I expected him to walk out, to cry, to rage, or to blame—or all of the above.

Instead, he admitted that he got on everyone's nerves and spoke of some of his worst offenses, which occurred at recess. His reaction took everyone by surprise and we scrambled to respond to his openness. One student spontaneously offered to sit with him at lunch for a week and help him with his eating habits. Another student offered to play with him at recess for a week so he wouldn't interfere and try to destroy everyone's games. Other students offered to take their turns giving Monty support—for a limited period of time. It was an astounding resolution with students stepping up to play the role of social coach. As the classes filed out, his teacher remarked to me that he had been an isolate for so long, he lacked all ability to interact normally with his peers.

Shortly thereafter, the two other fourth-grade classes in that school entered the carpeted area and we began anew the conversation about targets, bullies, and witnesses. I was debating whether to share with them the remarkable transformation that had just occurred. On the one hand, I felt the ethical necessity of maintaining the confidentiality of the session. On the other hand, I wanted to make them aware of the plan that had emerged, in hopes of engaging their involvement as well. While I was struggling with my dilemma, Monty suddenly appeared. He had asked his teacher for permission to share what had happened in his session with the other fourth-grade classes, and she compassionately granted his request.

To say that those students were stunned does not capture the moment. The image of that encounter between Monty and his peer group will stay with me forever. A hushed group of students stared in awe as Monty delivered his confession of annoyance. He talked about anger—theirs to him and his to them. He told them that he was sorry about all the problems he had caused and how happy he was that his classmates had offered to help him. His straightforwardness resulted in an even larger support group. The reality is that not many Montys, who've been emotionally mangled for such a long time, will handle their situation with such maturity and aplomb, but it might be well to share his story to encourage other children and their classmates to consider this "social skills coach" approach.

Self-Esteem

It's hard to imagine that a concept as praiseworthy as self-esteem has caused controversy. The debate involves those who say that a child cannot acquire self-esteem merely by being told that he or she is special. True self-esteem, they say, must be earned, and as *The Essential Curriculum* states: "It is our self-esteem which insures us against the possibility of becoming arrogant or self-righteous on the one hand, or hopeless and self-condemning on the other. It allows us to say to ourselves, that 'No matter what happens to me or around me, I will stand firm in the knowledge that my life and the living of it are of value. My inner self sustains me.'"

Parents can find infinite ways to help children earn their self-esteem, for example, by praising them for following rules, completing tasks, taking responsibility for their actions, etc. J. D. Hawkins, president of the National Association for Self-Esteem in Normal, Illinois, has stated, "If you are not personally and socially responsible, then your self-worth is built on a false reality and, therefore, it's not healthy."[48]

A beautiful example of the power of self-esteem comes from a family in Maryland. An eight-year-old boy was informing his mother that he was *always* chosen last at every sporting event at school. Often teams fought over who would have to take him. His mother was furious and vowed that she would go to his school to put a stop to the abuse. The son turned to his mother and said: "Mom, don't worry! It doesn't bother me. I always think of you and how much you love me for all of my good qualities and I figure that being picked for teams just isn't that important."

For schools, the task of helping each child discover abilities, talents, qualities, and skills is crucial. A widely read advice column reported a story that came to light when a soldier's body was returned to his family for final memorial. Among his personal belongings, folded carefully in his wallet, was a list of qualities his classmates admired about him. Many years earlier, a teacher had assigned all of her students to write something genuinely positive about each person in the class and this soldier had treasured that list enough to keep it on his person throughout his life journey. That column has inspired many teachers to make the same assignment, with variations on the theme. One teacher in Clay Center, Kansas, had each student write, "What I appreciate about . . ." each classmate on a Rolodex card. Then she attached all of the Rolodex cards for each student on a key chain so that each person had his or her own collection of delightful dangles.

Conflict Resolution

Educators and parents are intrigued with conflict resolution programs, which are gaining popularity around the country. Forty-nine percent of students who were contacted in a national survey said that conflict resolution was being taught in their classes.

I am frequently asked about the efficacy of such programs. A study published in *Children and Schools,* a journal from the National Association of Social Workers, reports the success of conflict resolution to curb less extreme acts of violence, such as verbal threats, name-calling, and insults. Debra Woody, LMSW-ASP, Ph.D., described a three-phase model program that involved everyone in the school. Phase one focused on the students, who received four-hour training sessions in communication skills, conflict resolution, negotiation, acceptance, and appreciation of diversity. The second phase included both faculty and staff, who received the same training as the students with additional emphasis on daily use of the skills. The third phase focused on follow-up discussions and activities, and each day, students received a "booster." At the end of the year, results indicated a more cooperative atmosphere throughout the school, no physically violent altercations, and students seemed less aggressive and were more assertive in resolving conflict through nonviolent means. They plan a fourth phase, which will bring parents into the training loop.

Some schools integrate dispute resolution programs by training peer mediators to facilitate conflict resolution sessions between students. Conflict mediation is a specific skill used by a trained mediator or team of mediators to assist two or more parties who are willing to work out a win/win solution. Even elementary school students can be trained to be effective mediators.

Several variables impact the effectiveness of these student mediation programs. The excellence of the training is foremost, but other factors include the quality of adult supervision, consistent opportunities for student mediation experience, the maturity level of the mediators, and the willingness of the student body to participate in resolution of disputes.

In our chapter on Resources, we list a catalogue that offers a variety of conflict mediation programs for reference.

Character Education

Esther Schaeffer, executive director of Character Education Partnership in Washington, D.C., shared the history of the character education movement. Our country's founding fathers believed that democracy was dependent on an educated citizenry and believed that character development should be a component of the education system. This idea prevailed until the 1960s and '70s when churning national issues such as the Vietnam War and the Civil Rights movement sparked great differences in social values. As a result, schools were under pressure to eliminate character content and leave values education to the family. By the late 1980s and early '90s, parents, school administrators, and leading academicians began in earnest to reconstitute the inclusion of character education in public schools as well as at home. There is no common lexicon of traits that defines character education. Schools adopt values that reflect parent concerns and are important in the community, but the virtues of responsibility, respect, honesty, and compassion are included in almost every list. Other traits that are often promoted are trustworthiness, fairness, loyalty, and kindness. Schools will frequently stress one word each month and bring a variety of speakers, programs, and projects into place to underscore the celebrated trait. Bullying prevention and character education go hand in hand to create a sense of caring and belonging for children, two concepts frequently identified by research as essential to successful development.

An exemplary resource is CHARACTER Plus, a comprehensive approach to character education, coordinated as a project of Cooperating School Districts of Greater St. Louis. It was started in 1988 as a collaborative partnership between the school, home, and community. CHARACTER Plus currently reaches 89 districts and 560 schools throughout Missouri and Illinois. It promotes a process that includes ten essential elements rather than a program or curriculum.

Respect for Differences

Unfortunately, many students bring prejudices to schools that they have learned in their homes. These biases can easily become the basis for bullying. Economics, religion, race, culture, and gender identity serve as the basis for the most common forms of discrimination, but intolerance in one area can spread into disdain for other differences.

Children pick up on prejudices that parents express indirectly—telephone or overheard conversations, jokes made at someone's expense, slang words used to describe an individual or group. By the time children attend school, they have already been exposed to deeply felt attitudes held by their parents and caregivers.

Schoolwide programs for children, parents, and staff about prejudice are becoming prevalent and can be very helpful. The Southern Poverty Law Center has a program called "Teaching Tolerance," a highly acclaimed, effective program that is used in many schools across the country.

The Midwest Center for Holocaust Education, in Overland Park, Kansas, has sponsored a number of powerful exhibits. This program collected oral testimonies of fifty local Holocaust survivors and conducted training programs for over four hundred teachers in Kansas and Missouri. They encourage student research through an annual essay-writing contest, and have coordinated presentations by survivors to nearly 100,000 students in order to imprint on young peoples' minds the ultimate consequence of prejudice. There are Holocaust survivors in many cities who realize that time is running out to share their experiences in a meaningful way with a generation that is far removed from the horrors of that time in history.

Even a small exercise can make a difference in the way children think about themselves and others. For example, one inventive Kansas fourth-grade, public-school teacher brings a wrapped package for every student at the beginning of the school year. Each package is completely different. Some are quite large, while some are small. She uses tissue paper, holiday paper, newspaper, bows, stickers, yarn, and a variety of decorations to make each one unique. Every student is invited to select a package and to discuss why it was chosen. When they finally open their box, the students discover the same candy treat inside each package. The teacher uses the activity to illustrate the fact that each of us comes in "a different package" and is attracted to certain outward appearances. Though we all have a distinctive wrapper, the teacher emphasizes that there is "sweetness" inside of everyone. She believes that learning how to get along is most important, so she spends a great deal of time talking with her children about these issues—not only to prevent problems from occurring, but to deal with them when they do erupt.

Assertiveness

Teaching children to stand up for themselves and to advocate for their rights is one of the best prevention strategies that adults can instill in their charges. Students intuitively realize that most bullies are cowardly and prefer classmates who cower to those who stand their ground. Assertiveness can be projected verbally and/or non-verbally. In our chapter on Strategies for Students, we discuss the differences between aggressive, passive, and assertive responses and give examples and scripts to underscore assertiveness. Some parents grapple with the fine line between assertiveness and disrespect. Assertiveness is taking a position for oneself that protects and honors the integrity of the self without dishonoring or diminishing someone else.

Anger Management

Anger can be a virtue if it is used wisely at the right moment, in the right way. It can warn us of danger and prepare us to take action to protect ourselves. Anger can also motivate us to right a wrong, but it can be a vice when it controls us or when we act on anger without thinking first.

One of the most profound lessons I ever learned about anger occurred when I took Jack Mandelbaum, a Holocaust survivor, to speak to a group of inmates at a Kansas Correctional Facility. The chairman of the inmate self-help program thought it would be invaluable for complaining incarcerated men to hear about imprisonment from the perspective of a former concentration camp prisoner.

Jack agreed to speak but as we drove to the correctional facility he expressed some trepidation about entering a site that would stir up so many memories. We went through the security check, arrived at the meeting place, and I introduced my friend to the assembled crowd.

Jack spoke very frankly of his two years of slave labor and three years in several concentration camps from the age of thirteen to eighteen. He lost his entire family and his youth was taken from him. Jack then observed that this institution revived no pain for him because it was a country club compared to the prisons he had known.

He observed that the men were wearing appropriate clothing and they were served three meals a day. They had access to health care and were permitted communication with their families. They had heat in the winter, and he was speaking to them in an air-conditioned room. Many of them had determinate sentences and hope that they would leave their confinement alive. He concluded by saying, "I had none of these things and I never did anything wrong!"

This account did not sit well with men who did not feel gratitude for their incarceration. One of them finally asked Jack what he did with all of his anger. Jack's reply that he wasn't angry, was met with fierce skepticism. Jack restated that he held no anger, but insisted that it was not because he was saintly. He went on to explain that if a Nazi guard from one of his camps was watching television at that very moment, drinking a beer and eating a knockwurst, any anger of Jack's would not affect the Nazi. The only person affected by Jack's anger would be Jack himself and the people that he loved, who would suffer the anger that he stored. He was not about to give his former Nazi guard one more ounce of his life.

Jack went on to say that his philosophy had literally been a life-saving position for him to take and he asked the question, "What good is it to be free in body and not be free in mind?" What an incredible lesson about the futility of holding on to anger, no matter how justified!

Relinquishing anger is not easy, though, and children do need instruction in handling the anger that will come up for them. There are many issues that trigger angry feelings—divorce, loss, exposure to violence (virtual and real), competition, and peer pressure to name a few. Here are ten suggestions for helping children deal with anger:

1. Encourage children to express their anger in words. Even if they express disrespectful anger at you, separate the two expressions, such as "It's okay for you to be upset and angry with me for not letting you do what you want, but it's not okay for you to talk to me that way."

2. Confirm that you really listened by repeating what they said and expressing some understanding of their feelings.

3. Discuss their reason for being angry. Is it because they are disappointed, frustrated, sad, or jealous? The more children can understand the source of their anger, the better equipped they will be to deal with it themselves.

4. Let them cool off. Put younger children in time-out until they can get control of their feelings. Advise older children that they need to take time to collect their emotions.

5. Recommend exercise. Help children dissipate some of the anger energy by engaging in some physical activity.

6. Offer suggestions for activities that have a calming effect—take deep breaths, soak in a warm bath, listen to soothing music, read a book, etc.

7. Focus on finding a creative solution.

8. Distract them by involving them in something that requires their attention and energy.

9. Share a personal example about how you learned to handle your anger in an appropriate way.

10. Suggest that they draw a picture or write a letter, poem, or story to describe their anger.

In truth, the most profound lesson children will learn about handling their anger will be observing and experiencing the way you handle yours!

Power

Power is a major factor in bullying. Bullies acquire destructive power at the expense of children who feel powerless. Children who obtain more power than they can handle, or who use power to abuse and exploit, are in peril of forming behavior patterns that will follow them throughout the course of their lives. They may become wife batterers or child abusers, abusive employers, difficult neighbors—people who thrive on troublemaking.

Children begin to understand the dynamics of power at a very young age. As one student said: "The first time my mother answered me by saying: 'Because I said so,' I knew what power was!" The quest for power is instinctive. I vividly remember an "aha" experience for my husband and me at a parent education meeting when our children were young. The psychiatrist on the program explained about the "Power Triangle." A child, he said, understands at a very unconscious level that mother and father hold the power—two against one, so to speak. Though children cannot articulate their impotent power status, they instinctively grasp that if they can split the two parents and persuade one to become their ally, they have shifted the balance and successfully reconfigured the triangle in their favor! Children in schools will act out this power triangle by manipulating a split between two close friends that results in one of the friends being reduced to the role of an outsider.

Our desire to have a sense of control and claim our space in the world are normal yearnings. There is nothing wrong with wanting to acquire and maintain power. It is quite natural for children to seek to be leaders or to be part of the "powerful" group in their school even though it must be obvious that the pyramid of leadership narrows.

Power is often perceived as only negative . It is often thought of in a pejorative sense: "power hungry," "corrupted by power," "power struggles." But power can also ennoble. Think of spiritual, military, and political figures who have combined power with courage and self-discipline in gallant ways. Think of all the heroes, both masculine and feminine, of 9/11 who used whatever personal power they had for the sake of others. Power over oneself—to control impulses, to resist destructive temptations—can be tremendously liberating.

Perhaps our most daunting task as adults is to teach targets, bullies, and witnesses the value of power for the greater good and the role they play in the design of building a generous, secure school community. Targets need to understand the power they can have to defend themselves against a bully, at best, or, at least, to withhold satisfaction from the bully. Bullies need to understand that exploiting others for power can lead to criminal habits, which will bring much heavier power against them. If they can use their affinity for acquiring power in admirable ways, they can reap tremendous rewards. Witnesses hold the ultimate power. By sheer numbers alone, they could assume control. But if you add collaboration, creativity, and courage to that leverage, the life lessons to be learned are incalculable.

I often share with students the compelling story of the fourth airplane on 9/11. On the first three airplanes that crashed that day, the passengers were unable to interrupt the tragic plan. Passengers on the fourth airplane had learned about the three previous crashes and understood their fate. Four male passengers who were witnessing a gruesome use of power collaborated to change the direction of that plane and possibly the destiny of our country. Witnesses who join forces to deflate bullies and support targets are our schoolyard heroes.

I wonder how many of our readers saw the heartbreaking image of a sobbing Andy Williams at his sentencing, who wished that he could take that infamous day back when he killed two students and injured thirteen. So many lives would be different today if witnesses at that high school in California had used their power then.

Problem-Solving

Much too often, children speak of the ineffective advice they have been given by adults to deal with a bully: "Just ignore it!" This counsel has obviously not worked for most targets, or bullying would have ceased to exist. When I ask children "What can you do to get a bully to leave you alone?" the first response is usually "Just ignore it!" But when I ask: "How many of you have ignored a bully and it worked?" only a few hands go up. When I ask: "How many of you have ignored a bully and it *didn't* work?" many hands go up. What we can learn from that exercise is that what works with one bully may not work on another one, so a student must have many arrows in his or her quiver. There are often many possible solutions to every problem, and the task is to continue various attempts until one succeeds! If adults recommend ignoring as the *only* solution and it doesn't work, a target may feel defeated. And, there are *many* ways to ignore. A school counselor in Belleville, Kansas, describes his "chin to the chest" theory as "If you lower your chin, the bully wins; if you lift your chin, then you can win." This idea was confirmed by a student at Scarsdale Middle School, who recounted how he had ignored his bullies all through elementary school, to no avail. During the summer before he began middle school, he told us, "I grew myself up inside and decided that I would determine who I was, not someone else." He surmised that he carried himself differently, reflecting the change in his opinion of himself. The concept of altering your body language works well when it comes from a genuine inner force, but it can also be rehearsed, much as actors can portray a character different from themselves. Vicki Price, our Salina, Kansas, trainer advises elementary school children to practice in front of a mirror—slouching versus standing tall, chin down versus chin up—and then to try out their new posture on their pet. "If you can't pull it off with your dog, it probably won't work with a bully," she advises.

Problem-solving skills should be introduced at an early age, long before a crisis occurs. There are infinite opportunities for parents to present problems to be solved regarding clothing, toys, food, bedtime, and TV at an early age, enabling children to develop a thinking process that can be transferred to greater dilemmas as they mature. Schoolwork, in itself, will present myriad chances for children to rehearse problem-solving strategies.

Learning how to analyze a situation through a variety of perspectives can be an invaluable gift from adults to children. Our daughter-in-law, Camille Fried, a fifth-grade teacher in Tillman Elementary School in Kirkwood, Missouri, uses the Socratic method to prod the thinking processes of her students. She will bring a piece of art, a newspaper article, a short story, or a video to her class that is geared for older students. It is important for the subject matter to be beyond their individual understanding. Once the item is displayed, she invites her students to think overnight about what they have seen and to write down any questions they might have. The next day, she facilitates a discussion, staying totally neutral and encouraging the students to explore all facets to make sense of what they have seen, rather than to come to an immediate answer.

Another element of this technique is to assign one student who does not participate in the discussion to be the *observer*. At the conclusion of the discussion, the observer reports on who participated, who held back, who was helpful to the conversation, who monopolized, who took the group off task. Camille is very enthusiastic about the growth in her students as a result of this exercise.

Empathy

Of the thousands of elementary and middle school students I have spoken with, I can count on the fingers of my hands the number of young people who have been able to give a definition of the word

119

empathy—including elementary and middle school students. Though most of them can define *sympathy*, a longer word than *empathy*, few have ever heard the word, much less have an understanding of the concept. Discussing and fostering empathy can begin very early, with the telling of nursery rhymes. How did Goldilocks feel when she was lost in the forest? How did the bears feel when they discovered a stranger in their home? Engaging children to put themselves in someone else's place—to "walk in someone's moccasins," as the Native American philosophy teaches us—cannot begin too young. Empathy is when my heart can feel your pain.

From conversations I have had with converted bullies, the most significant factor in their transformation was when they began to consider how their target might be feeling. The capacity for empathy exists, but practicing it on a daily basis is what can move it from being an inactive force in children's lives to one of active vibrancy.

Sexuality

While many of the taboos of sexuality seem to have fallen by the wayside and the mystery of sex has been replaced by a barrage of blatant sexual images in ads, TV, movies, CDs, and the Internet, it remains an uncomfortable topic for many parents to discuss with their children. We do know that children are intensely curious about their bodies at an early age. They like to touch their own bodies and the genitalia of others, if permitted. They soon learn that most adults are threatened by behavior or language that involves sexual body parts, so they create their own sexual "resource centers" on school playgrounds where whispered data is embellished, distorted, and passed on with great relish but with no accountability. The vulgar words, the body-part language, the dirty jokes, the stories that are shared on the playground and other places do a tremendous disservice to the candid, value-connected information that children deserve to hear from their families. The risks and effects of sexually transmitted diseases, date rape, AIDS, unwanted pregnancies, and sexual abuse that are unfortunately rampant in our society are too disastrous to ignore.

Here again, many schools are offering courses on sexual matters because young people are eager for information that is accurate and intelligently presented. Parents and schools have a crucial role to play in ensuring that students' questions about their bodies and their relationships will be answered honestly and appropriately. The use of denigrating sexual language must be emphasized again in this section because of the consequential deaths of so many young people.

Peter Miner, a middle school teacher in an inner-city school in New York City, has created a Sexual Respect curriculum that has earned high praise and testimonials from his students. His lessons raise their awareness that sexist and sexually harassing behavior are unworthy of people of intelligence and integrity. He also helps his students make a connection between the indignities of racial harassment and sexual harassment, between bigotry and sexism.

Many parents want to know how old their children should be to discuss sexuality. In our minds there is no magic age, but probably earlier than you think if you want to be the first presenter. The key is to use proper names for body parts from the very beginning, to respond to all questions without embarrassment, and to have comfortable conversations when the subject is appropriate. Children are very grateful to have been informed about sexual matters by their parents rather than to have their innocence publicly exposed at school.

Summary

Prevention is always preferable to intervention. The effectiveness of polio shots has obscured the existence of iron-lung machines, which were living prisons for people infected with poliomyelitis, prior to the discovery of the Salk vaccine. When we provide children with skills that can preclude bullying, we will save them and ourselves great heartache down the road. SCRAPES—social skills, self-esteem, conflict resolution, character education, respect for differences, anger management, assertiveness, power, problem solving, empathy, and sexuality information are just the kinds of tools that children need to have in their social and emotional repertoire. The beauty of such a plan is that while we are giving them the capacity to take care of themselves, we are building a generation that is better prepared to take care of the world.

CHAPTER SEVEN

STRATEGIES FOR STUDENTS

"I learned that if I am ever making someone feel bad, I should think what it felt like to be in their shoes."

—Alli, a student

This chapter, or parts of it, could be read to students to stimulate discussion about solutions or they could read it themselves. This chapter can be adapted for younger children. We have sections for children who bully, children who experience bullying, and children who witness acts of bullying. Many students shift among all three roles, so it is important to discuss strategies for bullies, targets, and witnesses with all children.

Dr. Karl Menninger, famed Kansas psychiatrist, states that children, like adults, develop behavior patterns that allow them to survive. When a child's basic security is not threatened, he or she is free to pursue higher goals; when he or she is under siege, he or she will resort to life-preserving actions. In his book *The Human Mind,* Dr. Menninger writes: "When a trout, rising to a fly gets hooked on a line and finds himself unable to swim about freely, he begins a fight which results in struggles and splashes and sometimes an escape.

Often, of course, the situation is too tough for him. In the same way, the human being struggles with his environment and with the hooks that catch him. Sometimes he masters his difficulties; sometimes they are too much for him. His struggles are all that the world sees and it usually misunderstands them. It is hard for a free fish to understand what is happening to a hooked one."

These words never rang more true than when Martin, a seventh-grade student, shared the following story with me. Serena, a girl in his class, had a serious hygiene problem and gave off a terrible body odor. At the beginning of the year, students avoided her, but as time went on, they started calling her names and eventually started tripping her in the halls. A teacher who observed the physical bullying assigned Martin to escort the girl in the hallways to ensure her safety. Martin was not keen on accompanying a foul-smelling girl from class to class, but the teacher gave him no choice. After spending so much time with her, he began to see her in a different light and discovered that she was a pretty neat person. One day he mustered up his courage and said to her: "If you would just take a bath, your whole life would change. Why don't you take a bath?" In response, Serena firmly declared that she would never take a bath. When he asked her why, she told him that not bathing was the only way she could keep her father from "coming on to her." This thirteen-year-old girl was struggling with her hook, and found a most resourceful way to survive.

Dr. Menninger would plead that we have to honor students like Serena where they are, to probe the invisible trap that explains the offensive behavior—and to give them hope. It is not only targets who are thrashing on fishhooks, there are also bullies who are frantically flailing, as well. The empathetic educator has the opportunity to help the student understand what he or she is doing and why he or she is doing it, and help him or her find a better way to do it.

Jan Roosa, Ph.D., a psychologist in Kansas City, has designed a format for self-understanding that helps children as well as adults deal with issues and dilemmas. He calls it SOCCSS—Situation, Options, Consequences, Choices, Strategies, Simulation. The process he created begins with defining the specific problem; considering a range of options in response; analyzing the consequences that might result, positive and/or negative; making choices based on sound thinking; developing an action plan and rehearsing it.

Using this method is a practical way to make a thoughtful decision, taking both reason and emotions into account. The following example is an illustration of how the process could work from a student's perspective. While it is not likely that a student who is a bully will volunteer this situation, it is an excellent case study to use as an example for understanding SOCCSS. Students can agree or disagree with any of the options and consequences that are listed and add others. Once this illustration is completed, students can offer their own authentic situations and proceed with the outline.

Situation

Define the problem: *I keep getting in trouble in school because I am a bully.*

Options

1: Take responsibility for my problem
2: Blame others for my situation
3: Try to understand the reason for my negative behavior
4: Talk to a counselor or an adult I can trust
5: Drop out of school
6: Control my impulses
7: Stop picking on other students
8: Keep my anger inside
9: Find ways to deal with my anger
10:Change my behavior

Consequences

Option 1: Take responsibility for my problem
Positive consequences
- Become more mature
- Will need to take some constructive action
- Gain respect for myself and from others
- Learn that I can't get by with inappropriate behavior

Negative consequences
- Have to admit that I am at fault

Option 2: Blame others for my situation
Positive consequences
- Don't have to admit that I am at fault

Negative consequences
- Frustrated because I can't change oother people's behavior
- Have no control over the solution
- Never be able to solve my problem

Option 3: Try to understand the reason for my negative behavior
Positive consequences
- Could I learn something about myself, i.e., do I need some attention, am I upset about a situation in my family, am I angry about something, why do I do the things I do, am I dumping my hurt on someone else?
- Develop a way to check out my feelings
- Learn how to be introspective

Negative consequences
- Makes me think about unpleasant things
- Have to work very hard to understand

Option 4: Talk to a counselor or an adult I can trust
Positive consequences
- Learn how to reach out for help
- Could get some helpful guidance
- My problem might get solved

Negative consequences
- He/she may not believe me
- May not have any good suggestions

Option 5: Drop out of school
Positive consequences
- Won't have to deal with problem

Negative consequences
- Won't graduate
- Could get in bigger trouble
- Have a hard time finding a job

Option 6: Control my impulses
Positive consequences
- Could get along better with students, teachers, parents, siblings
- Could learn self-control
- Feel sense of personal power

Negative consequences
- People will expect me to be perfect
- Requires too much self-discipline

Option 7: Stop picking on other students

Positive consequences

- Students won't be afraid of me
- Students might like me
- Make a new group of friends
- Won't have to worry about someone trying to get revenge
- Won't feel crummy about the way I treat people
- Won't get in trouble
- Won't get suspended
- Targets won't get angry with me

Negative consequences

- Bullies will start picking on me
- Won't have any fun in school
- Others won't think I'm tough
- Lose my personality
- Won't get any attention
- School will be boring
- My friends won't hang around with me

Option 8: Keep my anger inside

Positive consequences

- Don't have to talk about my feelings
- Be "cool"
- Won't get in trouble

Negative consequences

- Might explode and lose my temper
- Could get stressed ou
- Disguise what I'm really feeling,
- Have physical problems, e.g., h headaches, stomach aches intestinal problems
- Get angrier

Option 9: Find ways to deal with my anger
Positive consequences
- Won't feel so stressed
- Get involved in an exercise program, do something physical
- Learn how to soothe and calm myself
- Won't get in frequent fights
- Sleep better
- Be healthier
- Use anger to solve a problem or improve a relationship

Negative consequences
- Have to work hard to think of new ways

Option 10: Change my behavior
Positive consequences
- Create an incentive or reward for myself
- Learn how to set goals I can accomplish
- Feel proud of who I am
- Stay out of trouble
- Establish a new reputation
- Attract new friends
- Make better grades
- Look forward to a better future
- Give up blaming others
- Find positive ways rather than negative to get attention

Negative consequences
- Lose a sense of power
- People will question my motives
- Others will keep expecting me to act like I used to
- It's very difficult to change behavior

After brainstorming all of the Options and analyzing the positive and negative Consequences of each possibility, the next step is to make some Choices and plot some Strategies. The final step is Simulation—putting the strategy into action. This is how the diagram could look:

SITUATION: I get in trouble in school because I am a bully
OPTIONS: Take responsibility for my problem
        Blame other people for my situation
        Talk to a counselor or an adult I can trust
CONSEQUENCE: (positive) I could get some helpful advice
CONSEQUENCE: (negative) They might get me in deeper trouble
CHOICE: Choose someone I have confidence in to talk with
STRATEGY: Rehearse a conversation about my hopes and fears
SIMULATION: Role-play with a peer to try out a dialogue

The same process with a different option would look like this:

SITUATION: I get in trouble in school because I am a bully
OPTIONS: Drop out of school
        Control my impulses
        Find ways to deal with my anger
CONSEQUENCE: (positive) Learn how to release my anger in a
        physical way
CONSEQUENCE: (negative) Have to change my personality
CHOICE: Use my athletic skills to work through a problem
STRATEGY: Make up a list of possible physical exercises, such as:
        lift weights, jog around the block, shoot baskets,
        jump rope, skate board, roller blade, etc.
SIMULATION: The next time I get angry, do something physical
        to release anger instead of taking it out on some-
        one else

I spoke with Trevor, a sixth-grade student who attended a week-long camp for students with ADD and ADHD where this strategy was used. In addition to swimming, tennis, computer activities, archery, and other fun events, SOCCSS was introduced. Trevor found the SOCCSS sessions extremely useful. The campers were divided into small groups of four or five students who worked with the construct for part of every day, including the simulation. They tried out their ideas and then practiced them until they felt confident that they could make the information work. Trevor reported that he was very pleased with his success in dealing with bullies when he returned to middle school. For further information about Roosa's SOCCSS copyrighted construct, check the chapter on Resources.

Strategies for Students Who Bully Others

From our extraordinary conversations with bright, articulate young people, there are some themes that emerge over and over again. One is that bullies have problems and they come to school with a lot of feelings that they take out on other people. If you recognize yourself in this sentence, a smart thing to do would be to become more aware of your feelings. When you get upset about something that is going on in your life, try to sort it out by asking yourself some questions: "What am I feeling?" "Am I angry?" "Am I disappointed?" "Am I sad?" "Am I jealous?" "Am I hurt?" "Am I frustrated?" "Can I handle this myself?"

A fourth-grade boy shared this: "In second grade my father died and I lashed out and became a bully." A number of students have admitted a similar reaction to a painful event. Once you have sorted out what is really going on and have some understanding of the source of your behavior, take a positive action step.

If you are having a serious problem in your family—if someone is ill, if there has been a death, if someone has been injured in an accident, if someone in your family has been sent to prison—find an adult to talk to. When you keep things bottled up inside, you don't deal with them productively. A bright little girl in the third grade in a California school made this insightful comment: "I was having a problem and I didn't tell anybody about it. I just kept it inside and then one day I exploded. I didn't ever do that again, but now some kids think I'm a bully just because of that one time."

Learning how to calm and soothe yourself is a wonderful skill to acquire. Phil Jackson, former coach of the Chicago Bulls and current coach of the Los Angeles Lakers, had his team regularly practice imagining themselves in a special place where they felt safe. He wanted his players to have a way to calm and focus themselves when a time-out was called during an intense, adrenaline-pumping game. You can teach yourself the same strategy. Start by taking a few deep breaths. Picture a place where you feel safe—a favorite spot in nature, the porch swing at your grandmother's house, your bedroom, whatever comes to your mind. Close your eyes and take some time to imagine what it looks like. Use your other senses, too. Are there sounds or smells or physical sensations that go along with your safe place? If so, add them to your imagined experience. Spend five to ten minutes practicing going to your safe place everyday. Soon you'll be able to get the complete experience very quickly. Then think of the times in your life that it would help you to become calm and focused, such as when someone is taunting you or goading you to get in trouble, and use this strategy in those situations.

If you are bullying other people—your peers or your siblings—and you've given some thought to making a change, here are some suggestions that have come from students:

Learn how to handle your anger.
Ask yourself, "Why am I doing this?"
Get some help to feel better about yourself.
Try to stop picking on someone for just one day.

Recognize what you are doing.

Develop a hobby or skill to help you feel better about yourself.

Listen to a friend who has some good advice for you.

Talk to another bully and discuss your behavior.

Work really hard to control your behavior.

Try to get some attention by doing something good.

Get some help if your family is abusing you.

Pay attention to any consequences you are experiencing.

Form a "Bullies Anonymous" chapter.

Think about how you would feel if you were the victim.

A number of students who stopped being hurtful to others claimed that it was focusing on empathy that made the difference. They were so caught up in their own issues—anger, power, pain—they hadn't given any thought to the person on the receiving end. Once they connected with the feelings of their target, they found it hard to be cruel. If you put yourself in your target's shoes and you feel no empathy, your problem is more serious.

Something to think about is that no one ever forgets the name of his/her bully. That is hardly the way someone would wish to be remembered.

Strategies for Students Who Are Targets

If you are being bullied, realize that the bully's behavior is more about him/her than you! The following are suggestions that I have collected from classroom discussions all over the country:

Ignore.

Walk away.

Run away.

Get an older brother or sister to help you.

Stay near an adult.

Follow the Golden Rule.

Be smarter.

Tell the bully's parents.

Laugh it off.

Talk to a friend.

Avoid the bully.

Offer to help the bully with a subject they find difficult; for example, spelling, math.

Ask the bully to help you with a subject.

Tell an adult, parent, teacher, counselor, principal.

Get a group of friends to give you support.

Stand up for yourself.

Firmly say, "Stop that."

Be polite when you stand up for yourself.

Get involved in some activities that make you feel good about yourself.

Threaten a bully who might back off from strength.

Agree with the bully.

Compliment the bully.

Use humor.

Have a comeback: "Whatever you say turns to glue, turns around and sticks to you." "So?" "Thank you." "How nice of you to notice."

Take karate lessons or study another martial art.

Hide from the bully.

Involve a peer mediator.

Go to another school.

Be homeschooled.

Act "crazy."

Bore them; for example, a girl in Iowa said that when boys

bully her, she starts talking about makeup, shampoo, jewelry, nail polish, and they leave her alone.

Be firm, but not mean.

Ask a question: "Why do you want to hurt my feelings?" "Are you having a bad hair day?"

Surprise the bully—when you do the unexpected, you're in control.

Do something dramatic. (Four girls who were targets sang "Don't Laugh At Me" at a school talent show.)

Confuse the bully.

Calm your anger—then act.

Ask a witness to report the bullying to an adult.

Tell a police officer.

Fight back—as a last resort, and only when you feel at risk for physical harm.

As you look over the list, think about the suggestions that might work for you. Consider the possible consequences for each proposal. Perhaps you can add some additional ideas of your own.

I feel the need to respond to the suggestion to "Fight back." This is mentioned too frequently to disregard, but I have grave concerns about recommending fighting as a solution. I reluctantly include it with the caveat "as a last resort" because of a lengthy interview I had with Jack.

Jack's bully beat him up on numerous occasions and made public, vulgar comments about his height and his body parts. Jack used ignoring as his first strategy. The bullying did not stop. His second course of action was to tell his teacher. She advised him to walk away. The bullying continued. He tried to recruit some friends to help him but the bully spread weird rumors about Jack to those friends and threatened them as well. Jack decided to tell his parents. His father had been taunted about being short when he was young and learned then that ignoring didn't work, so both parents went to the principal to report the situation. The principal spoke with the bully and kept an eye on him. For a month the bully laid low, but then attacked Jack in the bathroom. The janitor entered, turned on the light switch, and saved Jack from serious injury, but Jack was too intimidated to report the incident to the principal. He tried to make a friend of the bully by helping him with his poor grades, but it took too much time to maintain the tutoring strategy.

One day, the principal saw him in the hall by himself and asked him about the bullying situation. Jack was very relieved that the principal inquired, because the bully was keeping an eye on Jack to make sure he didn't go into the principal's office. Jack suspects that the bully was contacted and this might have resolved the problem, except that the principal had to take a leave of absence, and the bully took advantage of the situation. Jack feigned illness to stay home from school, and after two days he did become ill!

Jack had no desire to fight. He wanted to believe that his problem could be solved without physical force. Eventually his father enrolled Jack in martial arts and told him not to start a fight but if necessary, to use self-defense. One day, while being attacked, Jack finally fought back and the bully backed down.

Reflecting on his long siege—all the steps he had taken and the final result—Jack thinks if he had fought with his bully in the beginning, it wouldn't have worked. He believes the bully would have thought he was too scared to tell an adult or would have recruited some buddies to teach Jack a lesson. Jack feels that by trying all of the other options first, he was letting the bully know that he was determined to make the abuse stop. When I asked Jack if he could imagine any other successful scenario, he wonders if the bully would have retreated if the bully's parents had gotten involved and taken away privileges from their son. He thinks the principal might have controlled the situation if she had not had to leave.

When fighting is mentioned as a strategy, I share a true story of two outstanding athletes who were competitors. "Witnesses" loved to stir up the rivalry by carrying tales back and forth between the athletes, and one day their instigation egged one of the athletes to challenge the other to a fight. At an agreed-upon time and place, they met for the fistfight showdown, except that one of them had a gun. A bullet drilled into the spine of one of the athletes, who is spending the rest of his life in a wheelchair. The other athlete is serving time in prison. Such potential lost—for both of them!

I asked Walker Adams, a bright thirteen-year-old student who is about to enter the eighth grade, to review the list and select the recommendations that might work best for him. After thoughtful consideration, he came up with the Walker Adams Theory of Bullying Counteraction: Cool Down, Confuse, Comeback, and serve as Consultant.

Cool Down

Do not react when someone does something to you! One day a boy threw eight paper clips at me. After the eighth paper clip hit my ear, I threw one back. He ducked, the one I threw hit someone else, and I got into trouble! I should not have reacted the way that I did. I should have figured out another solution.

Confuse

If someone starts messing with me, I come up with a random sentence like, "Do you think that global warming is going to destroy our planet?" They are so surprised and confused by my response, they leave me alone.

Comeback

Bullies are not very smart. If they were, they'd have better things to think about then making other people miserable. You have to put the bully in your position and make them the target but don't be cruel, just get the upper hand. Try to get them to laugh or smile. Teach yourself to think on your feet. For example, if someone calls you a "pussy," say "meow, meow."

Consultant

Advise the bully that they are going to have to give up the idea they can always be in control. There is always going to be someone who is smarter, prettier, tougher. You can't always get what you want, so learn how to handle yourself without trying to get all the power.

If you are being verbally abused, you can respond passively, aggressively, or assertively. Here are three examples to illustrate the difference:

Put-down #1: "You look like a tub of lard."
PASSIVE RESPONSE (unspoken): I hate being fat. Everyone hates me.
AGGRESSIVE RESPONSE (spoken): "I'd rather look like a tub of lard than look like you!"
ASSERTIVE RESPONSE (spoken): "I am definitely on the chubby side, but you should see the fried chicken I turn out!"

Put-down #2: "You sing like a frog."
PASSIVE RESPONSE (unspoken): I'm so embarrassed about my voice.
AGGRESSIVE RESPONSE (spoken): "I'd rather sing like one, than look like one, Kermit."
ASSERTIVE RESPONSE (spoken): "I'm just waiting until I turn into a handsome prince."

Put-down #3: "So how are you going to suck up to the
teacher today, nerd?"

PASSIVE RESPONSE (unspoken): I won't raise my hand in
class, even if I know the answer.

AGGRESSIVE RESPONSE (spoken): "I'm just glad I'm not
a retard like you."

ASSERTIVE RESPONSE (spoken): "I'm going to turn my
homework assignment in and hope I make a good grade."

John Stanfield has developed a program called Be Cool using
these three concepts, but he uses terminology that is much easier to
grasp. He describes the three kinds of responses as *Cold, Hot,* and
Cool. I wish I had thought of that!

Mary Beth Peterson, the counselor who contributed the continuum of joking, teasing, and bullying in chapter 2, uses the concept of
"fogging" as an assertive technique when someone is teasing you
about some *thing,* such as a new haircut, tennis shoes, clothing, etc.
It is not used when what is said is something that hurts your heart.
According to Peterson, when you "fog," you use such statements as:

Maybe so.
Possibly.
You could be right.
Could be.

Examples:

A. That's a dumb outfit to wear to a party.
B. You could be right.
A. People will laugh at you.
B. Maybe so.
A. No one will invite you to a party again.
B. That's possible.

The fogger knows what he or she can say as an assertive comeback. Usually the attacker has just two or three statements he or she wishes to use toward the victim. The target responds quickly and in a matter-of-fact way, which frustrates the attacker. Students enjoy practicing the technique, often with puppets or stuffed animals. The purpose of fogging is to have the bullying statements stop. The purpose is *not* to have the target win.

In a marvelous little book, *How to Handle Bullies, Teasers and Other Meanies,* Alice Cohen-Posey gives some wonderful advice about responding to a bully with a compliment, agreeing with the bully, or using a sense of humor.

While you are trying to decide which comeback to use the next time you receive a put-down, think about your computer. The two most important commands on the computer are "Delete" and "Save." You can choose to delete or save any comment that is addressed to you. Maybe the best comeback is to say: "Delete!"

Several years ago I trained Vicki Price, who works for Child Abuse Prevention Services in Salina, Kansas, to do the work that I do in her community. She has been doing student empowerment sessions with nearly every elementary school in Salina and has added some wonderful dimensions to this work. I observed her recently and was delighted with an idea that she uses with third- and fourth-grade students.

After leading a discussion with students about ways you can handle a bullying situation, she suggests that there are four words that can be helpful: "Stop bullying, it hurts!" Then she invites students to come up with four other helpful words, and they offer phrases like "Please don't bully me," "Why are you bullying?" "Don't be so mean," "Stop being a bully," etc. After collecting a wonderful list, she suggests that if it's hard to look a bully in the eye and say those words, just hold up four fingers and the bully will know what you mean. Students love using the four-finger secret code.

Another addition that Vicki added to the student discussion

groups is the use of scripts. She writes each part out on a piece of paper and assigns a role to volunteer actors.

Here is a script for you to try with a group of students. This role-play requires a bully, three targets, and three witnesses. Each student receives a one-line script, which they can read on the spot or practice before performing. After the parts are read, invite other students to make observations and/or improve on the script. Students could create an entirely new scenario, a new verbal bullying remark, and new responses.

> **BULLY:** "Your hair is so ugly!"
>
> **AGGRESSIVE TARGET:** "My hair may be ugly but it's not as ugly as your face!"
>
> **PASSIVE TARGET** (to herself): "I wish I didn't have such awful hair."
>
> **ASSERTIVE TARGET** (agree): "When I got up this morning and looked in the mirror, I thought the very same thing."
>
> **ASSERTIVE TARGET** (compliment): "I wish I had hair like you!"
>
> **ASSERTIVE TARGET** (joke): "I slept on a metal pillow last night and now my hair is full of static," or "This hair style looks great on my dog."
>
> **WITNESS #1:** "We don't treat people that way at our school."
>
> **WITNESS #2:** "You wouldn't want someone else to say that to you."
>
> **WITNESS #3:** "What is it in you that you have a need to do this?" (could also be an assertive response)

I learned this last response from Desmond Richardson, an extremely talented dancer who has performed with the Alvin Ailey Dance Theater among other renowned dance companies. He was harassed by his peers for being a dancer when he was in high school. His mother had instilled such a deep belief in himself that it never occurred to him that ridicule directed toward him was anything but a reflection on the bully. Because he understood that the verbal assaults exposed the inadequacy of the bully, he used this phrase consistently with great success.

Strategies for Students Who Are Witnesses

If you are a witness, here are some ideas for you to consider:

Challenge the bully.
Get a group of students to challenge the bully.
Befriend a troubled bully.
Tell an adult.
Include a target in your activities.
Don't laugh at the bully's put-down.
Don't join forces with a bully and give him/her power.
Don't repeat gossip.
Support a target in private.

When I do "witness training" with students, I ask them to rank these suggestions in order of greatest risk. Invariably, students rank "challenge the bully" as the scariest and "support a target in private" as the least scary. The rank order of the other suggestions fluctuates from class to class. One of the purposes of this discussion is to present a range of options for witnesses to consider that best fits their comfort level. My hope is that they will begin with one and as they gain confidence in their role, will attempt other strategies as well.

One creative fifth-grade student came up with an innovative idea for a "Guardian Angel" corps at his school. He believes that many students would be enthusiastic about the role of protector, and it would give witnesses more courage, if there were an organized, supervised school activity to help targets.

Many schools have developed "buddy" systems. In some schools, eighth-grade students are trained to be buddies to sixth graders just entering middle school. Buddy plans have been designed to ease the transition for students who are new to the school system. Specially trained buddies also work with high-risk students, and buddies serve as tutors.

One astute fifth-grade student in Cincinnati, Ohio, raised the following issue at the conclusion of a student empowerment session. She was concerned that we were revealing too much information to the bullies and, as a result, none of the strategies for the targets would work. I expressed admiration for her thoughtful conjecture but wondered aloud how we could separate the bullies, the targets, and the witnesses for private discussions when the roles overlap. Still, her question lingers.

Our best hope is to engage everyone, believing in the possibility that:

- Informed bullies will make wiser, not more devious, choices
- Informed targets will have more confidence in their ability to handle bullies
- Informed witnesses will deny bullies status and power and become "Guardian Angels"

The more we talk about changing the school culture, not just the behavior of the child, the closer we will come to breaking the pain chain.

CHAPTER EIGHT

STRATEGIES FOR PARENTS

"The hardest part of being a parent is when your child is being bullied in school"
—Howard, a parent

That sentence is a direct quote from a father who was my airplane seatmate. As I listened to his story, I recalled the creed I repeat at parent seminars: "If your child is being abused by another child or children, do everything you can to empower your child to resolve the situation him- or herself. If that doesn't work, contact the teacher; if that doesn't work, contact the principal; if that doesn't work, contact the school board; if that doesn't work, contact the parents of the bully; if that doesn't work, contact the bully; if that doesn't work, get a lawyer; if that doesn't work, change schools; if that doesn't work, move; if that doesn't work, home school. No child deserves to be abused by anyone." The point of the speech is to imprint in parents' minds that bullying is nothing less than peer abuse and that as parents or guardians, they must be unfailingly persistent in their determination to protect their children from abuse.

STRATEGIES FOR PARENTS

My fellow passenger told me that he raised three children in a rural community in the Midwest. The hardest part of parenting for him was when his youngest son, Nick, was bullied in school. Nick had a late growth disorder and when he was in the fourth grade he weighed only forty pounds. He was much smaller than all of the other students and there was one boy who made his life hell. He pushed Nick around, taunted him, picked on him constantly and made his life absolutely miserable. Nick didn't want to do his homework, and he didn't want to go to school. He was lonely and depressed. Nick's father went to the school to speak with his teacher and received no support whatsoever. In fact, the teacher made fun of Nick, as well. The next step was a meeting with the principal, who told the father that his son was going to have to learn to stand up for himself. "How," the father asked, "could a forty-pound youngster stand up to an eighty-pound bully who was twice his size?" The principal just shrugged.

The father went on to say that most of the information about his son's bullying experiences came from his older sister. Fortunately, she was very aware of what was happening to him at school, as Nick did not report the incidents to his parents. His antipathy to school and depression were the only clues they had to realize that something was wrong. His father was determined to do something for his son because he had had three older brothers who bullied him mercilessly until he grew big enough to fight back. "I remember all the anger I felt towards them. I remember how the anger carried over at school and when a bully picked on another student, I would beat him up. I got into a lot of trouble for that, and I realize now that I was really dealing with the anger at my brothers against whom I couldn't defend myself because of their size, their strength, and it was three against one."

There were two elementary schools in the small town where Nick and his family lived, and his parents' next strategy was to transfer Nick to the other elementary school. Because of his stature, he became an immediate target there, as well. The teacher and the principal were unwilling to do anything about the bullying at that school either. His parents realized that their son needed counseling for the abuse he was dealing with and found a good therapist for him. It was very helpful, but it couldn't compensate for the daily attacks on his self-esteem at school.

Somehow Nick survived elementary school, but not without a lot of damage to his personality. In middle school, Nick's parents encouraged him to join a community wrestling league. Opponents were matched on the basis of weight, not age or grade, and he did very well. In fact, there was a tournament where he came in first place. Coincidentally, his bully entered the same tournament in a different weight category and lost. This defeat enraged him, and he beat up Nick in the locker room after the match. When Nick's dad confronted the bully's father about the fight, the father just shrugged.

"With no support from the school, and no acknowledgment from the family of the bully, we felt that we had to move out of that town, which we did. In addition to the move, we took him to a doctor who prescribed some hormone shots that helped with his growth. In the next year he grew four inches, which made a tremendous difference in his self-concept and took the pressure off of the taunting. He joined a youth group at our new church and he discovered friends and support that he had never had. I don't know what would have happened if he hadn't connected with such a terrific group of young people. He's doing well now and has a good job. Even though our situation had a happy ending, I know that the early bullying experiences Nick suffered have left a mark. And I know that I still have a lot of anger inside of me because of what I experienced at the hands of my brothers and what my son experienced at the hands of a bully."

The home plays such a pivotal role because children have formed strong patterns of social interaction by the time they enter school. Core values that can prevent bullying from ever occurring need to be taught from the beginning. By the age of five, children will realize if cruelty is unacceptable in their family or not. If parents speak in demeaning ways to each other and treat their children disdainfully, a code of disrespect can become a norm that is transferred from home to school.

The majority of mothers and/or fathers who come to our seminars are parents of students who are dealing with bullying problems. We believe there are five kinds of interactions where parents can be helpful to their children:

1. Parents with their own children
2. Parents with other parents
3. Parents with other children
4. Parents with teachers and school administrators
5. Parents as advocates

The following questions are representative of the queries we often receive at parent meetings that fall into these categories and the corresponding answers represent our advice as well as the responses of several extraordinary people we have trained to do this work.

Parents With Their Own Children

QUESTION: *What should I say to my child who doesn't want to go to school because of the bullying he endures?*
ANSWER: First of all, be grateful that your child is confiding in you and express appreciation for the fact that he or she is willing to talk with you about his or her problem. Second, take the issue seriously and listen carefully to his or her report. Children are reluctant to discuss bullying issues with their family. Many children are afraid their parents will do something to make the situation worse. Others are concerned that their parents will become too upset and won't be able to handle the information. Still oth-

ers assume that their parents will just dismiss the problem and tell them to ignore the bully, which they have already tried, unsuccessfully.

A recent study by the Kaiser Family Foundation and Nickelodeon reported that children who discussed bullying problems with their parents said the conversations were infrequent and not very helpful. According to the survey, half of eight- to eleven-year-olds whose parents said they discussed their troubles with them didn't even remember the conversations.

The first strategy should be to empower your children to resolve the situation themselves. Ask them to tell you about all the methods they have used and the responses that followed. Ask them if the bully has ever picked on other children and how others have dealt with the abuse. Have they observed anyone who has succeeded in getting the bullying to stop? Find out where the bullying most frequently occurs. If it's on the bus, perhaps you can contact the bus driver to change your child's seat or to provide him or her with more protection. It might become necessary to find another means of transportation. If it's at recess, maybe a playground supervisor can be clued in to the situation or your child can spend recess in the library.

Ask your child what he/she suspects is the reason why the student bullies others? Children are incredibly insightful about the family and personal problems that provoke bullies to pick on their classmates. Perhaps you can help them to see that the bully is the one with the problem. One child psychiatrist found that parents were amazed at how quickly the problem could be solved when the target became convinced that he or she was not at fault and it was the bully who was the source of the confrontation. Giving up the self-blame that accompanies bullying may be all it takes for a target to break the pattern.

Talk to them about denying the bully the satisfaction of evoking tears or showing distress. Suggest that they make every effort to refrain from crying until they're in a place where the bully can't revel in his or her power. Let your child know, in no uncertain terms, that you believe that bullying is very hurtful and you are committed to seeing that it stops.

Role-playing can be extremely advantageous. You can get more clarity about the explicit bullying your child is receiving, plus it will give you an opportunity to use specific language that your child can adopt. Students in the throes of taunting feel helpless to find the magic words that will make it stop. They are eager for language tools, for scripts that will make a difference. Repeat the role-playing many times, using different verbal responses until your child clicks with some phrase and then rehearse, rehearse, and then rehearse some more.

Body language can be equally effective. Talk to your child about posture that sends a message of defeat versus posture that sends a message of confidence. Teach them the song from *The King and I*— "Whenever I am afraid, I hold my head erect and whistle a happy tune, so no one will suspect I'm afraid." Another suggestion is to enroll your child in martial arts such as karate, tae kwon do, or tai chi. We have heard wonderful reports from parents whose children blossomed when exposed to the centering and respect that are part and parcel of eastern movement influences. Be sure to check the program before you enroll your child. Some programs put more emphasis on the fighting aspect, while we would favor the programs that focus on flexibility, concentration, and strength building.

Explain that you are going to continue to look at this problem from all angles and work together to take steps to ensure that it stops. If the first attempt doesn't work, you will go back to the drawing board and come up with Plan B. And if that doesn't work you will try Plan C. Reassure your child that you are partners in the solution and discuss every possible strategy together—whether it's contacting the teacher, the principal, or the bully's parents. Listen to your child's concerns and objections. Don't dismiss them out of hand because you are older and wiser. Your child may have a much better understanding of the personality of the players and the subtle factors involved from their unique vantage point.

Most parents have ultimately been able to assist in defusing the abusive situation, while keeping their child in the decision-making loop. On several occasions, however, parents have admitted that when student empowerment attempts and all else failed, they confidentially contacted school personnel despite their child's adamant resistance. They knew it was a risk to betray their child's concern, but at that point, they felt it was a lesser risk than the ongoing torment.

When all efforts to eliminate bullying for your child at school have failed, consider homeschooling. Approximately 850,000 of the nation's 50 million children are being taught at home rather than in schools. A report released by the Department of Education calculates that 1.7 percent of American children were homeschooled in 1999. Parents choose homeschooling for a variety of reasons, many not related to bullying, but for families who have decided that the school environment is too stressful for their child, home tutelage is a viable option.

By all means, share stories of bullying that you experienced when you were growing up. Children love to hear about real events in your life when you were their age. Nothing is more reassuring to your child than to hear that you were a target, that your world didn't come to an end, and that you are this fantastic adult who functions with ease in spite of the hurts you received.

QUESTION: *If it's true that a lot of children do not tell their parents what is going on, how can I know if my child is a target or a bully?*

ANSWER: There are a number of signs to look for to determine if your child is being targeted or if your child is engaging in bullying behavior. Does your child resist going to school, make excuses to stay home? Have there been any changes in sleep patterns? Are they sleeping too much or sleeping too little? Waking up in the middle of the night with frightening dreams?

Are there any signs of depression, withdrawal, loss of appetite, lack of energy? Have they started wetting the bed at night? Has there been a sudden drop in grades and test scores? On the other hand, has your child become more aggressive, hurtful to siblings? There will always be normal competition between children and their siblings for your affection and attention, but when cruelty erupts, it must not be ignored.

Have there been instances of animal abuse—killing birds or squirrels, torturing cats or dogs? Abuse of animals is often the first indication that a child's anger or aggression is out of proportion. "Even if pets have not been hurt by their abusers, children who are the victims of abuse may seek to re-enact the abuse they have suffered by repeating these behaviors on other victims who are weaker and more vulnerable than themselves. Often the targets of this 'abuse reactive' behavior will be younger siblings or small pets." This is a quote from Randall Lockwood, Ph.D., Vice President for Research and Educational Outreach of the Humane Society of the United States.

Any of these might be warning signs that a bullying situation is affecting your child. Don't wait for your child to initiate a conversation on the topic. Tell them that you've been reading some material about bullying, and you want to check out some information with them. Inform them about the different kinds of bullying—physical, verbal, emotional, and sexual. Many students still consider bullying to be a synonym for fighting and don't believe that verbal, emotional, and sexual behaviors qualify as abuse between peers. Ask them if bullying takes place at their school. Begin with more general questions, like asking where it happens most frequently, and then gradually move to the more personal ones. Be sure to ask questions rather than lecture.

QUESTION: *My children treat each other terribly. Do all siblings do this to each other or is this bullying?*

ANSWER: Nearly every parent with more than one child has experienced the bully-target dynamic in his or her own home. We believe there is a distinction between "normal" sibling conflict and sibling bullying. Conflict between siblings should be considered abusive when the interaction becomes violent, when either sibling feels that he or she is powerless to stop the interaction, when the conflict persists over a period of time, and when the conflict is lopsided so that one sibling is singled out consistently.

Researchers suggest that sibling abuse can have damaging consequences, resulting in relationship difficulties, poor self-esteem, sexual dysfunction, depression, and other emotional problems in more chronic and severe circumstances.

Blended families often face additional challenges as stepsiblings learn to live together. A second marriage may mean that a child must share a room that once was his own, or that a child who once had the role of the oldest in the family now feels displaced by his or her new, older stepsiblings.

One theme that consistently surfaces, however, in our research and experience with families is the pain many siblings felt because they did not feel their parents moved to protect them from the physical, verbal, emotional, or sexual sibling abuse that they were certain their parents observed.

Adele Faber and Elaine Mazlish, authors of *Sibling Without Rivalry: How to Help Your Children Live Together So You Can Too,* offer some very specific advice and strategies. They believe that although it is difficult to tolerate the negative feelings siblings can express about each other, acknowledging these feelings openly results in more positive interactions between siblings.

The authors feel that parents can do much to reduce conflict between siblings by avoiding making comparisons, either positive or negative, between siblings. Similarly, parents need to guard against unwittingly locking children into set roles—such as the responsible one, the talented one, the stubborn one—that may limit all of the children in the family from developing to their full potential.

Parents should also avoid casting siblings as the bully or the target. Parents can interrupt this dynamic even after it has been up and running for years. Seeing children who bully as capable of being kind and compassionate, and seeing children who have been picked on as capable of being strong and self-reliant is an important step.

When I ask students which they think causes more pain—sibling bullying or peer bullying—this is what they reply:

"Sibling bullying is worse because . . . 'you have to live with your brother or sister for the rest of your life' . . . 'if your parents won't do anything about it, there's never any relief' . . . 'when my parents leave us alone, I'm at my sibling's mercy' . . . 'my sibling threatens to do terrible things to me if I tell on him, so I'm damned if I tell, and damned if I don't' . . . 'my sister never gets in trouble for bullying me so why should she stop?'"

"Peer bullying is worse because . . . 'it's more embarrassing because everyone knows about it' . . . 'sometimes you do get along with your brother or your sister but you never get along with your bully' . . . 'if the bully decides you're a target all the other kids join in with the bully.'"

In general, siblings should resolve differences on their own. When siblings are unable to do so, adults should intervene to open the blocked channels of communication so the children can go back to working it out themselves. Adults also need to intervene if the conflict escalates to an abusive level, separating the children and facilitating a more effective approach later on when tempers have cooled.

QUESTION: *My daughter is being shunned by a vicious clique. It's one thing to make someone stop punching or name-calling, but how do you insist that girls include your child in their group?*

ANSWER: Isolation, rejection, ostracizing, shunning can be much more difficult to deal with than physical, verbal, or sexual abuse. The "Thou Shalt Nots" are easier to address than the "Thou Shalts." At the time of your youngster's painful exclusion, any suggestion to make other friends may not register, but patiently encourage your child to discover that there are young people who are trustworthy, who have the capacity for loyalty, and who will offer friendship gifts that are not as transitory.

Michael Thompson, author of *Best Friends, Worst Enemies*, believes that one friend, just one dependable relationship can make all the difference for students struggling with childhood churlishness. Do all that you can to guide your child to explore other social groups. Encourage them to sign up for after-school activities, scouting groups, community service projects, reading clubs—any opportunity to be in touch with other youngsters and the hope of making that one connection that can soothe their sense of rejection and provide a positive peer relationship. Sometimes parents have to deal with their own sense of loss here. Parents have recognized that their own painful experiences from the past are brought to the surface when their children have trouble with peers. This can help them empathize with and support their sons and daughters, but it may also interfere. Parents may assume that their child's experience is just as theirs was, and they may be uncomfortable if the child chooses to handle it differently.

It can be a particularly painful struggle for parents if their child decides to maintain some kind of connection with students who are cruel to them. Other parents' discomfort runs in the opposite direction. Mothers often hold out hope that their daughters will be included in the group that is excluding them, especially if it's the popular crowd. Sometimes they are uncomfortable with their daughter's decision to focus on developing other friends.

We believe the most helpful approach is to try to understand how the situation looks to your child. Share your point of view, as you may see something that he or she is too close to observe. In the end, however, support your daughter or son in his or her efforts to work through a thorny situation.

When a child's ego is crushed by bullying, one possibility to renew his or her wounded spirit is to focus his or her energy into a skill—academic, artistic, and/or athletic. Many famous people have expressed the belief that their success is inextricably connected to the passion they pursued when their peer survival was at stake. They were determined to prove the "rejectors" wrong about their denigration. Nicholas Cage, Steven Spielberg, Julia Roberts, Mark McGwire, Robert Reich, and other celebrities have revealed stressful childhood experiences at the hands of their peers. Their success as adults should serve as encouragement to youngsters who feel too troubled by the moment to imagine a brighter future.

For a period of time, the family might have to serve as the social and emotional healing bandage that protects the wounds. Favorite foods, preferred activities, distractions, and genuine expressions of affection can buoy a saddened soul. But be especially sensitive to the embarrassment that can occur if your child is seen with you too often in a public setting. Particularly at the middle school age, it might be best to attend a movie theater together in another neighborhood.

Work to find the right balance in your relationship with your child. Don't overdo solicitousness. There is a difference between empathy and pity. Appreciate that you and your child might heal in a different rhythm. Sometimes children are more resilient than we expect. Don't let your anguish become a burden for your child.

By all means, consider counseling. A skilled therapist can bring objectivity to a problem and be of enormous benefit. Do not hesitate to use professional help to support your son or daughter in dealing with isolation or any form of bullying.

Parents With Other Parents

QUESTION: *My child is being bullied by a classmate. Do you recommend that I call the bully's parents?*

ANSWER: Contacting a bully's parent or parents can be a risky strategy. Most authorities strongly oppose this approach and advise parents to take the matter to a teacher or principal, instead. This advice is based on the concept that a third party might be in a better position to mediate any conflict that might arise. If the parent is someone you know, however, you might want to handle the situation personally rather than have them contacted by someone else. Parents have spoken of being hurt and embarrassed when a teacher called instead of the parent they knew quite well.

Even so, you should anticipate a range of possible responses. One might be the parent who is shocked to hear that there is a problem and expresses appreciation for the contact. More often the response might be a parent who denies any possibility that his or her child is guilty of abusive behavior. In a recent police department survey in Oak Harbor, Washington, 89 percent of local high thirty-eight school students said they had engaged in bullying behavior. Yet only 18 percent of parents thought their children would act as bullies.

There is a risk that the parent will become very angry and say hurtful things about your child. If you are still haunted by memories of a personal bullying situation when you were in school, denial, defensiveness, and criticism of your child might trigger a response in you that can inflame the situation rather than defuse it.

If you can envision yourself as a problem solver rather than an adversarial champion, the tone of your voice, as well as your words, will benefit the conversation. Tone of voice, especially on the phone when facial cues are not accessible, can be very revealing. When the pros and cons of parent-to-parent communication arose at one PTA meeting, Barry White, headmaster at Pembroke Hill Country Day School, supported the idea for the following reason. He said: "Make the call because you will get important information. If the parent listens respectfully and shares your eagerness to get to the truth and solve the problem, you're ahead. If the parent is belligerent and disrespectful, then you have a significant clue about that family culture and the kind of predicament your child is facing. Either way, it's a Win/Win situation."

At another parent meeting, a parent remarked that children need to observe adult role models resolving difficult issues. Contacting a bully's parent provides an opportunity to show children problem solving in action. In a new national PTA survey, 25 percent of parents support contacting other parents to deal with bullying.

At parent meetings, I will frequently raise the issue and ask: "If your child was bullying a student, how many of you would want the parent of the target to call you directly?" Invariably, all hands are raised. This gives permission and support for parents who, in their best judgment, choose to make such a call.

The following question always arises: "What about the parents who didn't come to the meeting, who didn't hear the discussion, who didn't vote?" We suggest that a column be included in the next newsletter to parents that describes the meeting, the issues that arose, and the results of the conversation.

With all of that said, we still recommend that you gather as much information as you can about the parents in question as you consider your decision. Are they known to be reasonable and civil in the way they have been observed at athletic events and/or social situations, or do they have a reputation for being defensive and easily angered?

One parent shared a most creative and highly successful strategy. She called the parents of the bully and invited their family to come for a holiday supper. The evening was a great success. The parents enjoyed each other's company, continued to share family events, and the bullying situation was eliminated by the change in the family social dynamics.

In short, consider all the possibilities before you make a decision. Just as we propose that you work with your children to find empowering strategies that coincide with their comfort level, go through the same process as you determine yours.

A most poignant, unusual solution occurred when a child called the parent of his bully. Max was seven years old when he reported a problem that he was having with a bully to his mom and dad and asked them to call the bully's parents. While his parents pondered whether to make such a call, their son reached for the school telephone directory and dialed his tormentor's phone number. To Max's relief, the father of the bully answered the phone. Max announced that he was so pleased to have a chance to talk with him because his child was picking on him and Max thought it would be very helpful if he would have a talk with his child and get the bullying to stop. (He did and it did!)

Parents With Other Children

QUESTION: *I've thought about contacting the child who is my son's bully? What do you think about that idea?*
ANSWER: We consider this to be a plausible strategy. If your child has tried a number of tactics and none of them have caused the bully to back down, consider talking to the bully yourself. It is best to get your child's permission to pursue this move. If such permission is denied, you have to weigh the options of intervening or remaining silent.

Three parents in different parts of the country have recounted very successful interventions with their child's bully. The first parent stopped the bully as he rode by the house on his bike and informed him that she was going to call his parents if there was one more instance of bullying and, indeed, the bullying ceased. In the second situation, a mother accompanied her child into the school, asked her son to point out the bully, and then instructed her child to leave the scene. She approached the bully and spoke very firmly to him. She told him to stay away from her son and that if she ever heard of another incident, she was going to locate him at school and take him to the principal's office. That bullying situation stopped immediately. In the third case, a father waited after school for the bully to emerge. In front of a crowd of students, he told the bully that punching his son amounted to assault and battery, and if the bully ever touched his son again, he was going to have a lawyer file suit against him and his family. In each of these successful cases, the formula consisted of being respectful; remaining calm, but firm; presenting the facts; and stating a plan of action.

If you choose this strategy, consider the fact that the bully might be a child in distress. When your own child is hurting, it is difficult to be empathetic with your son's or daughter's tormenter, but the possibility exists for you to make a connection with a child who is in need of compassion.

Parents With Teachers, Counselors, and School Administrators

QUESTION: *I want to contact our daughter's teacher, but I don't want the teacher to become upset with me and take it out on my child. What should I do?*

ANSWER: Most school bullying problems are best resolved when the students, the parents, and the faculty are aware and engaged in the solution. Parents and teachers must work together to curtail the power of bullies. Keep in mind that most teachers are parents, too.

Peer power issues are complicated and sometimes delicate because some parents are eager for their children to be popular. Many bullies gather a certain amount of status and popularity because of the power they accrue, and parents are not inclined to interfere when their children's standing is at stake. If mature adults can be corrupted by power, imagine what can happen with a ten-year-old or a teenager. Children cannot be expected to develop their own code of fairness. Adults must take responsibility to set limits for children who overstep reasonable boundaries.

Explain to the teacher that you have worked with your child to deal with the situation directly, but the attempts have not been productive and you have reached the conclusion that adults must become involved. The teacher may or may not know that bullying is occurring, because bullies are very clever about abusing their peers when adults are not present. Collect as much accurate information as you can acquire from your child and write down the facts as you know them. If you know of other parents whose children are also a target, you might want to join forces. Your first approach might be to make an appointment with the teacher to share what you have learned and ask the teacher if he or she has noticed any corroborating evidence. Be prepared for the possibility that the teacher has never observed the bullying and/or the teacher sees your child through different eyes—perhaps as the provocateur. Be willing to hear another opinion because it might be valuable data, even though not what you anticipated. There is also the possibility that the teacher might have a bias and his or her view might not be accurate. Remember Eddie Haskell from *Leave It to Beaver?* Haskell was charming to adults, concealing the mean-spirited, biting personality he showed off to his peers.

If the teacher is responsive and willing to play a role, the best scenario is when a teacher can catch a bully in the offensive act and intervene immediately. This will require the teacher to be on alert for a troublesome situation and more aware of subterfuge.

Another action step the teacher can pursue is to contact the parent of the bully or bullies. The teacher might have established a relationship with that person and can bring facts to their attention in a tactful way. The teacher might recommend involving the school counselor or social worker, if there is one, or perhaps the principal. Continued communication between parent and school personnel is important to track the outcome or lack of one. It is very important to discuss how and when that communication should occur to keep expectations of each other in proportion and to assure follow-up that is agreeable to all parties.

If your child is in middle school, where there are many teachers, it might be preferable to contact the counselor and/or the principal initially. It might be advisable to contact the vice principal or the principal under any circumstances because the bully might be in a different grade, or the teacher may have handled the situation poorly.

If you find the teacher to be uncooperative and dismissive of your report, you need to take the problem through the chain of command, whatever that may be—principal, superintendent, or the school board. Always present yourself as someone who sees the school as a helpful partner and ally, rather than an adversary, until proven differently.

Keep a written record of any conversations you have with your child, the bully, the teacher, the bully's parents, the counselor, the principal, the school board member or any other relevant party. Make notes about the questions or comments you make and the corresponding responses. It is very important to be accurate and to confirm what you hear from the other person, adult or child. When feelings are running high, sometimes it is difficult to absorb someone's responses objectively. Take the time to repeat what you hear and ask if you have heard the reply correctly. Let them know that you are taking notes for accuracy rather than trusting your memory. Document, document, document, and date it! You never know how important the documentation can be until you really need it.

Parents As Advocates

QUESTION: *My child is in kindergarten and we aren't having any problems, yet, but what can I do to avoid or prevent bullying from ever happening?*

ANSWER: There are many steps you can take as an advocate to make your schools and community the safest environment for your children.

Become familiar with your school culture through involvement with the PTA or other parent organizations. Organize a Parent Seminar on the topic of school safety and/or bullying, and invite an expert on the topic to make a presentation. At the least, attend the parent meetings that are planned for your benefit. Offer to chaperone field trips; volunteer for playground, cafeteria, or hallway supervision; assist with school events; and support your principal and staff. Volunteer to help in the classroom where you can really witness the dynamics firsthand.

Network with other parents. If your child is describing bullying situations with classmates or even with a teacher, check with other parents to see if they are collecting the same stories. It is easier to effect needed change when you have leverage. If you have been accused of being overprotective, similar stories from other parents can add weight to your concern.

Think of all the carpools you drive. What if you made it a rule that in your carpool, no one would put anyone down? What if you insisted that in your car, everyone would feel safe because you do not allow people to hurt each other? What if your home, your carpool, your style of supervision became known as a place where kindness and respect were valued and appreciated?

Use your role as scout leader or den mother to address the issue of bullying with your youth groups. Devote a meeting to the topic and then reinforce the important concepts throughout the year. Do the same thing with faith-based youth groups. Surely scouting and religious tenets would sanction ethical behavior between peers.

Collect data. Clip articles from newspapers and magazines. Recruit friends and neighbors to join you in the research. Interview young people and adults about their experiences to become knowledgeable about the issues. Persuade your local library to become a resource center for videotapes, books, pamphlets, catalogues, and other reference materials on bullying. Identify local experts on the topic to speak to community organizations. Maybe you will become the expert!

Volunteer to serve on a committee that is developing bullying prevention policies at your school. Become involved in some of the larger issues that impact on bullying, such as media violence, access to weapons, Internet bullying, etc., and be sure to recognize, celebrate, and acknowledge individuals and groups who are making a difference, including students. Two outstanding mothers/advocates are Nancy Barrow and Barbara Rodriguez, with the Lee County Medical Society Alliance in Ft. Myers, Florida. They have begun a three-year plan to have every school counselor in their county go through our BullySafeUSA Training Institute. They have networked with public, private, and parochial schools. Through the alliance, they have built partnerships with volunteers, the superintendent of schools, a community hospital, the media, and corporate supporters.

We need nothing more than the reports of several tragedies at youth athletic events to convince us that sporting activities are rife with feelings that can get out of control. Bullying can occur between players, between players and opponents, between coaches and players, between parents and coaches, between parents and referees, between parents and parents, and between parents and players, and we've heard stories about every situation, including appalling deaths.

The Saint Barnabas Health Care System has collected some important data in the process of developing a Rediscovering Youth Sportsmanship program: 45.3 percent of young athletes have been called names, yelled at, or insulted while participating in sports; 17.5 percent of young athletes say they have been hit, kicked, or slapped while participating in sports; 15 percent of parents at youth sports events display obnoxious, unruly, or unsportsmanlike behavior; 70 percent of children drop out of organized sports by age thirteen.

One of the most constructive advocacy stories we heard had to do with a father who was bullying his son at a soccer game. The coach of his son's team had a wonderful philosophy. His goal was not to win games, but to give children a love of the sport, to give them skills and to teach them the benefits of teamwork. Consequently, he let every boy play in every game. The bully's son was not an excellent athlete. His coordination left a lot to be desired but it didn't matter to the coach who played him on a rotating basis. The boy's father was distraught with his son's lack of prowess. Whenever the boy would miss a kick, his father would scream at him from the stands. He called him names, berated him loudly so that everyone could hear, and screamed instructions at him. The other parents were horrified at the father's behavior but felt helpless to put a stop to it. They called a meeting to discuss the situation and decided not to confront the father, fearing that it could make the problem worse. Instead, whenever the boy came on the field, all of the parents cheered him on. They would yell: "You're doing a good job," "You're trying your best," "Hang in there, don't give up," and *their* voices prevailed. That is parent advocacy at its finest!

Another innovative approach came from a female coach who was dismayed by the irate behavior of some fathers at their daughters' soccer tournament. She invited the fathers to play against their daughters at the next practice. As they huffed and puffed across the field, they came to realize the physical demands of the game and their own athletic flaws. They were perfect spectators when they returned to the stands at the next game. Every time adults and children gather together, it is a precious opportunity for adults to demonstrate and epitomize standards of behavior we would wish them to emulate.

Paula speaks about the sense she had growing up of living in a "community container." Looking back, she feels fortunate that other people in her community, in addition to her parents, would reprimand her if she disobeyed the neighborhood norms, would remind her of expected behavior, and would compliment her when she was polite and mannerly. It wasn't just Mom and Dad that coaxed, cajoled, disciplined, and encouraged. She was grateful for the village that shaped her development.

CHAPTER NINE

STRATEGIES FOR TEACHERS & EDUCATORS

*"Without a safe learning environment, teachers
cannot teach and students cannot learn."*
—National Center for Education Statistics

Stories of the Courage to Teach: Honoring the Teacher's Heart, by
Sam M. Intrator, presents the narrative stories of twenty-five
effective teachers woven together with concepts about great teaching. In return for the important commitment teachers make to
our children, Intrator prods us to give teachers the support they
want and deserve—such as respect, more time with their colleagues, better pay, and more emphasis on teacher-driven lessons
and less on standardized curriculum and testing. Standardized
testing has become a source of contention in many states and
communities, because teaching to the test takes time away from
teaching the curriculum.

Teachers today are under enormous pressure to raise the test scores of their students. In Iowa and North Carolina, teachers are given a bonus if test scores increase. When scores become higher, there is even greater pressure to attain the next level. The priority of test scores is good news/bad news for bullying. The good news is that when bullying goes down, test scores go up. The bad news is that teachers don't have as much time to work on the consistent reinforcement and classroom discussions essential to affect bullying behaviors.

Even teachers who are conscientious about bullying issues don't realize how much abuse occurs out of their awareness. A study by Wendy Craig from Queen's University and Debra Pepler from York University, determined that 71 percent of teachers say they almost always intervene in bullying situations, while students say that teachers intervene only 25 percent of the time. Pepler and Craig's observations indicate that teachers intervene in 14 percent of classroom episodes and in only 4 percent of playground episodes of bullying.[49] This discrepancy is not necessarily a reflection on the detachment of educators as much as it is a testimony to the almost Machiavellian means employed by bullies to thwart detection. There are infinite opportunities for students to bully their peers when adults are not around or their backs are turned. Even when educators and administrators are diligently attentive to bullying situations, the possibilities for abuse on buses and playgrounds and in bathrooms, cafeterias, locker rooms, hallways, and classrooms are limitless.

Teacher Issues

We cannot close our eyes to the deaths and injuries of those teachers who have been victimized in school shooting incidents, as well as to random killings that have occurred. While no profession is immune to potential threats, we cannot ignore the fact that teacher shortages pervade school systems all across the country and that salaries for educators have not kept pace with competitive professions.

In California, the legislature passed a law limiting classroom size as a strategy to increase educational opportunities for primary school students, kindergarten through third grade. When teachers were pulled from higher grades to fill the mandated K–3 slots, the school districts were often faced with the task of hiring instructors for the replacement classes who did not meet state teaching standards. Is a warm body in a classroom of twenty-five students preferable to a qualified teacher in a classroom of thirty-five students? Obviously, numbers alone do not solve the problem.

Schools are dealing with a shortage of substitute teachers as well. Lee Shulman, president of the Carnegie Foundation for the Advancement of Teaching, says: "We've lost not only our pitchers, but also our relief pitchers and the entire bench." The Department of Education predicts that the nation will need more than a million new teachers by 2010. Some schools are preparing for this challenge by recruiting teachers from overseas, hiring people from other fields who are switching careers, and even luring teachers with bonuses and offers of college-loan reimbursement and low-interest mortgages. Clearly, as our society struggles to recruit and maintain effective teachers, creating safe schools should be one of the strategies.

What Teachers Need

In discussions with teachers about bullying problems, teachers consistently indicate that they want support from their principal and the school administration. There is nothing more demoralizing to teachers and counselors who are dedicated to dealing with peer issues, especially before they become serious problems, than to have a principal who will not back them up at a time of challenge. The influence of the principal on the school atmosphere is indisputable. I knew of one elementary school where all the ingredients were ideal—a gifted, dedicated faculty that worked beautifully as a team; involved and supportive parents from a community that honored education; diverse students with high expectations for themselves and each other; and a principal who had earned the respect and affection of the students, teachers, and parents. When a new principal was appointed, in spite of all the factors that had been imbedded in the culture of the school for many years, this seemingly impenetrable, solid system began to disintegrate. The teachers, who had been included in policy decisions and were proud of the open communication lines that were a signal feature of their school, were reduced to receiving administrative memos. As the principal played favorites and gave assignments based on those who did or did not question decisions, the teachers moved into a self-protective mode and the Technicolor haven that had defined the structure of the school converted to a black-and-white, adversarial bunker within one year.

A school principal who understands that learning, academic achievement, and test scores—areas for which the principal is held accountable—are inextricably tied to student safety will take steps to make bullying prevention a high priority. There are many children who cannot concentrate on school subject matter when their fears are all-consuming. Their poor test scores label them as mediocre students rather than identify them as capable students who are dealing with stress, whether at home or at school.

At one conference I attended, Michael Dorn, a presenter from the Georgia Emergency Management Agency (GEMA), described how they had put elements in place that had dramatically reduced, and in some cases eliminated, school violence in certain areas. Dorn reported that they had built fences around the schools and metal detectors were installed at every entrance. All students and teachers wore identification badges and there was a dress code. Dogs were brought in to sniff lockers for drugs, there were surprise locker searches, surveillance cameras were mounted in the hallways and on the buses, and a uniformed police officer was on campus at all times.

A team of high school students, who were attending the conference, observed that it sounded more like being in a prison than a school. The GEMA expert smiled knowingly and said that they were just ahead of the curve. He asked us to remember how annoyed we were when airports first put in metal detectors and now, he asked, would you consider boarding a plane if there were no metal detectors? As more and more precautions are taken to protect our social, political, travel, and business institutions from attack and subversion, schools will conform to the modus operandi of the day. Students need to hear that the more responsibility they take for ensuring school safety for everyone, the more latitude they will have in their environment. Conversely, the less responsibility they take, the more restrictions they will have to endure.

Some schools have already put very restrictive, zero tolerance policies in place. Other schools have concentrated on team building and instilling feelings of success. Still others focus on incentives and rewards for positive behavior. Different policies can bring about similar results. The system that fits the style of the principal is more likely to succeed.

Even when the principal is less than ideal, there is Mrs. Farmer. Mrs. Farmer is an eighth-grade teacher at a Midwestern public middle school and is glowingly described by her students. They reported that at the beginning of the school year, most teachers spend the first three days on "orientation," which consists of information about textbooks, homework assignments, and grading systems. Mrs. Farmer, however, spends the first three days discussing the need for dignity and respect. When students are taunted or laughed at when they ask or answer questions, she claims that the opportunity for learning is stifled. Her highest priority is an atmosphere where students feel safe to raise their hands and ask their curious questions.

Mrs. Farmer shares personal stories of bullying experiences that she observed when she was a student and as a teacher. She stresses the values of compassion and support. Her students use words like "sanctuary" when they talk about the chaos in their lives and the relief they feel when they enter her classroom. There are thousands of teachers who create sacred havens of physical and emotional safety for our children, and their students are blessed. Every teacher *can* provide such safe havens, and they must be encouraged to do so.

What Students Need From Teachers

Students are in need of S.O.S. from teachers—Skills, Observation, and Support.

Skills

Students want to feel capable of handling bullying situations themselves. They are eager for opportunities to learn skills that can really work. This training should be given to all students because of the interchangeable roles in students' behavior.

Skills for Targets

The skills should include strategies to deal with students who are bullying them physically, verbally, emotionally, and sexually. Targets need language ideas, scripts, and role-playing opportunities to act out possible scenarios. They need a list of options to consider, to understand the difference between aggressive, passive, and assertive responses. Students who seem to attract bullies need to understand the behaviors or body language messages they convey that make bullies more likely to harass them.

Targets need to understand that many bullies are very much like the Wizard of Oz—a fierce and intimidating facade but a troubled and vulnerable coward behind the curtain. Targets need to understand that no child deserves to be abused, and there is some adult in their lives who will take their anguish seriously and be in their corner until the bullying stops.

There are a number of books and workbooks that have been published on the topic of strategies and skill training that are teacher/counselor friendly. Two of my favorites are: *Get Connected*, three teacher guides, grades K–2, 3–5, 6–8, by STOP Violence!, and *The Bully Free Classroom: Over 100 Tips and Strategies for Teachers K–8* by Alan Beane. More specific information about skills for targets is given in chapter 7, "Strategies for Students."

Skills for Bullies

Bullies need to understand that bullying will not be tolerated and that consequences will occur when they are hurtful to others. When bullying behavior is accepted as the norm, it encourages other students to join in the fray. Emphasizing empathy, respect, responsibility, and other components of character education is essential. Basic social skill training can go a long way in curbing disruptive behaviors. Teachers can insist on basic manners in the classroom that should have been instilled at home. While bullies may prevail in the confines of a school, ultimately individuals who relate to others through fear and intimidation face a lonely and unhappy future when they can be more easily avoided. We owe it to bullies to help them recognize this truth, as the implications for their future relationships are profound.

REACTIVE BULLIES—Studies suggest that students who bully in reaction to perceived provocation from others can benefit from social skills, anger management, empathy training, and inspiration. Inspiration could include a suggestion such as: "It looks like you've put other people in charge of your behavior and then you pay the price. You think that if someone else starts something, you have no choice but to finish it and then you get in trouble. You deserve to find other ways to handle these situations that don't cost you so much."

PROACTIVE BULLIES—Researchers are understandably skeptical that calculating, mean-spirited, vicious bullies will respond to empathy training or social skill enrichment. Callous bullies need to experience the consequences of their behavior. The recommended course of action for these students is setting boundaries, establishing limits, and determining and carrying out consequences. The more they abuse without penalty, the more their behavior will become entrenched. I have heard many prisoners confess that leniency when they were juveniles didn't alter their criminal activity but just prolonged harsher sentences at a later time. That is a strong recommendation for bullying intervention that is timely, persistent, and appropriate for the offense. Consequences do not imply absence of compassion and concern. Counseling, intensive therapy, assignment to an alternative classroom for students with behavior disorders, or even psychiatric hospitalization should be considered.

ELITIST BULLIES—These students tend to be self-centered and egotistical. They are filled with themselves and feast on the power given to them by their peers as well as adults. Our recommendation for these students is opportunities for service learning such as tutoring disadvantaged or disabled students and/or some kind of community service that exposes them to people and circumstances from a different perspective. Elitist bullies have tremendous leadership potential. Empathy opportunities can also work here. A perfect example is the case of a group of cocky high school student athletes from a community where sports were monumental. A teacher came to the thoughtful conclusion that they might benefit from visiting children in a cancer ward, so she made arrangements at the local hospital for them to appear. A nurse who observed their conversations with the children became irate at their selfishness. The athletes used their time with the patients to boast about their trophies, their championships, and their many accomplishments. The nurse pulled one basketball player out into the hall and reprimanded him for his obvious disinterest in the children. She instructed him to go back onto the ward and ask the children questions about themselves. She insisted that he shift from focusing on himself to investing in children who were dealing with life-threatening ilnesses, painful treatments, and homesickness. It was a life-changing, defining experience for the young man. He came back to visit with children in the hospital after the teacher's experiment was concluded. He made a special point to seek out the nurse who had given him a transcending point of view and turned his life around.

All students can benefit from making a contribution to their community. Volunteerism has proven to reduce the school dropout problem. Volunteering changes the way young people feel about themselves and it changes the way others see them. Volunteering can change their lives and it can change the world they live in. Since September 11, 2001, young people have turned to volunteerism in exciting ways and are making significant contributions to issues of peace making and violence prevention.

Ron Poplau, a sociology instructor at Shawnee Mission Northwest High School in Kansas, created a community service credit course for high school students. The first year, seventeen students signed up for the classroom course, called Cougars Community Commitment. The program is now in its fifth year and attracts over three hundred students—five classes each day, limited to thirty-five students per class. Students work in the community, interact with senior citizens and younger children, and raise funds for worthy causes.

Another wonderful program that encourages youth volunteerism is the Youth Service Alliance, created and directed by Mary and Tom Bloch. This program is in 156 schools in the greater Kansas City area. Over four thousand students have been recognized for completing fifty to one hundred hours of community service, and twenty-eight have received $1,000 college scholarships. (See www.ysagkc.org.)

Youth Service America is a national resource center and alliance of more than three hundred organizations committed to increasing the quantity and quality of volunteer opportunities for young Americans. SERVEnet is a program of YSA. Through the program's Web site, www.servenet.org, users can enter their zip code, city, state, skills, interests, and availability and be matched with organizations that need volunteers.

Youth Volunteer Corps of America and Canada draws young people from diverse ethnic and socioeconomic backgrounds and involves them in community problem solving through structured volunteer service during the summer and school year. David Battey and Monica Meeks have been instrumental in the design and implementation of this enriching program.

The International Youth Foundation has extended youth community building to the international scene. Rick Little founded the program, which is currently operating in sixty countries. Contacts for all of these programs are listed in the Resource Chapter.

Farheen Haider, a Muslim student at Pascack Valley High School, New Jersey, transformed her bullying experience into the creation of Origins—a twenty-student in-school group focusing on raising awareness about individual bias specific to cultural differences. Following the World Trade Center bombings, she also set up a support group for kids who were being targeted. "I wanted anyone who was afraid to have a place to talk about his or her fears. Our society teaches us to be wary of those that are different and that's what I want to change, one person at a time. I feel this is the purpose of my life."

Skills for Witnesses

When we conduct classroom programs, we ask students for suggestions about actions a witness might take. They have offered a range of ideas from challenging the bully, telling an adult, reaching out to a target in private, getting a group to challenge the bully, withholding power from the bully, and including the target in group activities, among others. After all of the suggestions have been solicited, we ask the students to consider which ideas seem the riskiest, and which ideas fit with their comfort level. Every suggestion comes up for discussion, and the end result is to urge witnesses to engage in at least one action step of their choice. We cannot make this statement too often—empowering witnesses to take action is one of the most crucial solutions to bullying!

During a discussion about the role of witnesses with a group of fifth and sixth graders in the school gym, a young girl sitting in the upper stands of the bleachers timidly raised her hand and asked: "What if someone is picking on a girl, and she's not my friend. In fact, what if I don't like her, do I have to stick up for her?" The group became unusually silent. The discussion about bullying had become a forum on ethics. I had never been asked that question before, and as usual, I looked to the wisdom of the group for the answer.

A boy in the front row said, "Yes."

"Why?" I asked.

And the reply came: "Because she's a human being."

If you had been there, I suspect you would have had tears in your eyes, too. In Plattsburg, Missouri, where young people are struggling with all the angst that comes with preadolescence, in a world that bombards them with more violent messages that ones of moral spirit, I was deeply moved by the honesty of the question and the beauty of the answer.

Observation

Bullies are quite clever about tormenting their peers out of sight of adult scrutiny. Adults on school premises will have to be diligent about looking for abusive behavior. Here is a list of actions that students would like teachers and other staff members to take.

Monitoring

When teachers are assigned to playground duty, students notice that the teachers tend to congregate in a cluster rather than distribute themselves to the outlying boundaries where bullying is likely to occur. Because the playground is one of the most tempting areas for peer abuse, many schools are hiring playground aides and involving parent volunteers. (We have a section on playground interventions in chapter 10.) Teachers need to leave their classrooms and stand in the hallways in between classes. Passing periods are fraught with abuse. Students get shoved into lockers; have their book bags yanked; are tripped, pushed, shoved, and taunted. For many students, crowded hallways are dangerous places, and the presence of watchful adults is a key to maintaining safety.

Discerning

Students want teachers to be more attuned to the slights, the derisive laughter, and the ostracizing that is taking place in the classroom, the hallways, and the playground. Students who are avoided and isolated must first come to an adult's attention before sensitive but effective measures can be affected. Physical education instructors, especially, need to notice students who are always the last ones to be picked for teams. This humiliating experience, repeated in class after class, needs to be eliminated. Many gym instructors are

177

creating new ways to determine team formation to the great relief of those youngsters who do not excel in athletics. The competitive nature of sports tends to exacerbate put-downs. Ann Stewart, a physical education teacher at Basalt Middle School, Colorado, uses a deck of cards to determine teams. Students randomly pick a red or black card, and this process is repeated each day. Stewart emphasizes cooperation rather than competition.

Supervising

On a number of occasions students have spoken of the terrors that occur when the teacher leaves the classroom. The absence of the teacher can become a ripe opportunity to harass a target with impunity. When a teacher once asked a student panel that we had organized, "What advice do you have for us to be helpful to you?" a fifth-grade boy replied in all seriousness, "When you have to go to the bathroom, take the bully with you." If at all possible, find an adult that can supervise the classroom when you must leave. And be sure to discuss your expectations, rules, and the code of conduct with a substitute teacher.

In a recent professional workshop, one teacher had the courage to ask the panel of students what goes on when the teacher's back is to the class. The students were brutally honest and the assembled teachers gasped at the described behaviors—verbal and nonverbal—directed at students and the teacher.

Support

An article written by Bob Chase, president of the National Education Association, contains the following statement: "Every time an adult does not speak out or intervene when witnessing the bullying or harassment of a student, they are complicit in the abuse."

TEN WAYS TO OFFER SUPPORT

1. Establish clear rules and consequences regarding unacceptable behavior, and enforce them.

Engage students in a discussion about what constitutes bullying and condense the conversation into a manageable set of rules and consequences that everyone understands and accepts as a code of conduct in the classroom and/or school. Post the rules and the consequences where they are visible at all times. If intervention when a rule is broken does not occur, the code of conduct is relatively worthless. A teacher who gives an appropriate consequence for every violation raises the sense of security for all students tremendously.

2. Deal with verbal abuse before it escalates.

Students wish that teachers would "intervene at the words, not the weapons." It will require much more vigilance on the part of teachers to make an issue of put-downs, but students truly yearn for that kind of involvement. Often they will request that teachers do something about the "little problem" before it can become a crisis.

3. Mobilize witnesses.

Support should include motivating witnesses who are aware of bullying situations to play a positive role by reporting to an adult, standing up for a target, and, at least, withholding support for bullies. It is important to stress the difference between tattling and reporting. As several students have suggested, "Tattling is when you are trying to get someone *in* trouble. Reporting is when you are trying to get someone *out* of trouble." It might take a while before the class members grasp the concept of tattling versus reporting, but it is worth putting the question into practice each time a student divulges information, until the difference becomes very clear.

4. Take bullying reports seriously.

One of the most common complaints we hear is about teachers who dismiss a report from the target or a witness, without hearing how traumatic it is for the target. A typical piece of advice to students is to "ignore the bully." When students muster their courage to speak with an adult, they want more than such a simplistic response. "Ignoring" is almost always a defense they have already employed. They are looking for a more sophisticated conversation. Parents should not be rebuffed when they report bullying situations to teachers. Parents have to depend on teachers to protect their children when they are being abused at school.

5. Realize the challenges of making change.

Bullies fear that their friends will desert them if they are not tough. They are afraid that everyone will call them a wuss. Some students won't give bullies a second chance, won't believe that a bully is sincere when he or she *does* make an effort to change. Targets are often skeptical, thinking the new behavior of a bully might be a trap to catch them off guard. Talk with your students about the challenges of making changes and the importance of recognizing and honoring those students who choose to transform. Gilman School, a private elementary school for boys in Baltimore, Maryland, brought me back to their school a year after I had first worked with their students, and as I went from classroom to classroom, the students complimented those who had made an obvious change in their behavior. At a school assembly, there was further acknowledgment. Awards to students who excel in athletics and academics are commonplace, but tributes to students who work hard to relinquish longstanding negative habits are rare.

6. Guarantee confidentiality.

Teachers need to assure students that confidentiality will be respected and that when a witness reports a bullying incident, the identity of the reporter will not be revealed to the bully. While most teachers would never jeopardize the reporter by revealing his or her name, students are extremely fearful of retribution and need verbal reassurance before they put themselves at risk.

7. Avoid embarrassing the student, whenever possible.

One teacher told of a cue that she agreed upon in advance with a student who had behavior problems. To reduce the number of times that she reprimanded him, she offered to give him a signal to let him know that she was displeased, without calling him by name. Without making an issue of a situation, without interrupting the classroom session, she would pull on her ear as a sign of disapproval. The student liked being part of a secret code between himself and the teacher and appreciated her willingness to give support rather than punishment.

Another way to avoid embarrassment for students is to stop having them grade each other's papers. Information about the number of mistakes a classmate makes, spreads quickly. A case on this issue made it to the Supreme Court. The parents sued the school district, claiming invasion of privacy. On appeal, it went from the circuit, to the state, to the federal, and ultimately to the Supreme Court before it was dismissed. Though many teachers feel the need to have students grade each other's papers because of time factors, and the courts support their right to use that process, sensitive teachers might appreciate the added pressure that comes with classmate grading. It can put a burden on the students who do extremely well along with the students who do poorly.

8. Utilize classroom leaders.

Invite a select group of class leaders to quietly become creative classroom advocates. Charge them to find ways to raise the status of taunted and isolated students. One example that I learned about occurred when the homecoming queen asked a "nerd" to dance with her at the prom and irrevocably changed his social status. There are many ways that leaders can use their power for the good of others. Such an assignment can not only benefit the target, but can set a pattern of constructive use of power for students who have previously used it only for personal enhancement.

9. Speak to bullies and targets separately.

As we have learned from the domestic violence community, the abused spouse is extremely fearful and reluctant to report all the factual details of abuse in the presence of the abuser. It is preferable to meet with the bully and the target separately to gather data. It might also be important to learn if there were neutral witnesses to the bullying situation and to meet separately with them as well. Be aware that cohorts of the bully might give prejudicial information. At some point, you might find it beneficial to bring the bully and target together, but certainly not in the beginning.

10. Reinforce the classroom code of conduct.

Make frequent references to the code of conduct that the class has agreed upon. Use literature to point out aspects of empathy or cruelty. Use math problems to bring statistics about bullying into relevance. Use current events to illustrate bullying between national leaders and their citizens, bullying between countries, and bullying situations that get resolved. Integrate activities into the classroom that promote character education, kindness, and respect. Be sure to enforce agreed-upon consequences, consistently and fairly, when infractions occur.

All across the country we have learned about class discussion groups, which are referred to by various names—home room, class councils, class meetings, and religion classes in parochial schools. Some of these groups are determined by schoolwide policy; others are the decision of the classroom teacher—especially at the elementary school level. Some schools or teachers prefer to schedule these discussions first thing in the morning, to clear the air of issues that can contaminate the rest of the day. These meetings are usually limited to thirty minutes. Some teachers have decided that it is more practical to conduct such classes at the end of the day, when the approaching dismissal bell serves to bring closure to a wide-ranging conversation. Teachers employ various discussion tools—some structured, some not—to engage their students in topics that are important to building a sense of community or family. Bullying situations of all kinds occupy these group meetings. Every teacher who has spoken to us of this ritual, whether it is conducted on a daily or weekly basis, is enthusiastic about the problem-solving nature of the experience.

During a BullySafeUSA Training Institute, an insightful teacher observed that if you take bullying and negative behaviors away from students, you need to fill the void with something appealing and positive. In Kansas City, Missouri, they have done just that. For the past ten years, two school counselors who serve on the STOP Violence! Board, Jacque DeJesus and Shelly Busby, have saturated their schools with Kindness is Contagious, Catch It! activities. One such activity requires teachers to install two transparent jars in the classroom—one labeled "Put-Downs" and one labeled "Put-Ups." Every time a student receives a put-down or a put-up, they drop a token into the appropriate jar. Each week the jars are emptied, and the assignment begins again. The students enjoy seeing the change in the contents of the jars. This visual documentation of peer interactions encourages kindness, rewards caring, and has a transforming influence on the class culture.

The critical issue for teachers to realize is that peer abuse situations will occur without your knowledge or awareness. Children are quite adept at concealing bullying events, especially in unsupervised areas. Your classroom is a supervised area, a sanctuary for students who are forced to run the gauntlet on the playground, in the bathrooms, in the locker rooms, on the bus, and in other worrisome places.

Summary

Students need S.O.S.—Skills, Observation, and Support. Be firm about the code of conduct you expect and enforce it fairly and consistently. Confront the smaller offenses before they escalate. Don't allow anyone to giggle or snicker when a student gives a wrong answer or asks an obvious question. Create a sense of community, at least, family, at best, for the young people in your charge. Be alert to any sign of intimidation, rejection, and/or humiliation.

Students are reluctant to report bullying incidents. They would prefer to handle their problems themselves, but they need skill training to do it. There are skills designed to reach different kinds of bullies—proactive, reactive, and elitist. There are skills that can empower targets to stand up for themselves or, at least, deny bullies satisfaction. Mobilizing witness power is an extremely efficient use of your time.

Teachers deserve support, as well, from principals, superintendents, and school board members. If the administrator is disinclined to tackle the bullying issue, teachers must become the pivotal advocate. Counselors and parent groups can be valuable resources.

Test scores, academic achievement, and classroom management have a better chance of soaring when children test their wings in sacred learning space.

CHAPTER TEN

STRATEGIES FOR SCHOOLS

"There are two kinds of schools: Those that have
faced a crisis and those who will."
—Ronald D. Stephens, executive director,
National School Safety Center

Fire drills are not the only drills that occur on school campuses these days. School safety and preparedness for violence have become priorities of the first order. Potential threats have made violence prevention workshops at school administrators' conferences quite popular as schools formulate policy decisions to provide for the safety of students and staff. While metal detectors will become more commonplace to provide external protection, pain detectors for internal protection from senseless cruelty are sorely needed to bring about the desired security.

Some experts have recommended smaller classrooms as a strategy for school safety. A federal study that followed 72,000 teens from seventh through twelfth grade, beginning in 1994, found that the size of the class was not as important, however, as having the classroom managed by a caring adult. In fact, the single most important factor affecting students' sense of well-being and their chance of engaging in risky health behaviors was the presence of a caring adult, whether students attended private, public, parochial, urban, suburban, or rural schools. According to Robert Blum, director of the Adolescent Health Center at the University of Minnesota, "school environment has as much or a bigger impact on what happens to kids as what is taught in the school."

A caring environment should include a concern for the ethical climate. When educational institutions show moral resolve, there is hope for a kinder school culture. It bears repeating, the transcending bullying prevention vision goes beyond changing individual actions and seeks to change the culture where behavior is influenced.

Many schools are moving forward to create a caring environment with policies and programs to reduce peer cruelty. In our workshops we recommend six elements for a comprehensive bullying prevention and intervention school program.

1. School bullying prevention and intervention policy
2. Team approach
3. In-service training for faculty and staff
4. Parent involvement
5. Student empowerment sessions
6. Reinforcing concepts throughout the year

1. School bullying prevention and intervention policy

It is essential that schools adopt a policy statement that is "owned" by everyone in the system. Ownership can come about in a number of ways. The need for a committed principal who makes bullying prevention and intervention a high priority cannot be overstated. Mobilizing the staff and the students is the crux of a successful program. Writing a policy is one thing; enforcing it fairly and consistently is quite another.

Schools that have policies about bullying that are widely disseminated, consistently applied, and justly enforced are finding reductions in suspensions. Phil Hackett is principal of the Edwin H. Greene Intermediate School in Cincinnati, Ohio, home to nearly 900 fifth- and sixth-grade students. In the 1996–1997 school year, Hackett reported that there were 327 office referrals for discipline problems. The following year they adopted a clear, concise policy statement— Respect Yourself, Respect Others, Respect the Environment.

In addition to the adoption of the policy, in 1998–1999 Hackett introduced the Discipline With Dignity program along with BullySafeUSA, the antibullying student empowerment and teacher training sessions that Paula and I conducted. The school counselor created a year-long follow-up program, which will be summarized at the end of this chapter. During that school year, office referrals dropped to 167, and by the 1999–2000 school year, office referrals dropped to 33. Hackett believes that their program works because every member of the staff holds students to those values.

Increases in test scores can also be a result of bullying prevention. Stuart Twemlow, M.D., was research director of the Peaceful Schools Project of the Child & Family Center, The Menninger Clinic, Topeka, Kansas. He developed a bullying intervention program, Creating a Peaceful School Learning Environment (CAPSLE), for elementary schools in Topeka, Kansas. Following implementation, Twemlow's research showed dramatic reductions in serious disciplinary infractions and suspensions along with increased academic achievement. In one school, composite scores rose from the 40th percentile to the 58th percentile, and in a replication program in another elementary school, the composite Metropolitan Achievement Test scores rose significantly.[50] Twemlow believes that academic success, though not a direct focus of the program, emerges naturally from an environment that is conducive to learning premises.

2. Team approach

It takes a team to teach a child! Creating a culture of safety and kindness in a school requires every adult who comes in contact with children to take an active role on the bullying intervention and prevention team. Every day, every member of the staff sends a message about the values of the school by the language he or she uses and the way he or she interacts with students. The key is consistency and saturation! Saturation occurs when everywhere a student turns, the rules are enforced. If this does not occur, students will quickly learn to work the system, taking advantage of those staff members who slack off on enforcement instead of conforming to the policy.

The exciting aspect of a team approach is not just shared responsibility, but shared appreciation for the gift that each adult brings. Ideally, team members should include the principal, vice principal, teacher, counselor, school nurse, bus driver, secretary, custodian, school resource officer, playground supervisor, cafeteria worker, librarian, and teacher's aide. These staff may not be available at every school, but we are highlighting all of them because they represent the ideal.

Principals

The principal is the principle factor in the life of a school. The principal has responsibility for the students, the faculty, the staff, the parents, and the community served. He or she needs to be a leader, a mediator, a disciplinarian, a communicator, a counselor, a delegator, and a decision maker. It is the principal who sets the tone for the climate of the school, walking a fine line between being inclusive, valuing staff opinions, being open to conflicting ideas, and being the ultimate authority that is accountable for the decision at hand.

The principal determines the priority issues, whether to be pro-active or reactive about bullying prevention and intervention, whether to have a policy owned by everyone or the absence of a policy that leaves the players to make their own rules. The principal must be prepared to run interference between a teacher and a parent, a teacher and a student, a teacher and a teacher, and all other combinations imaginable.

Each year, a principal can choose a focus that the staff needs to take to heart. A current issue for many schools is diversity. Diversity can include language, economics, race, religion, and/or culture; children with special needs and disabilities; and gender identity issues. Diversity fits with bullying prevention so well because schools have a unique opportunity to teach people about tolerance and acceptance. If a charismatic principal emphasizes building a true sense of community within the school, a lot of the bullying will stop on its own.

The principal walks a tightrope between being a disciplinarian and being a friend to students. A principal in Baltimore wanted students to feel comfortable about coming to see him. If a student is seen going into the principal's office, it is usually an indication of wrongdoing. To counteract that perception, he announced at the beginning of the year that a large jar of candy would be sitting on his desk, and if anyone ever felt the need for a sweet, they were welcome to dip into the jar. Once that practice was put in place, he had access to many more students on an informal basis.

Principals realize that when a child is sent to his or her office because of an offense that has occurred on the playground or in the classroom, it is a significant opportunity to combine discipline with learning, not just punishment. It can be an opening for coaching that allows a child to remain in the school environment rather than a suspension that further isolates a child from needed supervision.

It is the principal who will organize and value the team approach.

Counselors

Counselors can be treasures to the school system. When school budgets are cut, often it is the counselors who get cut. Fortunately, most schools realize that counselors are not a luxury. They are essential. Counselors can be an important liaison to the principal because they have their fingers on the pulse of the school. They know the problem students and the students who have problems. They are also quite familiar with the teachers who are having classroom difficulties.

Ann Cole, M.S., and Kimberly Clements, M.A., write about school counselors as change agents, construction project managers who facilitate the development of critical building blocks that provide the necessary foundation for student attainment of personal, social, academic, and career skills that will enable children to be successful and productive members of society.

Counselors must be advocates—advocates for students, for teachers, for parents, and sometimes for a schoolwide program.

ADVOCATE FOR STUDENTS—Students will confide information to counselors that they may withhold from everyone else. The confidential information may be about issues in their families, such as abuse, drugs, illness, and divorce. It may be about tormenting from other students, or it may be about bullying from the teacher. In one school a teacher made comments to a boy such as: "Your medication must not be working today!" The counselor, the student, and teacher met together with the teacher's permission and agreed upon a contract not to refer to the student's meds. They also developed a positive plan to use when the student has a difficult day. When the student is feeling edgy, he gives the teacher a body cue and then is allowed to visit with the counselor. Counselors are on the front line of the pain chain that dominates the lives of so many children.

ADVOCATE FOR TEACHERS—Teachers who are having difficulty getting along with parents of their students frequently turn to the counselor for support to affirm a strategy the teacher is trying with the student. Counselors will sit in on parent-teacher conferences and can bring another voice to the discussion about a child who is a bully or a target. Counselors can offer therapeutic advice about a student with a particular difficulty due to personality, health, and/or family problems. Counselors can be a liaison between teachers and the principal of the school. Counselors can offer highly beneficial role-playing sessions for students when teachers are not comfortable with that format.

ADVOCATE FOR PARENTS—Many parents have found a sympathetic ear from a counselor when a teacher or even a principal is unwilling to deal with a bullying situation. Even though they may walk a delicate line as employees of the school system, counselors can offer support to parents when they are stressed.

ADVOCATE FOR A SCHOOL PROGRAM—Counselors attend conferences that offer a wide variety of topics. They learn about guidance curriculum, issues facing families, speakers, videos, books, current research, and so forth. and bring back exciting information and ideas to their schools. I have been invited to work in many schools because the counselor identified bullying as a serious issue to the principal and was enthusiastic about our program.

Counselors not only identify programs, they implement them. They have excellent working relationships with the parent-teacher organization in their school to partner on ideas. They reach out to community artists, who bring incredibly stimulating projects into the school. They have contacts with not-for-profit organizations, skilled parents, and professionals who bring expertise on specific subject matters. They encourage service learning and organize volunteer efforts to engage students in contributing roles.

Many schools have prevention/intervention specialists or school social workers who perform many of the roles we've attributed to counselors. The following are two examples of specific bullying programs implemented by counselors.

The counselor at the Edwin Greene school, Cheryl Borden-Thomas, has developed a yearlong program, using our Kindness is Contagious and On Target to Stop Bullying materials. In addition she has added literary components, skill training, and student involvement. Cheryl meets once a week with every fifth- and sixth-grade class in the school. She uses fiction and nonfiction literature to illustrate issues related to bullying. She has orchestrated mock trials to demonstrate the consequences of bullying behavior. Every morning students participate in a Responsive Classroom meeting, a concept recommended by the Northwest Foundation. During this home room time, the principal, while delivering the morning announcements, will bring up a subject related to respect, and home room teachers will follow up with a short discussion. The discussion might center on positive energy, overcoming resistance to change, or making amends. This approach, which focuses on saturation and constant reinforcement, has made a significant impact on the school climate.

Becky Sandy, who works half time as counselor and half time as music teacher at Sellman School in Cincinnati, attended our professional workshops and was inspired to design a comprehensive plan using an activity guide, On Target to Stop Bullying, coauthored by Mara Weyforth and me, based on *Bullies & Victims*. Sellman School serves 345 students, grades four though six. The school is middle to upper middle class, with about 2 percent of the population being African American, Asian, or Hispanic. Becky began by using a survey in On Target to Stop Bullying to tally students' perspectives on bullying at their school. The survey results persuaded the principal, Roger Slagle, to fully support a schoolwide strategy. A brainstorming committee met and, after analyzing data from the survey, decided to have more teachers station themselves in the hallways between classes to reduce problems in that area. Becky conducted forty-minute bullying presentations every two weeks, using On Target to Stop Bullying activities including role- playing sessions with all students. The teachers attend these sessions and follow up during the intervening days.

The parent survey in On Target to Stop Bullying indicated that there were special problems in the fifth grade. As a result, a workshop was offered and parents attended in large numbers. The parents were upset because of some incidents, both physical and verbal, that had taken place during the fifth-grade girls' basketball games. Concern was also expressed about problems on the playground.

The principal made duty assignments and the teachers responded by giving up their lunch hour to provide additional supervision on the playground and the cafeteria. A NO TAUNTING PROMISE was developed and displayed in every classroom. A copy was sent home to the parents, and every morning, there was a discussion of some part of the promise on the public address system. There are a number of such pledges.

One of the parents, who had expertise in mediation, Tina Neyer, volunteered to go into classrooms to work with students on conflict resolution and communication skills. She made a presentation to the parents to ensure their support for the terminology and concepts that she was teaching. Funding from the PTA and local businesses enabled expansion of the program. With a $4,000 grant from the Ohio Department of Education and the Ohio Commission of Dispute Resolution and Conflict Management, a trainer will conduct special in-service workshops for teachers.

Becky continues to teach the activities from On Target to Stop Bullying, extending each one and emphasizing common language and common terms to be used by every adult in the building. The staff takes a team approach, and each member of the team is respected for the special role that he or she plays. For example, Becky meets with the bus drivers before school starts, and then once a month at a school safety session. Problems with students are discussed and resolved. The gym teacher uses birth dates, telephone numbers, or other random methods to sensitively select teams so that students who are not athletically skilled are not left to be chosen last. The custodian monitors hallway and bathroom situations, and the school secretary is respected for quelling many situations before they become major problems.

Becky and her principal are keeping tabs on the effectiveness of their program. Four months after the program was put in place, Becky conducted the survey again to learn where there had been successes and where problems still occurred. She plans on going to the middle school to meet with the seventh-grade team who will be receiving their sixth graders. The goal is to effect continuity for the students entering the challenging middle school culture. There will also be meetings with the staff of the elementary school to plant seeds of bullying prevention in the primary grades.

Becky and her team even have a connection with the high school. High-school students contribute to community service by doing recess duty. A "One on One" program matches up high school students with Sellman students who would benefit from special tutoring and contact with student role models.

Individual success stories are accumulating. A delighted parent called Becky to thank her for the change in her child's report card. The mother credits the bullying prevention program with raising her student's grades from Cs and Ds to Bs and Cs. Students who were once coming for counseling sessions on a daily basis have been empowered to deal with bullying situations. One student recently came into Becky's office to announce, "I'm learning how to solve my problems, and now I'm helping others!"

School Nurses

The old image of the school nurse as someone who waits in her office for a child to come in for a bandage or to be checked for head lice is completely out of touch with today's reality. Today's nurse does everything from classroom teaching about hygiene, hand washing, and blood protection for AIDS prevention to case management with families around health issues to supervising medication for students with ADD and ADHD to making home visits. In some schools, bullying programs have been introduced and carried out by the school nurse.

The nurse has a unique opportunity to experience relationships with families who are dealing with hearing and vision problems, asthma, diabetes, eating disorders, epilepsy, cancer, attention deficit disorder, Tourette's, Asperberger syndrome, allergies, and other special illnesses. Because of her health background, the nurse can inform classroom discussions about various illnesses that are affecting the student population. These informative talks can be generalized, or they can be instructional in dealing with specific students' health issues. Frequently, it is left to family members to come into the classroom to explain their child's illness, disorder, or challenges.

Another sensitive area is euphemistically called Family Life Education. It is the school nurse who is most often assigned to teach information that deals with matters of sexuality, puberty, harassment, child abuse, family roles, and parenting education.

Students who are suffering from abuse at home or at the hands of their peers will often seek out the school nurse for protection and comfort. The school nurse can make "rounds" on the playground, in the cafeteria, and in the bathrooms and pick up on behaviors that require attention. She feels trusted by students, parents, the faculty, and the administration to be a neutral person on the campus, serving as both a resource and a supervisor.

Bus Drivers

Here is an exercise to test your capacity for empathy! Close your eyes and imagine that you are a bus driver. Your hands are on the steering wheel; you are negotiating stoplights, stop signs, oncoming traffic, and residential stops; you are constantly checking your side-vision mirrors, making sure that students are safely anchored beyond the curb when departing the bus; and you are maneuvering in and out of lanes. At the same time, there are forty to seventy children behind your back, frequently taking advantage of their freedom from a school authority figure. Student passenger behavior can include shouting, screaming obscenities, throwing spitballs, shoving students against seats and windows, mooning cars behind the bus, fighting, sexually harassing others, terrorizing younger children, demanding that someone give up his or her seat, sticking a foot in the aisle to cause tripping, throwing books in a person's face, grabbing a student's books, tearing up a person's homework, hanging out of windows, and throwing items out of the windows, not to mention directing abuse at the bus driver. Stay with this mental image for one minute. Keep in mind that, for the bus driver, completing the route can take an hour or more.

Students have reported to me that in some areas, there are contests to see how many drivers they can provoke to resign during a semester. One boy bragged about the five drivers who had given up the job on his route, only to be topped by another student who gleefully spoke of eight drivers who had resigned—one in tears. Some bus drivers, out of complete frustration, have turned the bus around and driven back to the school grounds, waiting there until the students have settled down. A more disturbing report tells of one desperate bus driver who slammed on the brakes at every stop sign, throwing the passengers into the backs of the seats in front of them, as a means of control.

Is it any wonder that this country is facing a bus driver shortage? In one community I visited, the shortage is so acute that school begins and ends on two different schedules because one bus driver has to make two complete rounds to compensate for the lack of available employees.

In Cincinnati, Ohio, I had the opportunity to meet with members of the Indian Hill Transportation Department. During the course of a lively discussion, I learned why this group was recognized by the state of Ohio for its outstanding service. The department has an official liaison who serves as a communication link between the bus drivers and the schools they serve. All complaints, suggestions, and important student issues are channeled through the liaison who is admired by both the drivers and the school staff.

At the beginning of every school year at a public school in Cincinnati, great efforts are made to connect the bus drivers with the parents on their route. The Indian Hill Transportation Department holds an open house at the bus depot. Parents are invited to inspect the buses, and there is an opportunity for anyone who wishes to drive the bus around the parking area to do so. Parents are encouraged to share information and concerns with the drivers and asked to accompany their child at the bus stop the first day or two of school so that drivers can make a visible connection between parents and their children.

The bus drivers hold monthly meetings to discuss issues and solutions. They talk about student conversations that are cause for concern. The liaison can transmit at-risk information to the school counselors, who can be counted on to use the communication appropriately.

The more experienced drivers mentor newer drivers, and the system enjoys an extremely low turnover rate. Most of the drivers had been working for the system for more than ten years; one or two had been driving for twenty-five years or more. Some of them had carried the parents of their current passengers when they were in school. One of the drivers commented that if appropriate passenger behavior is deeply ingrained in elementary school students from the very beginning, it can prevent problems that flare up at the secondary level.

A word of caution about the liaison: In one southern city, I met with two groups of bus drivers. The liaison for one group was a fair-minded, respected advocate for the drivers who was equally appreciated by the school administration. The other liaison was an employee of the bus system whose intimidation of the drivers made them fearful for their jobs and, consequently, squelched open communication and complaints of any nature.

An article in the *South Florida Sun-Sentinel* reports that Broward School District officials in Broward County, Florida, are taking a hard look at setting conduct rules on school buses that will result in consistent discipline measures for various categories of misbehavior. Bus drivers had complained about the inconsistencies from one school to another and requested policies that specify real consequences for students who cause havoc.

In response to the issues raised by the bus drivers, the Broward School District developed a policy that will go into effect for the 2002–2003 school year. A Code of Student Conduct on buses outlines a Level One offense, which includes eight misbehaviors, three of which are "being disruptive, distracting, or disobeying the bus driver." A Level One infraction results in a one- to ten-day suspension from school bus transportation. Repeated offenses result in suspension or possible expulsion from school. A Level Two offense is specific to opening a school bus emergency door and exiting when the bus is stopped, without direction by the school bus driver. Level Three specifies six misbehaviors, including "threats against the bus operator or passengers on the bus" and "fighting on the bus," which result in suspension and/or possible expulsion from school. Vandalism offenses also require restitution for related damages.

Many school districts are outfitting their buses with surveillance cameras. The bus drivers whom I have spoken with are enthusiastic about the presence of camera equipment, and one of them recounted the following story. After receiving a report of a serious bullying attack on a school bus, the principal contacted the parents of the offenders. Their children and they, in turn, denied any complicity. The principal invited the bullies and their parents to a meeting in his office and revealed that the incident in question had been captured on videotape. Consequences for the students were implemented.

Another issue we have heard about is behavior problems that occur on the bus when teachers accompany students on field trips. Confusion about who maintains authority for discipline can reign unless there is a clear policy agreed upon in advance. Teachers may have different expectations than the bus driver and not be aware of the rules that the bus driver enforces. Sometimes the presence of additional adults can be very helpful, but at the same time there can be contradictions in procedures that result in chaos.

Since most student surveys identify the school bus as a major site of bullying, it behooves school districts to have consistent conduct policies and consequences in place that are implemented and enforced, to consider the position of a school bus liaison position for the drivers and the schools they serve, to place surveillance cameras on buses, to have ongoing discussions with students about the necessity for appropriate bus behavior, to have clarity around authority when teachers travel on field trips, and to include a bus driver, or liaison, in staff meetings. Bus drivers have an enormous responsibility and deserve to be included in important discussions and decisions.

Playground Supervisors

Whenever student surveys on bullying are administered, the playground usually heads the list of hot spots for occurrences. Because students identify recess and the playground as the most treacherous place for cruelty to occur, many schools are beginning to focus on recess periods as a critical opportunity to defuse bullying situations.

Some Canadian researchers have filmed bullying incidents that have taken place on school playgrounds, and those clips have been shown on a number of national television programs. The menacing behaviors, the physical attacks, the assaults are painful for viewers to watch, much less for children to experience. On many school playgrounds, there is too much action occurring over too large an expanse to be adequately monitored. It is hoped that the presence of playground supervisors will greatly reduce peer problems, but the Canadian film clips illustrated that seemingly benign contact between children can be fraught with menacing behaviors.

Following is a list of interventions that have come to our attention in schools across the country. Although no school that we know of has put all of these strategies in place, many schools find benefits when one or more of these ideas has been implemented.

GREATER ADULT SUPERVISION—Trained playground aides whose job description includes intervening and preventing bullying are a great addition to the school staff, but many schools cannot afford playground supervisors. In most cases, the responsibility falls to teachers. Teachers who have playground duty should be instructed not to cluster together in the center of the recess area but to monitor the perimeters.

Volunteers can be recruited to assist with playground supervision—parents, retired members of the community, high school students, etc.

OPPORTUNITIES FOR STRUCTURED AND UNSTRUCTURED RECESS—Nonathletic students, who are often excluded from the informal but competitive teams that form, can have the options of unstructured time or an opportunity to participate in structured but noncompetitive activities like New Games, a concept where each exercise or game has a Win/Win goal.

PLAYGROUND CONFLICT MANAGERS—Many years ago, a program was developed in California to train elementary school students to help their classmates deal with spontaneous conflicts that occur on the playground. When they complete the training, they are identified by a special vest and can be called upon by peers to settle disputes that erupt during the recess period.

SAFETY ZONE—A certain area of the playground is staked out and marked with a flag that declares it to be a safety zone. An adult is always available at the safety zone for any student or students who feel the need of protection. The mere existence of such an area makes a statement about concern for student protection.

ELIMINATION OF AGGRESSIVE GAMES—This injunction has stirred quite a bit of controversy, but many schools feel it is important to send a clear message that no game, such as dodgeball, can be used as an excuse to throw a ball as hard as possible at someone's body. The game of tag is coming under question, too. Whether these games become banned or not, the discussion about reducing aggression between peers is a positive sign.

ELIMINATION OF COMPETITIVE GAMES—Some schools are taking the position that students have opportunities to participate in competitive sports during physical education, after-school programs, and through organized leagues, and that recess should offer alternative activities where children can release energy without the pressure of winning or losing.

POSTING OF PLAYGROUND RULES—Clear rules and expectations are posted in various sites and discussed regularly with students so there is no confusion about what behavior is expected and what interactions are appropriate and inappropriate.

ALTERNATIVE ACTIVITIES—At Brooks Elementary School in Windsor, California, the PTA has set up an alternate recess program. Every Friday, parent volunteers offer board games and activities such as bingo, Jenga, bead-stringing projects, knitting, and arts and crafts in a room set aside for this purpose. Their intent was to offer an option to a small group of children who might prefer being indoors to the terrors of the playground. Out of 450 students who share recess, 125 students flock to the Activity Room and are asking for the program to be expanded to additional days per week.

School Secretaries

Never underestimate the impact of a skillful school secretary on the climate of a school. For many parents and visitors, the secretary represents the initial impression and the sense of receptivity at the school. School secretaries can be an anchor in a flood of swirling problems—lost articles, forgotten lunches, unsigned release slips, irate parents, heartbroken students, early school closings because of weather, demands from the superintendent's office, frequent tardy reports, and hoards of data issues—the cheerful resource person for all things large and small.

The secretary is invaluable to the principal. She can be a buffer for an angry parent; a calming, soothing listener who handles daily problems; and a voice of reason who prevents crises. She can be a comfort (and a bank) to a distressed student who forgot his or her lunch money and an empathetic listener for a teacher who has a family member in the hospital. Secretaries have to be on top of important personal information about the staff. If the secretary receives an emergency call from the day care center of a teacher's child, the situation requires immediate response without pushing a panic button.

An important topic on a secretary's agenda these days is understanding custody issues. Secretaries need to be current on laws relating to custody matters as well as the particulars in a family. Secretaries have to be on high alert about a noncustodial parent who may wish to pick up their child at school.

Specifically in bullying cases, secretaries may have to deal with a student sent to the office for disciplinary reasons when the principal is out of the building or in a meeting. Likewise, "lingering" is a significant clue for secretaries. A student who lingers at the office can be a student who is trying to avoid recess. A student who is lingering in the cafeteria for the same reason may welcome an invitation to sit in the office. As one secretary put it: "We are just like mom for a thousand children and two thousand parents."

Custodians

Custodians see students from a slightly different angle. They are more likely to come in contact with students in the hallways, the cafeteria, the locker rooms, and the bathrooms. Custodians see the kids pushing each other into lockers, sometimes literally. Custodians can tell stories about the students who not only get pushed up against the locker but slammed and locked into the locker. The student's only recourse is to scream until someone, usually the custodian, releases them. Students will often confide in custodians because they see them as problem-solvers. Custodians may have to intervene and report bullying behavior when they see students picking on someone. Sometimes a custodian is the only adult who is aware of specific bullying. A custodian that I interviewed said that she tries to work with both the bullies and their victims. She says, "Bad kids need as much help as the good kids." Students are often surprised when she intervenes, but she is willing to confront the incident because she cares.

Bathrooms can be dangerous places. We have heard countless stories of students who will suffer all day with a full bladder rather than risk a possible attack in the bathroom. For boys the attacks are more likely to come in the form of "swirleys" (having your head dunked in the toilet while it's being flushed), beatings, having your genitalia ridiculed, or being jumped for your lunch money. For girls the bathroom can be treacherous because of the graffiti. Custodians will make sure to remove vulgar statements scrawled on the walls as soon as possible. Some of the more common epithets following a girl's name are: "slut," "bitch," "whore," and worse. It is important to note that this report came from an affluent suburban school.

Locker rooms are another site of vandalism and torment. A

source of enjoyment for some bullies is to hide a student's clothing while he is showering, or to snatch his towel and snap him painfully with it. Athletes have been known to devise cunning, cruel initiation rites that take place in the locker room, and victims dare not report the incident lest they be accused of being wimps, unworthy of being members of the team.

It is frustrating for custodians who report these incidents when no action is taken. A positive situation occurred when a custodian and a teacher conferred about a student who had gotten in trouble on numerous occasions. The teacher assigned the student to stay after school under the custodian's supervision. The bully was given mop duty, resulting in some positive outcomes. The custodian insisted that the floors of the classrooms be spotless, which meant that they had to be mopped several times in order to make every smudge disappear. The custodian engaged the student in conversation during the mopping, and even though the mopper's arms were quite sore, he appreciated having an adult take an interest in him, make demands on him, and praise him when he finally completed the task satisfactorily.

A custodian that I interviewed believes that students ridicule in-school suspensions. She went on to say that, "Emptying wastebaskets and cleaning blackboards will never bring about the results of one hour of mop duty. After they've mopped one room three or four times, they take detention more seriously." In fact, the student's mother thanked the custodian for making a difference in her son's life. The combination of reaching out to him in a personal way and assigning a consequence that he did not relish repeating, brought about a marked change in the boy's troublesome behavior.

Custodians would probably welcome an opportunity to meet regularly with faculty and administrators to report incidents of bullying known only by them. They would like to share the information and have it taken seriously by those in authority.

Cafeteria Workers

Another group of employees that has valuable observations to share is cafeteria workers. They have no authority over grades and provide comfort food in a nurturing environment. Cafeteria workers can tell a lot about students through their eating habits. They can spot the kids with eating disorders, the ones who are caught in food extortion abuses, the isolates who eat alone every day.

On Monday mornings, after a difficult weekend at home, students will come in for breakfast and disclose painful problems in their families. Many children come to school hungry for more than food. They will talk freely and openly to the women who feed their empty tummies and their famished souls. Cafeteria workers will give second helpings to someone they know needs an extra serving of affection and confection. Sometimes workers offer a "job" to lonely students who are dropped off at school very early. They are known for their comforting hugs and many an apron carries tear-stains along with streaks of gravy.

Cafeteria workers observe lunchroom cruelty, such as taking or demanding someone's food.

An example of a food extortion incident is the case of a boy with a speech problem who was taunted by a group of boys. The target was intimidated to bring extra money every day to buy snacks for one of the bullies. In another case, when a student brought his tray to a table and sat down, everyone else at the table stood up and moved their trays to another table. The humiliation of such public rejection is long lasting.

Food servers should receive training on antibullying policies along with other staff members and be encouraged to give feedback to faculty and administrators about slights and problems that occur in their territory.

School Resource Officers

This national program started in the 1960s in Arizona and expanded at middle schools and high schools after the Columbine shootings in 1999. There are 15,000 school resource officers (SROs) across the country. School resource officers are specially trained police officers assigned to schools. In one Kansas school district, four officers rotate among twenty-seven elementary schools.

The National School Safety Center (April 2001) describes an SRO as an educator, a role model, a youth advocate, a law enforcement officer, and a liaison with the community. As educators, SROs can speak to students about current statutes, legal issues, drugs and substance abuse, consequences for a person who is an accessory to a crime, how to use the legal system when necessary, protection rights, bullying, abuse, and other essential matters. An SRO can be an active role model within the school, someone who listens and responds to students' needs and who deals with situations calmly, effectively, and confidently. SROs serve as youth advocates when they stand for fairness and justice and speak on a student's behalf when needed. They enforce the rules of the school and offer security for the building and the people therein. SROs can be a valuable liaison between the school and the community. They can share important information with parents, other law enforcement officers, health officials, and policy makers and can bring perspective to students about safety precautions.

Deputy Scott Thirkell, an SRO at Southeast of Saline Elementary School in Salina, Kansas, started a program that recognizes students who have shown courtesy, kindness, respect for others, and good citizenship. Every two weeks, pupils who have been nominated by their classroom teachers eat lunch with Officer Scott at a special table set with a tablecloth and a special dessert. They receive a certificate of recognition, a picture of their lunch group, and a copy of the group picture is enlarged and displayed on the cafeteria wall for the rest of the year. Being part of "Officer Scott's Lunch Bunch" is much more than a reward for good behavior. It helps to shape a peer norm that promotes courtesy and responsibility at school.

Having a positive, personal relationship with a law-enforcement official can be a major breakthrough for some teenagers who are more inclined to see an officer as an adversary than a resource. Some SROs also serve as DARE officers, and in either role they add a meaningful dimension to the support network our children deserve. A number of SROs have taken our training and facilitate bullying prevention workshops. Randy Wiler, a DARE officer in Leawood, Kansas, developed a bullying prevention and intervention Web site at the request of Kansas Attorney General Carla Stovall. Information is available at www.kbpp.org and www.ink.org/public/ksag.

Librarian

An enthusiastic librarian in Alabama found a way to become an intrinsic part of the schoolwide mobilization to prevent bullying. She set up a display of the books that had bullying themes in a prominent place in the school library. Then she created a book review contest as an incentive and invited students to read the selected books and write a critique about them. She was interested in discovering if the book captured the reader's interest, if it identified a solution, if it would be of more interest to girls or boys or both, if it were more relevant to a particular age group, and/or if it focused on a particular type of bullying. The best reviews were posted on a bulletin board, the winners were announced in the school newspaper, and literature became a visible bullying prevention component.

Another kind of contest could be to create a unique bookmark. One student at Stephen Mack Middle School in Rockton, Illinois, came up with a very clever idea. On one side of his bookmark he wrote STOP horizontally and PAIN vertically. The letters stood for Problems, Anger, Insults, and Negativity. On the other side he wrote BE horizontally and KIND vertically. This stood for Knowledgeable, Inclusive, Nicer, and Decent.

Librarians can be a resource for teachers and students who inquire about books that address peer cruelty, promote empathy, and inspire kindness. The library is a safe place for students who want to confide in an adult about a bullying problem. A troubled student would not arouse suspicion by talking to a librarian, who could alert a counselor about a conflict that needs attention.

Special Education Resource Teacher

In 1975 the Individuals with Disabilities Education Act was passed, mandating that students with disabilities must be educated alongside other students in the "least restrictive environment." As a result, many schools established special education classrooms or special education centers within their buildings. The Shawnee Mission, Kansas, School District has five thousand special education students, almost all of whom attend their neighborhood schools. Inclusion facilitators were employed to ensure that the transition for students with disabilities would go smoothly when the program was initiated. They worked with parents, school staff, and students.

An example of a very successful situation, reported in the *Kansas City Star*, involves Stephen Rouse, who has Down's syndrome. Stephen did very well in elementary school, thanks to the extremely supportive school administration and teachers who used Stephen's presence in the classroom to teach other students compassion and patience. Middle school was destined to be more socially challenging. The middle school had never had an inclusion student, and adolescent students are much harder on each other. Consequently, Judy Bennet, the inclusion facilitator, organized a Circle of Friends for Stephen beginning in the fifth grade. Six students—four girls and two boys—were selected to live up to their name in his last year of elementary school and to be available to him during the succeeding years.

The group often met on weekends and after school. They went to movies, attended concerts, shared family vacations, and visited Stephen at his job. When Stephen enrolled in first grade, his parents did not imagine that thirteen years later, he would graduate from high school with a B average and attend college away from home.

Stephen's support from his family was immeasurable. Their willingness to enroll their son in a pioneering program was a life-changing decision. The faculty's dedication to Stephen was extraordinary, but the Circle of Friends lifted him to heights not otherwise possible. What a glorious concept!

His parents, teachers, and administrators believed in him, but without a peer group who believed in him, his future could have taken a different turn. The applicability to other students with challenging situations is exciting to contemplate. Since that first arrangement with Stephen, Bennett has organized many Circles of Friends for children with special needs and has high praise for the program.

Other Adults

A moment of praise for school crossing guards. In Kansas City, Missouri, a school crossing guard not only ensured the safety of all the children crossing a major thoroughfare, but he smiled and waved to each and every driver passing by. Maxee Dupree became a community icon, a symbol of kindness to early-morning commuters who observed that his smile was better than a fresh cup of coffee. At a Kindness Dinner, held annually in Kansas City, Missouri, an award is given in Dupree's memory to three adults nominated by students for their kindness. A recent winner of the "Kindest Kansas Citian" recognition was a school crossing guard who was honored by a student for his cheerful greetings and concern for each and every child.

When everyone that children come in contact with during the day uses the same words, intervenes in the early stages of bullying problems, reaches out to both bullies and targets, and consistently holds children accountable for their behavior, the potential for transformation is awesome. The success is in the saturation effect. Saturation occurs when every student is aware of the policy and realizes that everywhere they turn—bus, playground, cafeteria, bathroom, library, locker room, hallways, classrooms—the policy is enforced. If some adults insist on the policy and other adults dismiss it, the students spend their energy playing the system rather than conforming to the code of conduct.

3. In-service training for faculty and staff

An ideal in-service training is a full day of course work attended by administrators, teachers, bus drivers, cafeteria workers, counselors, custodians, librarians, playground supervisors, secretaries, school nurses, school resource officers, special education teachers, and any other members of the school staff. Everyone should receive the same information, but not necessarily at the same time. Smaller groups work better. It is very important that teachers and counselors feel free to discuss all matters pertaining to bullying.

The Maine Project Against Bullying reports that 71 percent of the teachers or other adults in the classroom ignored bullying incidents. When asked, students uniformly expressed the desire that teachers intervene rather than ignore bullying. It is crucial to engage the faculty to actively intercede at the first sign of harassment.

The content should include definitions of bullying; the four kinds of bullying; the role of the bully, target, and witness; current research, including the significant finding about the impact of a caring adult on students' chances of engaging in risky behaviors; classroom strategies; empowering students; strategies for working with individual students; parent issues; and resource materials. This is the subject matter covered in our BullySafeUSA program.

Teachers Who Bully

The subject of teachers who bully needs to be addressed, uncomfortable though the topic may be. In defense of students, I offer Exhibit A: a communication I received on my Web site. I am including it as it came to me, without grammar, punctuation, or spelling corrections.

> I wanted some information regarding a teacher who is the bully in her class room to students as young as I. I am depressed and get sweats right before I go into her classroom. My mother and the principle is aware of this teachers lacks but the teacher still abuses us in her class, the principle said that is very hard to get rid of a teacher even if they know that this teacher is not fit to teach, this teacher has files of complaints from kids and parents but nothing is been looked on. Am I the only kid in the world that has a teacher who bullies? Are my classmates now, before me and after me will have no choice to just deal with the abusive ways, because it is just too much work or details to go through just to discipline a teacher, it is just not fair. This teacher has been teaching more than 25 years as my mom had her once and it was an unpleasant experience for her too and now I am experiencing it. I just feel very strongly that this is so unfair, that teachers can do to us and say things that hurt our feelings and that is okay, if we the student did any of that disrespect to the teacher we encounter almost an world war III from the principle, teachers, and parents while this teacher do to us and just laughs. I don't want nothing to with science anymore, I also don't respect teachers as much as I did, I always respected them like a second parent but this teacher changed almost all my thinking of my mind. Can you help me? Do you have any materials I can share with my classmates and may be help the principle to do something about our problem?? This teacher is a pro-bully for she have

been doing it for almost 30 years . . . 20, 30 thousands had to endure her and more, I pray for my teacher, to STOP . . . She makes us cry every time . . .

Several suggestions to deal with this problem have emerged as a result of numerous discussions around the country. One school began with the premise that every adult who has contact with students needs to be a role model for respectful behavior. With that principle in mind, it was determined that if any staff member observes another staff member bullying a student, he or she is to document the incident—time, place, specifics—and send the memo to the principal. If the principal receives a number of such memos, he or she would have specific evidence to warrant a conversation about the observations.

Another solution occurred at a Midwestern elementary school following an in-service workshop that I conducted. Three teachers shared a pod in the corner of the building with a fourth teacher who was known for bringing disruptive students out in the hall and verbally abusing them. Prior to the workshop, it had become the practice for the three teachers, on such occasions, to close their doors and ignore the bullying. The next time an incident occurred, however, the three teachers chose to leave their classrooms and stand as silent witnesses to the student's abuse. The strategy worked and the offending instructor never engaged in such behavior again.

An additional solution evolved when educators observed that teachers who bully are usually new teachers reacting to overwhelming frustration or tenured teachers who are very set in their ways. The latter category seemed rather discouraging, as poignantly expressed by the student who communicated with me, but teachers who had learned the ropes of classroom management expressed a willingness to become a mentor and share effective techniques for maintaining order with beginning teachers. Many schools automatically match new teachers up with an experienced "buddy" to prevent stressful issues from arising. Collegial coaching is a concept that helps faculty members develop successful mentoring behaviors. The following Web site offers extensive resources on the topic: www.northern.edu/ois/Mentor.htm.

Counselors can be helpful. They are trained to deal with difficult problems but they appreciate being involved as early as possible, before the situation gets out of hand. One counselor had the student put the bullying complaint in writing, then presented the letter to the teacher in a private conversation. The teacher modified her behavior.

At a meeting of administrators when this topic arose, a principal pointed out that it is the responsibility of the principal to handle these matters, and counselors should not have to assume the task of intervening with bullying teachers.

An unexpected solution came when Mary Fischer, a BullySafeUSA colleague, was conducting a student empowerment session. Toward the end, a teacher who had been listening intently to the definitions and descriptions of bullying spontaneously apologized to her students for her bullying behavior. The forgiving students, who were so touched by her repentance, rushed to give her hugs and a tearful conclusion was had by all. Mary reports that the atmosphere of the classroom completely changed, and the teacher, her students, and their parents enjoyed a splendid year.

Teachers appreciate structured opportunities to brainstorm and consult with each other. They are grateful for teacher-friendly resource material, activities, films, and videos that are recommended by pleased users.

A counselor or school nurse who has gone through the in-service training could conduct training sessions for substitute teachers, team members who were absent, and staff members who, for various reasons, were not included in the in-service workshop.

4. Parent involvement

One of the most difficult challenges for school systems is actively involving parents. It certainly is the most frustrating part of the work that I do for schools. Schools will contract with me to do a parent seminar on bullying, announce the meeting date, send home a flyer, and set up a roomful of chairs anticipating a large crowd. I always urge them to move the meeting to a smaller room and put up fewer chairs because I have stood before many a scant group. Most parents of the bullies never seem to appear. It is parents of the children who are suffering who are most likely to attend. The largest parent meeting I ever addressed was at Our Lady of the Sacred Heart, a first- through eighth-grade parochial school, in suburban Cincinnati, Ohio.

When I walked into the gymnasium and saw 250 seats that had been dutifully arranged in rows, my heart sank. To my delighted surprise, at 8:00 P.M. there was a warm body occupying every chair, and we had a most productive meeting. A parent task force was organized as a result of the meeting, and a number of parents lent their support to the ongoing integration of bullying prevention activities. When I asked for an explanation of such great parental attendance, the principal, Barbara Adelmann, informed me of the following elements that were put in place:

1. A note went home to every parent stating that one parent had to attend an important meeting on the subject of school bullying.
2. Teachers were not allowed to give any homework assignments that evening.
3. All sports events were canceled.
4. All sports practices were canceled.

5. Students were informed that they could attend school out of uniform the following day if at least one of their parents attended.

I realize that schools where students wear uniforms or have a dress code have an advantage with element number five, but another incentive, such as permission to wear a cap, could serve as a motivator. The first four elements send a very strong message about the priority of the issue for the school.

Parochial and private schools seem to have an advantage in engaging parents, but public schools have combined a bullying presentation with a spaghetti supper, a dessert buffet, and/or childcare services and had good results. For insurance, plan to have the school's choir sing several songs at the *conclusion* of the program. Some schools have advertised the parent meeting as a presentation on school safety, rather than bullying, in hopes of attracting a wider audience.

A strategy being used more often is to use the newsletter that goes out to parents as a source of information about bullying issues. Some newsletters are using a question-and-answer format to bring the more serious problems to the attention of the parents. Involving parents, especially parents of bullies, continues to be a challenge. We salute those schools that make a determined effort to bring families to the table to complete the educator/student/parent triad. Changing the deeply imbedded culture around peer abuse will require the synchrony of all three components.

An award-winning, exemplary program of parent involvement takes place at Washington Elementary School in Santa Ana, California. I saw the program in action when I worked there and met with Cathy Kazanjy, the family literacy coordinator. Washington is an urban, year-round school, preschool through fifth grade. Spanish is the first language for the majority of the children; 87 percent of the students are learning English as a second language, and 85 percent fall in the federal poverty level for free and reduced breakfast and lunches. In 1996, one mother asked if she could read to her daughter in the classroom because they had no books at home. From that one mother, the program has grown to over 600 moms, dads, grandparents, older siblings, aunts, and uncles. Whoever walks their child or children to school, stays to read for the first twenty minutes of the day.

Once a week in the evening is family literacy night. Two hundred parents and children take optional courses together in computers, math and literature, science and literature, poetry, and healthy cooking, to mention a few. A family center on the school campus is home base for volunteer family members who assist with safety patrol, literacy book clubs for adults, projects for teachers, a revolving student library, school fairs, and holiday celebrations.

Kazanjy says that: "Immigrant parents care so much about their children's education. It is our responsibility as educators to open our doors and invite parents in on a time schedule that works for them."

5. Student empowerment sessions

Adults must become more proactive in confronting bullying and enforcing antibullying policies, but ultimately it is the students themselves who will determine the kind of environment they share. There are too many opportunities for students to ignore the rules when adults are not present, so we must find a way to reach their minds and their hearts.

Students have a great deal to say about the issue. They have stored up heavy concerns about bullying, and when given the chance, a flood of feelings, thoughts, suggestions, observations, and healing ideas streams forth. My favorite action is conducting student empowerment sessions and training others to do this powerful work, as well.

I continue to be awed by students' collective wisdom and inspired by their creative responses. If you want to learn about bullying, there is much to be fathomed from researchers, educators, curriculum designers, authors, and the Internet, but the very best sources—the real experts—are the students themselves.

6. Reinforcing concepts throughout the year

There are innumerable ways to emphasize respect, kindness, compassion, and wholesome conduct between young people, but it must be sustained in order to achieve corrective performance. Dan Olweus, the pioneer researcher from Norway whose efforts showed a 50 percent reduction in bullying in two years, focused on a saturation effect—actively involving teachers, parents, and students. His concepts are currently being replicated by a number of school districts in the United States.

Yoga, Dance, and Meditation

In California, where budget cuts have eliminated most physical education teachers, yoga is becoming institutionalized as part of the school culture in many schools. The Accelerated School, an acclaimed charter school in Los Angeles, introduced Yoga Ed yoga sessions for all of its students in 2001. In San Francisco, Tony Sanchez, founder of the United States Yoga Association, has trained sixty classroom teachers citywide in hatha yoga. Students describe the benefits of yoga as helping them to calm themselves down when they feel stressed, enabling them to focus, helping them to handle their angry feelings, and allowing them to feel proud of themselves for taming their bodies. Test scores were three times higher when the students had yoga sessions at least once a week.

Laughter has been praised by philosophers, extolled by Norman Cousins in his book *Anatomy of an Illness,* and is now a form of yoga called Hasya. It was developed in 1995 by a physican in Bombay, India, as preventive medicine for the maladies of life. The therapeutic value of laughter has been recognized for years at workshops in the corporate world as well as for society's caregivers. Laughter can be cathartic, can reduce tension, can be healing, can diffuse anger, and can bring about bonding. It has physical and emotional benefits that can be brought into the classroom.

Richard Brown, chairman of the early childhood department at Naropa University in Boulder, Colorado, recommends daily meditation for students and teachers. Brown believes that when teachers are nurturing themselves, they can take better care of their students and that the simple act of emptying the mind even for a few seconds is one effective way to control aggression.

In Baltimore, the Park School offers dance classes—a combination of modern, ballet, and jazz—as part of their curriculum. I observed one of these sessions and saw the enthusiasm that was generated. The instructor uses some gentle warm-up techniques and creates a sense of trust and closeness so that students can share thoughts or concerns with each other. The major part of the session is devoted to exuberant dancing and learning complex patterns, which helps to develop concentration. When structured effectively, dance has an amazing liberating effect that can lead to release of pent-up feelings and cathartic experiences.

Dance therapists across the country work in classrooms with students, and two of them have created movement programs specifically around bullying issues. Lynn Koshland is working in Salt Lake City, Utah, and Rena Kornblum has been working through the Hancock Center at the University of Wisconsin, in Madison. Kornblum has published a book and accompanying teacher's guide for educators, parents, and, of course, dance therapists to address bullying prevention by engaging children in movement activities. Some children learn best visually, some auditorally, but the kinesthetic sense of learning is very exciting and reinforcing. Information about this excellent material is listed in Resources.

Theater

Two plays, *The Wrestling Season* and *Bang Bang You're Dead,* are powerful dramas that could (and should) be produced in every high school in our country. *The Wrestling Season,* by Laurie Brooks, deals with rumors and innuendo that surface in a typical high school locker room with devastating consequences. The play is a metaphor for the conflicts, pressures, betrayals, and complex friendships experienced by most teenagers. *The Wrestling Season* was commissioned by the Coterie Theater in Kansas City, Missouri, and was developed at The Kennedy Center's New Vision/New Voices and New York University's Program in Educational Theater. See Resources for further information.

Bang Bang You're Dead, a one-hour, one-act, fictionalized drama, written by playwright William Mastrosimone, is the powerful story of a student who has been convicted of killing five students at his school and his parents. It is based on the real-life case of Kip Kinkel, a fifteen-year-old high school student from Springfield, Oregon, who was subsequently sentenced to 112 years in prison. The play takes place in his jail cell as the students that he shot come back in his mind to ask him why they had to lose their lives. I have seen it performed twice by high school students, once on a mostly bare stage and another time at a community theater with sets and lighting, and was profoundly moved on both occasions.

Mastrosimone has made it available on the Internet so that any school can perform it without paying licensing fees. A condition of this accessibility is that all performances be free. A telling moment in the play comes when the central character, in response to a poignant soliloquy from a victim who recounts all the important life events that she will never experience, states that he thought he was just playing "bang bang you're dead," that he thought he could just press the restart button and start all over again. A question-and-answer session follows the performance, capturing the impact of performing the play on the actors as well the audience. I strongly recommend this play for the upper elementary (fifth and sixth grades), middle schools, and high schools.

A play for elementary school students, *A Town Called Civility*, was written by Claudia Friddell, a teacher at Gilman School in Baltimore, Maryland. Sal, the main character, learns lessons in kindness from the locals in the western town, Civility. A sequel, *Respect in the West*, centers around respect and includes some gold miners and Native Americans. The Native Americans help show the gold miners respectful behavior. See Resources for further information.

Youth Courts deserve a serious look as a reinforcing strategy. In 1993, a core group of lawyers, educators, and community members, concerned that first-time juvenile offenders were not being held accountable in the traditional justice system due to budget constraints, developed the plans for a youth court in Oakland, California. When a youth commits a misdemeanor, the local police department may refer him or her to Youth Court. First-time offenders are represented by youth attorneys and tried by juries of their peers. Sentences are designed to hold youths accountable for their actions while providing a positive, meaningful experience. Once an offender successfully completes his or her diversion sentence, he or she is restored record-free to the community. Two thousand cases have been handled so far. The value of teen courts is not only the lessons learned by students who participate, but also the docket relief. There is always a minimum sentence, a written apology, restitution, and community service. The case is reviewed in sixty days to check for compliance, to see if there is a need for extension or the diversion is cancelled and a petition is filed for delinquency. The recidivism rate for the Youth Court program is the same or better than other diversion programs.

Restorative Justice is a similar concept that also serves as a diversion program. In Salinas, California, the program is under the direction of Cheryl Ward-Kaiser, who had been a witness to the murder of her husband and the rape of her daughter by a terrifying teenager. Out of her struggle to come to terms with the unbearable pain from that indelible experience, she decided to work with juveniles. Her motivation was to reach troubled youngsters before their bitterness and hostility turned them into killers.

Restorative justice brings a juvenile offender and his or her victim together to discover if there is any possible way for the culprit to redeem himself through mutually agreed upon restitution. An example of a successful case involved a boy who had trashed a woman's home, destroying furniture, clothing, heirlooms, plants, dishes, photo albums—no contents of the home were left unscarred. For the woman, the greatest loss was the photo albums. Shortly after the trashing, her only son was killed in an automobile accident, and she had no visual memory of him. The young criminal was genuinely touched by her pain and vowed to restore her loss as best he could.

Over the next six months, he contacted every family in the community who had had a child that had been in school with her son. He asked them to please look through their photographs for any pictures of the deceased young man. By the end of the year, he was able to gather enough photographs to fill an album and presented it to the tearful mother. Could a minimum prison sentence bring about the conversion of heart and mind that this young man experienced?

Another excellent program is Junior Judges, created by the Young Lawyers Association in Texas. "Junior Judges: Helping Kids Make Smart Choices" is a curriculum project, with an accompanying thirty-minute, MTV-style video, aimed at fourth-grade students. The project teaches students how to make smart decisions in tough situations such as cheating, destroying property, bullying, stealing, drugs and alcohol, gangs, and weapons. Members of the Texas Young Lawyers Association volunteer their time to go into classrooms with the video that has seven vignettes to provoke discussion.

"Mediators Achieving Peace: A Direction Away From School Violence," a project of the State Bar of Texas, trains middle school students to be mediators. Students at Shawnee Mission East High School,

Kansas, formed an I Will Campaign; 1,500 students signed a pledge that says, "I will think of how my words affect others; I will clean up after myself; I will choose to make a difference . . . my WORDS and my ACTIONS have the POWER to positively AFFECT others." As part of the campaign, students write notes to fellow students recognizing acts of kindness. One of the major purposes of the student organization is to encourage students to break away from cliques and expand their social environment.

What if our society could inherit a generation of young people who had developed skills in resolving conflicts; honoring respect, compassion, and empathy; reaching out beyond insular groups; and creating a safe environment for themselves and others? We would not just be eliminating bullying but generating a standard of behavior that would impact the way they raise their families and contribute to their communities.

Effective curricula have been developed, films and videos produced, activities designed, stories written. From a dearth of material in the 1990s to a profusion in this century, educators will not want for resources. The formula for success is in the insistence on follow-through. That insistence is dependent on at least one passionate champion within the system who believes that change is possible and understands the commitment required. That believer must think beyond changing behavior, which in itself is challenging enough, and focus on changing the culture, a more demanding vision.

Imagine a school where students encourage each other to learn; praise each other's accomplishments; respect individual choices in clothing, music tastes, hairstyles, personal goals, and cultural and literary interests. Envision a school where teachers spend their time challenging eager minds, inspiring creativity, preparing young people for productive futures, freed from time-consuming discipline enforcement. Picture a school environment where bantering, conversing, and interacting do not lead to pain, rage, and revenge. This is not a utopian ideal. This scenario is possible, but unlikely to happen unless the vision is shared and put in place by all members of the school community.

CHAPTER ELEVEN

POLICIES AND LEGISLATION

"You have to be the change you want to see in the world"

—Gandhi

In Norway, motivation to take up the cause of bullying prevention was stirred by a series of three suicides. In the United States, it took a rash of homicides to arouse concern for childhood cruelty. Not only a rash of homicides, but the killings had to involve multiple shootings and take place in the suburbs in order to capture our attention. Since Columbine, a number of national and state organizations have been deliberate about collecting information, sorting through masses of data, ideas, and concepts, and presenting resolutions, position papers, and recommendations to deal with bullying.

The May 2001 newsletter of the National School Safety Center listed a number of states that had passed legislation since 1999 in an effort to provide safer schools for children. Alabama, California, Colorado, Georgia, Massachusetts, Mississippi, Missouri, Nebraska, New Hampshire, New York, North Carolina, Ohio, Oklahoma, and Pennsylvania were mentioned as states that put policies and guidelines in place to deal with crisis intervention, emergency responses and procedures, potential hazards to safety, disorderly and disruptive behavior, and performance evaluation. In 1994, Vermont was the first state to adopt an act relating to harassment policies in schools, although the Minnesota State Board of Education had adopted a model religious, racial, and sexual harassment and violence policy in 1988. That policy is printed in its entirety in our first book, *Bullies & Victims*. Colorado and New Hampshire were among the first states to refer to bullying in their bills, and Missouri was one of the first states to attach monies to a violence prevention framework that recommends character education, conflict resolution, problem-solving, prejudice reduction, cultural diversity, sexual harassment reduction, gang awareness, activities that foster a sense of belonging, interpreting body language, practical options for dealing with anger, dealing with abuse, the relationship of alcohol and drug abuse to violence, and media literacy.

The National Conference of State Legislatures compiled examples of recent state enactments that are not inclusive of all legislative actions but highlight legislative responses that deal with bullying, harassment, and hate crimes. The sixteen states referred to, as of this writing, are: California, Colorado, Connecticut, Georgia, Illinois, Louisiana, Mississippi, Nevada, New Hampshire, New Jersey, Oklahoma, Oregon, Vermont, Washington, and West Virginia.

Most of the legislative responses require the state's Department of Education, school districts, and/or school boards to develop model policies on the prevention of bullying. Georgia requires the implementation of a character education program at all grade levels. Louisiana requires students expelled for fighting to pay for and attend conflict resolution classes with their parents. New Hampshire requires school employees to report any information regarding bullying behavior to the school principal and provides immunity to any school employee who makes such a report from any cause of action arising from a failure to remedy the reported incident.

Washington State attached a budget appropriation to its policy mandates. $500,000 from the general fund is appropriated for anti-bullying and antiharassment training at the school district level. Washington also included language that encourages students, employees, and volunteers to report reliable information to an appropriate school official while also declaring that no school employee, student, or volunteer may engage in reprisal, retaliation, or false accusation against a victim, witness, or one with reliable information.

The state of Illinois amended its school code by mandating a parent-teacher advisory committee to develop, with the school board, policy guidelines on pupil discipline, including school searches, and a time frame for furnishing a copy of the policy to the parents or guardian of each pupil.

The Colorado Bullying Prevention Act was signed into law on May 2, 2001. The law amends the Safe Schools Act by adding a provision requiring each school district to include a specific policy in the district conduct and discipline code concerning bullying prevention and education. Additionally, the law requires that the school's policy concerning bullying prevention and education, including information related to the development and implementation of any bullying prevention programs, be submitted annually to the Colorado Department of Education and be available to the public.

Most state laws have been specific about covering bullying situations on school grounds and school-sponsored events. New Jersey, Oklahoma, Colorado, and Oregon cover behavior on school buses and the last three include bus stops as well.

In many ways these state mandates echo the history of child abuse legislation. Each state passed its own child abuse statutes, including different definitions, provisions, and data collection. This fragmented system has made it extremely difficult, even twenty-five years later, to obtain a completely accurate picture of child abuse and neglect at the national level. This foretells a murky future for the collection of peer abuse data. However, these legislative enactments do recognize the significance of bullying and its impact on students.

Opposition to such legislation has been voiced. The newspaper *Education Week* reports that some states are running into conflict with Christian Coalition groups who oppose antibullying bills, contending that they are a cover for gay-rights efforts that could eventually force schools to teach about homosexuality in a positive light. Opposition is also coming from those who fear government intrusion and think that such matters should be determined at the local level. Others are concerned that laws could usurp the role of parents in teaching their children how to treat other people respectfully.

Dr. Deborah Prothrow-Stith, a professor of public-health practice at Harvard University and an expert on violence prevention, is concerned that state laws will become the "zero-tolerance fad of today" and will focus on punitive tracks rather than preventive approaches where the real focus needs to be.

After New Hampshire secured legislation, the antibullying mandate got bogged down in the implementation stage. A technical advisory in the law said schools had to report every incident of bullying, which school administrators found unrealistic. Despite the cumbersome challenges, the commissioner of education believes the provisions of the bill have been met and have spurred most school districts to adopt antibullying policies. The governor of Washington exercised a partial veto of the reporting requirement, citing it to be too burdonsome on schools.

The Safe School Initiative Final Report from the U.S. Secret Service and U.S. Department of Education identifies ten key findings from their review of the case histories of the thirty-seven incidents of targeted school violence. These findings offer implications for schools and communities in developing strategies for preventing targeted violence in schools.

- Incidents of targeted violence at school rarely are sudden, impulsive acts.
- Prior to most incidents, other people knew about the attacker's idea and/or plan to attack.

- Most attackers did not threaten their targets directly prior to advancing the attack.
- There is no accurate or useful profile of students who engaged in targeted school violence.
- Most attackers engaged in some behavior prior to the incident that caused others concern or indicated a need for help.
- Most attackers had difficulty coping with significant losses or personal failures. Moreover, many had considered or attempted suicide.
- Many attackers felt bullied, persecuted, or injured by others prior to the attack.
- Most attackers had access to and had used weapons prior to the attack.
- In many cases, other students were involved in some capacity.
- Despite prompt law enforcement responses, most shooting incidents were stopped by means other than law enforcement intervention.

The Commission for the Prevention of Youth Violence was established to bring together physicians, nurses, and public health experts to examine the problem anew. Agencies represented on the commission are: American Academy of Child and Adolescent Psychiatry, American Academy of Family Physicians, American Academy of Pediatrics, American College of Physicians–American Society of Internal medicine, American Medical Association, American Medical Association Alliance, American Nurses Association, American Psychiatric Association, American Public Health Association, and U.S. Department of Health and Human Services.

An Executive Summary states: "More school suspensions and more prisons are not the answer. The answer, rooted in public health, is prevention." The summary goes on to identify seven priorities and key recommendations.

PRIORITY ONE: Support the development of healthy families

PRIORITY TWO: Promote healthy communities

PRIORITY THREE: Enhance services for early identification and intervention for children, youth, and families at risk for or involved in violence

PRIORITY FOUR: Increase access to health and mental health care

PRIORITY FIVE: Reduce access to and risk from firearms for children and youth

PRIORITY SIX: Reduce exposure to media violence

PRIORITY SEVEN: Ensure national support and advocacy for solutions to violence through research, public policy, legislation, and funding

The Health Resources and Services Administration (HRSA) Maternal and Child Health Bureau is developing a multiyear campaign that will combine a variety of communications messages and activities designed to reach nine- to thirteen-year-old youths to help prevent bullying. The effort will be guided by sound research about the causes and impacts of the aggressive behaviors that characterize bullying. The National Bullying Prevention campaign will reach out to a variety of potential partners, from education to media to community-based organizations. It is designed for national launch in September 2003 and is to be sustained for years to come.

National Organizations

The American Psychological Association has been a leading pioneer in addressing youth violence. Other organizations have joined the effort— the American Medical Association, the American Medical Association Alliance, the National Education Association, the American Academy of

Child and Adolescent Psychiatry, the American Association of School Administrators, the National Parents Teachers Association, and others.

At the 2001 annual meeting of the American Medical Association, a resolution was introduced by the American Academy of Child and Adolescent Psychiatry and the American College of Preventive Medicine and adopted. It asked that the AMA:

- Encourage appropriate public and private funding agencies to support research on bullying behavior and anti-bullying interventions;
- Through the Council on Scientific Affairs, review the available research on the efficacy of intervention programs designed to reduce bullying;
- Work with specialty societies, state and local medical associations, the AMA Alliance, public health agencies, departments of education, and other interested parties in preparing and disseminating materials that will help schools, teachers, parents, and others to address bullying at the local level; and
- Evaluate survey instruments that can be used to measure the incidence of bullying.

Subsequently, the Council on Scientific Affairs made the following recommendations, which were adopted as AMA policy:

1. That the AMA recognizes bullying as a complex and abusive behavior with potentially serious social and mental health consequences for children and adolescents. Bullying is defined as a pattern of repeated aggression; with deliberate intent to harm or disturb a victim despite apparent victim distress; and a real or perceived imbalance of power (e.g., due to age, strength, size) with a more powerful child or group attacking a physically or psychologically vulnerable victim

2. That the AMA work with appropriate federal agencies, medical societies, the Alliance, mental health organizations, education organizations, schools, youth organizations, and others in a national campaign to change societal attitudes toward and tolerance of bullying, and advocate for multifaceted age and developmentally appropriate interventions to address bullying in all its forms.

3. That the AMA advocates federal support of research (a) for the development and effectiveness testing of programs to prevent or reduce bullying behaviors, which should include rigorous program evaluation to determine long-term outcomes; (b) for the development of effective clinical tools and protocols for the identification, treatment, and referral of children and adolescents at risk for and traumatized by bullying; (c) to further elucidate biological, familial, and environmental underpinnings of aggressive and violent behaviors and the effects of such behaviors; and (d) to study the development of social and emotional competency and resiliency, and other factors that mitigate against violence and aggression in children and adolescents.

4. That the AMA urge physicians to (a) be vigilant for signs and symptoms of bullying and other psychosocial trauma and distress in children and adolescents; (b) enhance their awareness of the social and mental health consequences of bullying and other aggressive behaviors; (c) screen for psychiatric comorbidities in at-risk patients; (d) counsel affected patients and their families on effective intervention programs and coping strategies; and (e) advocate for family, school, and community programs and services for victims and perpetrators of bullying and other forms of violence and aggression.

5. That the AMA advocate for federal, state, and local resources to increase the capacity of schools to provide safe and effective educational programs by which students can learn to reduce and prevent violence. This includes: (a) programs to teach, as early as possible, respect and tolerance, sensitivity to diversity, and interpersonal problem-solving; (b) violence reduction curricula as part of education and training for teachers, administrators, school staff, and students; (c) age and developmentally appropriate educational materials about the effects of violence and aggression; (d) proactive steps and policies to eliminate bullying and other aggressive behaviors; and (e) parental involvement.

6. That the AMA advocate for expanded funding of comprehensive school-based programs to provide assessment, consultation, and intervention services for bullies and victimized students, as well as provide assistance to school staff, parents, and others with the development of programs and strategies to reduce bullying and other aggressive behaviors.

7. That the AMA urge parents and other caretakers of children and adolescents to (a) be actively involved in their child's school and community activities; (b) teach children how to interact socially, resolve conflicts, deal with frustrations, and cope with anger and stress; and (c) build supportive home environments that demonstrate respect, tolerance, and caring and that do not tolerate bullying, harassment, intimidation, social isolation, and exclusion.

The American Medical Association has produced "Connecting the Dots to Prevent Youth Violence: A Training and Outreach Guide for Physicians and Other Health Professionals," authored by Lyndee Knox, Ph.D. It is an extraordinary document and a tremendous contribution to the field.

The American Medical Association Alliance is the proactive volunteer voice of the AMA. It is the largest, most influential organization representing physicians and their spouses. Stop America's Violence Everywhere (SAVE) was launched in 1995. Under the

SAVE umbrella are two paths of action: SAVE-A-Shelter, which supports battered women and their families and SAVE Schools from Violence, with a priority on bullying.

Alliance members have distributed more than 70,000 copies of "I Can Handle Bullies," an eight-page activity book that generates a dialogue about bullying, its effects on children, and strategies to overcome the consequences. Other user-friendly workbooks for students are: "I Can Be . . . ," "Hands Are Not For Hitting," "I Can Be Safe," "Be A Winner," and "I Can Choose." In addition, the Alliance has created a Hands Are Not For Hitting place mat with teaching suggestions and a thirty-piece Solving the Violence Puzzle that helps to start a dialogue about violence among eight- to eleven-year olds.

Shakila Ahmad, past president of the Cincinnati, Ohio, Medical Association Alliance, was the first member of the Alliance to invite me to work with schools, educators, and parents in her community. Since then, fourteen local Alliance chapters and three Alliance state organizations have invited me to conduct workshops in ten states. Paula, who is an Alliance member, and I have conducted four workshops at the annual Confluence for Alliance leaders. Alliance members are highly motivated, effective activists for children in their communities. As their national president, Patti Herlihy, said: "Bullying is such a timely and important public health issue. As advocates for America's health, it is our responsibility to be at the forefront of this issue so that we can make our schools a safer place for children to learn, play and grow."

Herlihy makes an excellent point by speaking of bullying as a public health matter. Not only does it fall into the public health domain, but the response should follow the public health model. An example often used to explain the public health model is the problem of dysentery. When people in villages contract dysentery, the public health model is to put in a sewer system. Treating one ill person at a time is another model. With bullying, we must do both. We cannot sacrifice individual children while we work to change the school culture, but we must begin working to change the school culture to prevent children's suffering.

There will never be a bullying prevention inoculation. Our solution will not come from a laboratory, it will have to come from us. Donna Stone, a cherished friend and mentor, founder of the National Committee to Prevent Child Abuse (now Prevent Child Abuse America) was fond of saying: "Anything is possible, the impossible just takes a little longer."

The National Education Association, the American Association of University Women (AAUW), and the national PTA organization have become vital and important disseminators of information about peer harassment. They are leading the way and inspiring other significant groups to become involved.

State Attorneys General

Many attorneys general have taken leadership roles in the cause of bullying prevention. Through my work, I am familiar with the efforts of four of them.

Jane Brady, the attorney general for the state of Delaware, made bullying prevention a priority, beginning in 1997. Her office developed two bullying brochures—one for students and one for teachers and administrators. The deputy attorney general, Rhonda Denny, travels around the state sponsoring school assemblies, making presentations to school faculties and PTAs, and training education students at various local colleges. At the school assemblies, students are asked to sign pledges, in which they pledge not to bully other students, to help those who are bullied, and to include students who are often left out of activities. Denny says, "Some people were surprised when the Delaware Department of Justice initiated bully prevention programs in schools in 1997. However, if you think about it, the word 'justice' has always included the notion that we should protect those who for one reason or another have difficulty protecting themselves. Children who are targets of bullying precisely fit that bill. If we look the other way when we know bullies in school are targeting young children, and only become involved once the children grow older and a crime has been committed, then we have failed to catch the cancer of injustice in its early stages, allowing it to metastasize, and making treatment difficult at best. The earlier we address the problem, the more chance of success in the end."

Students who are arrested for misdemeanors that occur in a school, and are first-time offenders, are often assigned to a school diversion program. These programs in Delaware are designed to recognize students with bullying problems. The attorney general's office has written worksheets for the students to deal with bullying problems, which are frequently related to their crimes. The office is currently creating a Web site with helpful resources for school employees.

In Kansas, Attorney General Carla Stovall contracted with Randy Wiler, a twenty-two-year law-enforcement veteran and DARE officer with special expertise in bullying prevention and intervention, to create a bullying prevention Web site.

Christine Gregoire, attorney general of Washington, and Ken Salazar, attorney general of Colorado, have been actively involved in the legislation that has been adopted in their states and champion the rights of children to have safe havens for learning.

When Attorney General Gregoire served as president of the National Association of Attorneys General, she decided to ask parents, teachers, and kids for their observations about youth violence. She held a series of national and state "Listening Conferences." Gregoire reported that "Kids changed our view. Without exception, whether in urban or rural settings, kids were unanimous that one of the main causes of violence is bullying and they blamed themselves and parents." Consequently, they issued a national report entitled "Bruised Inside," a quote that came from a student response: "If you stick me with a knife or shoot me with a gun, I go to the doctor and get patched up. If you 'diss'on me, you leave me bruised inside and I don't ever recover." Washington has legislation that calls for all schools to have a No Tolerance for Bullying policy and mandates teacher and student training across the state. Attorney General Gregoire says: "I think that children have a right to expect that they will be safe and secure in their homes and schools. When they felt unsafe in schools, we as a nation had to step up and acknowledge that bullying is a life or death matter."

Ken Salazar is determined to convert the tragedy of Columbine into a statewide immersion in bullying prevention. He believes that bullying impacts school safety and academic achievement and that "we have a moral obligation to address this challenge with a sustained commitment." His office works closely with every school district in the state and supports creative initiatives such as the Aspen Center for Integrative Health, which is making a major commitment to bringing our BullySafeUSA project to Aspen and nearby communities. Betsy Fifield, chairman of the venture, says that the Aspen Center for Integrative Health is committed to prevention and that translates into investment in children.

School Policies

School boards, school districts, and individual schools have been developing policies related to bullying. These policies include issues around sexual harassment, zero tolerance, and school dress codes among others.

Sexual Harassment

Minnesota was one of the first states to adopt a comprehensive policy prohibiting harassment and violence. The Minnesota School Boards Association in July of 1993 declared that, "It shall be a violation of this policy for any pupil, teacher, administrator or other school personnel of the School District to inflict, threaten to inflict, or attempt to inflict religious, racial or sexual violence upon any pupil, teacher, administrator or other school personnel."

An example of a sexual harassment policy comes from Saint Michael Lutheran School in Ft. Myers, Florida. The principal is Robert Ziegler. The school has a forty-two-page parent/student handbook that covers every possible process and procedure affecting school life.

> Sexual harassment of or by any student shall not be tolerated and may result in disciplinary and/or legal action, including possible expulsion.
>
> Sexual harassment has the purpose or effect of creating a negative impact on an individual's performance or of creating an intimidating, hostile, or offensive environment and includes but is not limited to:
>
> 1. Verbal conduct such a derogatory comment, unwanted sexual advances, sexual jokes, etc.
> 2. Visual conduct such as derogatory cartoons, drawings, pictures, gestures, etc.
> 3. Physical conduct such as leering, assault, blocking normal movement, touching an individual's body or clothes in a sexual way, etc.
> 4. Threats and demands to submit to sexual request.
> 5. Retaliation for reporting a violation or participating in an investigation.
>
> Teachers will discuss this policy with their students at the beginning of the school year in age-appropriate ways and will assure them that they need not endure any form of sexual harassment.
>
> Anyone at Saint Michael Lutheran School, who is subject to or witnesses sexual harassment, should immediately report such conduct to the teacher, the principal, the assistant principal, or the pastor."

The AAUW released a report on June 6, 2001. Harris Interactive surveyed 2,064 students in grades eight to eleven. They found that four students out of five personally experience harassment, girls only slightly more than boys. Disturbingly, these statistics have hardly changed since 1993, when Harris conducted a similar survey for AAUW, although the gender gap closed somewhat. Boys today are slightly more likely to be harassed, girls slightly less. More dramatic change has occurred. Today 69 percent of students, compared to just 26 percent in 1993, say their schools have a sexual harassment policy, while 36 percent, compared to just 13 percent in 1993, say their schools distribute materials on the subject. But despite school policies and procedures, students continue to harass other students and rarely tell adults when it happens.

Zero Tolerance

The federal government weighed in on the issue of school safety and weapon-free schools in the mid-1990s. The Gun Free Schools Act requires that each state receiving federal funds under the Elementary and Secondary Education Act (ESEA) must have put in effect, by October 1995, a state law requiring local educational agencies to expel from school for a period of not less than one year a student who is determined to have brought a firearm to school.

Each state's law also must allow the chief administering officer of the local educational agency to modify the expulsion requirement on a case-by-case basis. All local educational agencies receiving ESEA funds must have a policy that requires the referral of any student who brings a firearm to school to the criminal justice system.

Reacting to the federal injunction and the horrors of school shootings, Zero Tolerance policies have gone into effect in school districts all across the country. Administrators feel compelled to take an unequivocal position to ensure the safety of their students. Zero Tolerance can include more than weapons—such as guns, knives, bombs, razor blades, and/or pepper spray. It can encompass sexual misconduct, threats, fights, and drugs, as well. The rationale for the policy is that schools need to have strict rules that can be clearly understood by every member of the school community and consistently enforced. A 1999 study concluded after four years of implementation that schools using zero-tolerance policies are less safe than schools that have not implemented such policies. One theory is that already alienated students who crave attention may be encouraged by the presence of metal detectors and cameras to commit violent acts simply for the recognition.

On the positive side, Zero Tolerance has exposed a significant number of weapons that might have posed a dangerous threat to the security of school populations. The policy has alerted scores of students and staff to potential harm and prevented untold tragedies.

In an article by Lis Suhay in the *Philadelphia Inquirer,* Sean Duffy, president of the Commonwealth Foundation Charter School Resource Center in Philadelphia, is quoted as saying that zero tolerance "is a national disaster in education. A lot of children are going to be scarred by these rigid interpretations by overwrought bureaucrats." Newspapers have reported numerous examples of zero tolerance situations that have overreached the intent of school safety procedures. The following examples illustrate the problem. A girl who offered some Midol tablets to a friend who was having menstrual cramps was suspended. A boy who had been on a Boy Scout camping weekend and forgot to remove his scout knife from his backpack was also suspended. TV and radio talk shows expressed outrage for days about the case of the boy in first grade who kissed a girl in his class and was charged with sexual harassment. An honor student in Ft. Myers, Florida, was jailed over an incident involving a kitchen knife that had accidentally fallen under the seat of her car during a weekend move. In a similar incident in Bedford, Texas, a sixteen-year-old honor student was expelled when a bread knife was discovered in the student's pickup truck. He had been performing a good deed by packing up some household items belonging to his grandmother to take to the Goodwill store, and the knife was accidentally left in his truck. An appeal hearing was set, but school officials said they must abide by the state's policy. But Adrienne Sobolak, spokeswoman for the Texas Education Agency, pointed out that expulsion could be shortened because the student had a knife, not a gun.

Criminal charges in one community were even filed against two eight-year-old boys who were playing with a paper gun. Examples such as these have prompted some schools to repeal their zero tolerance policies in favor of a course that allows them to make decisions based on individual cases. The zeal to insure weapon-free schools has put some administrators in an untenable situation, eliminating the latitude to use common sense in particular circumstances. More and more educators are backing away from the "mandatory sentencing" approach in spite of their safety concerns and finding ways to manage policy infractions.

Further discourse on this issue appeared in the *St. Louis Post-Dispatch*, January 14, 2002. The article states that harsh discipline for students who bring weapons to school appears to be losing popularity in Missouri School Districts. While all Missouri schools have zero-tolerance policies for weapons, punishment varies. "Initially the public misunderstood zero tolerance and thought it meant that any weapon from nail clippers to a revolver would mean a student would be expelled," said Cahokia Superintendent Jed Deets. Deets added that students in middle school and high school would face expulsion for having a weapon, while younger children would face suspension and counseling. "Zero tolerance is here to stay, but it has to be administered with common sense," said Larry Humphries, a superintendent of Hazelwood School District. "You have to deal with individual students and parents."

While the federal law requires expulsion of any student who brings a weapon to school, it allows school administrators to modify punishment on a case-by-case basis. Jody Stauffer, director of student discipline in Parkway, Missouri, said she considers the student's age, the type of weapon, what the student intended to do with the weapon, and whether the child had the mental capacity to do harm.

Frank Zimring, a law professor at the University of California at Berkeley, believes that zero tolerance policies will make children more reluctant to tell on their friends.

The controversy will continue and errors in judgment will be made, but parents and communities will clamor for enforced policies that promise a secure environment when they send their children off to school. What role can lawmakers play with these contentious issues? An article published by the National Conference of State Legislatures poses three responses:

> First, they can ensure that even troubled children stay in school. Legislatures in Rhode Island and Missouri developed alternative education resources for disruptive students, while at least 37 other states have either authorized or required school districts to create their own programs.
>
> Second, lawmakers can learn from experience. The day before the Springfield, Oregon, school shooting, 15-year-old Kip Kinkel was caught with a firearm in school. When law enforcement officials lacked any basis to keep him in custody, he was released. The next morning, he went to school and shot 27 other students with a semiautomatic rifle. Oregon policy makers responded to the tragedy by enacting legislation requiring law enforcement to hold students possessing firearms for up to 72 hours, pending a psychological evaluation.
>
> Finally, legislators can learn valuable lessons from tragedy, but purely reactive policies can go too far. Most legal conflicts develop when school officials apply state law too broadly, disciplinary policies disregard circumstances, or students are kept out of school."

School Uniforms/Dress Codes

Another policy that gained favor among school systems was the insistence on school uniforms. Parochial schools and many private schools adhere to commonality of dress and adopted such a policy long before it was seen in the context of school safety. In 1994, Long Beach, California, was the first big-city school district to adopt uniforms. When school fights dropped by 51 percent, overall school crime rates dropped 36 percent, sex offenses decreased 74 percent, weapons offenses decreased 50 percent, assault and battery offenses decreased 34 percent, and vandalism decreased 18 percent, word spread quickly across the country. Dick Van Der Laan of the Long Beach Unified School District explained, "We can't attribute the improvement exclusively to school uniforms, but we think it's more than coincidental." The principal of a middle school in Seattle reported that, "The demeanor in school has improved 98 percent, truancy and tardies are down, and we have not had one reported incident of theft." In a document published by the U.S. Department of Education, these testimonials and others from schools in Memphis, Baltimore, Norfolk, Kansas City, and Phoenix affirm the value of uniforms in creating a less competitive, more academically focused atmosphere.

Some experts suggest precautions when mandating school uniforms, such as allowance for religious expression and parental rights to nonparticipation. Some parents have objected to mandatory uniforms, saying the policy violates students' constitutional right of free expression. Many schools that adopt a mandatory uniform policy choose clothing items such as khaki pants or skirts and solid-color shirts—white or navy. Collectively, students grumble about the loss of personal expression, but privately, many students express relief from the obsessive fashion competition that dominates the preteen and teen culture.

Many schools find it easier to set a dress code than to deal with definitions, infractions, and the distractions surrounding inappropriate clothing such as spaghetti-strap tank tops, skirts and shorts that are too short, see-through blouses, and sagging pants. Some schools keep a supply of belts on hand and do insist that males accommodate to a reasonable belted waistband where underwear is not exposed. Reports have circulated about bullying, robbing, and, in some cases, even students being killed for their leather jackets, jewelry, and expensive athletic shoes.

But according to an article in the *New York Times,* September 13, 2002, by Kate Zernike, many schools are backing out of enforced uniforms because it has become a huge distraction. When families could opt out, it created confusion. A middle school math teacher said, "It increased friction, it increased discipline problems, having to worry about who was wearing what. It wasn't worth the fight." Schools in Florida, Kansas, and New Hampshire are abandoning the requirement. However, in Utah they are attempting to make it work by eliminating the opt-out provision.

Because problems associated with clothing come up so frequently in bullying discussions with students, a dress code is one element of a strategy to reduce opportunities for taunting. This issue will continue to churn up strong opinions on both sides.

Mission Statements

Mission statements can reflect the heart and soul of a school's commitment to take peer abuse seriously. The process of creating a clear mission statement will help the school community define its approach to the whole issue and determine the action steps to follow.

Carole Lander, a counselor at Claymont School, in the Parkway School District in St. Louis County, Missouri, was instrumental in creating a succinct mission statement for their school that incorporates many elements:

> To make Claymont a place where every child and adult is safe and feels that they belong:

1. Hurtful teasing and bullying will not be allowed at Claymont.
2. The students and adults will help each other by speaking out against hurtful teasing and bullying.
3. Students and adults will treat each other with respect and kindness.

Parent Responsibility

Some states have tried to deal with the issue of school violence by holding parents responsible for the violent acts of their children.

The National Center for Juvenile Justice reports that by the end of 1998, thirteen states had enacted laws making parents criminally responsible for failing to supervise their problem children. The penalties range from court-ordered family counseling, community service, and fines (from $25 to $1,000) to imprisonment. Other states have chosen to impose civil rather than criminal penalties. The penalties in civil cases are more focused on restitution and parent involvement in treatment and probation programs. It seems obvious that insistence on participation in family counseling offers more return on society's investment than sentencing parents to prison. There is a strong case to be made, however, for parent accountability when parents fail to take responsibility for their children's violent outbursts. Is it possible for children to store arsenals of weapons in their rooms, to make diabolical plans, and to exhibit a history of behavior problems without raising any flags from engaged parents?

The answer is not as easy as it seems. Don Bross, M.D., with the C. Henry Kempe Center for Child Abuse and Neglect, poses a number of challenging questions. Should parents be charged with neglect if their child brings a weapon to school? Is the parent of a nine-year-old to be held to the same conditions as a parent of a seventeen-year-old? What happens once a child is identified as a bully at school? When should the child be considered a delinquent? On what basis can we force parents to put a child in treatment? Schools want to hold parents responsible, and parents want to hold schools responsible. Should decisions be made by the legal system? Do we want to clog our courts with these cases? Should children be charged with assault, and if so, what is the minimum age? Should standards vary from community to community? What if divorced parents disagree about intervention approaches? What if married parents disagree about intervention approaches? What are other questions that should be raised? How should we organize a national forum for discussion of these complex issues?

Policies and Issues in Other Countries

France

In France, schools require student insurance, which runs about $7 a year. After increasing incidents of schoolyard attacks and a barrage of complaints from parents, French insurance companies are offering bully protection. Two large French insurance firms pay hospital bills if students are attacked at school or on the way. The coverage reimburses students for everything from stolen textbooks to ripped clothing. The companies will not reimburse students for stolen cash or cell phones. According to Carolyn Gorman, spokeswoman for the Insurance Information Institute in Washington, a family's homeowner's or renter's insurance policy covers such risks.

Japan

Japan has had serious student suicide problems related to bullying. Concern for suicides coupled with the tragic stabbing of eight students at an elementary school near Kyoto, has led school officials to take some dramatic and drastic steps. Teachers are being enrolled in self-defense classes and furnished with tear-gas canisters, and, in some schools, simulated attacks have been staged to prepare students to protect themselves in the event of violence.

United Kingdom

Some of the most important research on the topic of bullying has been conducted in Canada and the United Kingdom. Connie Blair, wife of Prime Minister Tony Blair, has become a spokesperson for the issue. Delwyn Tattum and David Lane wrote one of the first books on the subject in 1989, *Bullying in Schools,* about bullying in the United Kingdom. We were panelists at the International Congress on Child Abuse and Neglect in Chicago in 1992 and grateful for the handful of people who attended our session.

Bullycide—Death At Playtime, coauthored by Tim Field and Neil Marr, has stirred a great deal of interest in the United Kingdom. The coauthors coined the term *bullycide* to describe suicides of bullying victims. They claim that sixteen children in Britain are pushed to suicide each year because of bullying. An article in the *Daily Mail* contains a report from Childline, a telephone service available to children. A spokesperson claims that bullying eclipsed every other issue as the subject that most children call in about—even sexual abuse. In 2001 the service received 20,269 calls about bullying, mostly from children in the ten- to sixteen-year age group, and from children up and down the income spectrum.

Kidscape, an antibullying child-protection charity in England that receives 16,000 calls a year from concerned parents, says that three clear and worrying trends have emerged in the past five years.

1. Bullying has become increasingly violent.
2. Bullying is starting younger than it ever did, in the four-to six-year age group.

3. Bullying among girls has become much more physically violent and sophisticated, involving technology such as text messages and e-mail.

Ireland

Dr. Mona O'Moore in the Education Department of Trinity College in Dublin set up the Anti-Bullying Research and Resource Centre in 1996. In addition to a broad range of services, the Centre conducts an annual Awareness Week where various classes and events are run to increase knowledge of what bullying is and what impact it can have. Competitions in art, poetry, prose, and drama are held on the theme. During the week, a staff development day is held to deepen teachers' understanding of the issue and to solicit suggestions on how to proceed. There is also an evening event for parents, school management personnel, and the wider community to enlighten and inform them on the subject and involve them in the drafting of the school policy.

The Centre strongly recommends the development of a whole-school, proactive, and constantly evolving policy on bullying. The policy should include:

- A clear definition of bullying and the forms it takes
- A statement that bullying is unacceptable behavior and that it will not be tolerated
- A statement that pupils should support each other by reporting all instances of bullying
- A statement that all reports of bullying will be investigated and be dealt with sympathetically
- A clear statement on how the school will handle an alleged case of bullying

I presented a workshop on bullying prevention and intervention again at the International Congress on Child Abuse and Neglect in Denver in 2002. In addition to interest from attendees in the United

States, participants spoke of serious bullying problems in the Bahamas, Estonia, and Croatia. The head of the Child Abuse Federation in Croatia talked to me about the cultural changes that have affected bullying in his country. The war has produced a change in the nature of bullying, especially with young males. Aggression is seen as honorable and necessary to defend one's territory, and boys who bully see themselves as having the characteristics of heroes.

CHAPTER TWELVE

CHALLENGES FOR THE FUTURE

"Bullying is the most enduring and underrated problem in American schools today."
—National School Safety Center

"Ultimately it is up to us—the adults—to stop children from hurting each other. More to the point, it is up to us to stop children from being hurt in the first place." So states a report from the Commission for the Prevention of Youth Violence, December 2000. Our noble task is to break the pain chain of bullying in the twenty-first century. To accomplish this, we must divide our heroic work into manageable pieces.

Recognize Bullying Is Peer Abuse

First and foremost, we believe that identifying bullying, or peer abuse, as a form of child abuse is the number-one challenge. Until the cruelty of children to each other is taken as seriously as the cruelty of adults to children, the issue will never receive its due attention. Data from the child abuse field indicate that 3 million reports of suspected abuse and neglect of children in the United States are received annually. Less than 1 million of those reports are confirmed. In response to that appalling figure, every state has a statute pertaining to child abuse; mandated reporters; protective services workers to investigate suspected reports; a foster care system; permanency planning and adoption services; trained medical, legal, and law enforcement personnel to deal with abuse cases; and, depending on the communities, support groups for parents, therapeutic treatment access, telephone hotlines, prevention programs, etc. The Office on Child Abuse and Neglect, funded by the federal government, sponsors national conferences attracting thousands of professionals, volunteers, and civic leaders to share cutting-edge information about violence against children. In spite of this array of resources, child abuse reports continue to increase.

It is obvious that altering child abuse statutes to include peer abuse is not the answer if that were to mean adding the responsibility for bullying issues to overburdened social service agencies. The first step is language acknowledgment; the second step is to determine the most effective way to deal with bullying. The current lack of a structure in place is no excuse for minimizing the problem.

Bullying data indicate that more than 5.7 million children are bullies, targets, or both, and yet there is no central system within the federal government to retrieve standardized reports. And there is no such thing as standardized data. Definitions of bullying vary from state to state, from school district to school district. Some bullying is criminal, some is not. One of the most formidable problems is the overwhelming amount of information that is available on the subject. The Internet offers seemingly limitless surveys, reports, statistics, policies, programs, curriculum, legislation, studies, etc., but there is no agency responsible for filtering this plethora of material on bullying in a focused way to rally public interest effectively. Excellent agencies such as the National School Safety Center and Safe and Drug Free

Schools address bullying through a larger agenda of youth violence prevention and school safety, but no agency or national organization focuses solely on bullying. Prominent professional organizations are signing on and producing extremely valuable reports. Too much information can be as detrimental as too little if there isn't a central resource in place that can require standardized data and disseminate information upon request.

The Anti-Bullying Centre at Trinity College in Dublin, Ireland, would be an interesting model to observe. We have learned so much from Dan Olweus and his pioneering work in Scandinavia. There is much that we could learn from Ireland, too.

Affect Policies and Legislation

"Legislation is a step in the right direction but passing laws won't make the behavior go away," says Bill Modzeleski, director of the national Safe and Drug Free Schools. To really make a difference, Modzeleski believes we have to create cultures and climates that don't encourage and support unacceptable bullying behaviors. For starters, he continues, we have to persuade parents, educators, and policy makers that (a) bullying is a serious problem, (b) bullying is a complicated problem, and (c) it's well worth the effort and time it is going to take to deal with it.

Ron Stephens has been director of the National School Safety Center (NSSC) since 1984. The NSSC has been publishing special materials on the topic of bullying and disseminating invaluable information through workshops and training sessions for almost twenty years. The National Conference of State Legislatures tracks current legislation and is an excellent resource for state laws pertaining to bullying.

For the most part, however, it is up to each individual school district to determine its approach to the problem. Many school boards are adopting specific policies. The following example is the policy of the St. Tammany Parish School Board in Covington, Louisiana:

BULLYING

Bullying is a form of aggression, and it occurs when a person(s) willfully subjects another person (victim), to an intentional, unwanted, and unprovoked, hurtful verbal and/or physical action(s) at any school site or school sponsored activity or event. Bullying may also occur as various forms of hazing, including initiation rites perpetrated against a student or a member of a team. Examples of types of bullying may include, but are not limited to:

A. Physical bullying includes, but is not limited to punching, shoving, poking, strangling, hair pulling, beating, teasing, kicking, punching, or excessive tickling.

B. Verbal bullying includes, but is not limited to such acts as malicious name calling, teasing, or gossip.

C. Emotional (psychological) bullying includes, but is not limited to rejecting, wronging, extorting, defaming, humiliating, blackmailing, diminishing personal characteristics such as race, disability, ethnicity or perceived sexual orientation, manipulating friendships, isolating, or ostracizing.

D. Sexual bullying includes, but is not limited to many of the actions listed above as well as exhibitionism, voyeurism, sexual propositioning, abuse involving actual physical contact, or sexual assault.

Personnel at all levels are responsible for taking corrective action to prevent bullying at any school sites or activities.

Allegations of bullying shall be promptly investigated, giving due regard to the need for confidentiality and the safety of the alleged victim and/or any individual(s) who report incident(s) of bullying. An individual has the right to report an incident(s) of bullying without fear of reprisal or retaliation at any time. Retaliation is defined as meaning "to pay back (an injury) in kind." When a person is accused of having behaved in an inappropriate fashion, especially bullying, the common reaction of that person is to be angry and want to pay the "alleged victim" back (retaliate). Retaliation must not occur and will not be tolerated.

Proven allegations of bullying can have serious consequences for the party deemed guilty including verbal or written reprimand, in-school or out-of-school suspension, disciplinary reassignment, and/or expulsion.

Victims of bullying have responsibilities. Victims should clearly tell the bully(ies) to stop. If bullying persists, don't ignore the incident(s) and, immediately report the incident to someone at school. Tell your parent(s). If the bullying continues after you have clearly told the bully(ies) to stop, make a written record of the incident including dates, times, witness or witnesses and parties involved in the incident. Report the incident immediately to an adult who has authority over the bully(les); for example, a teacher, guidance counselor, assistant principal or principal. Avoid being alone With the person(s) who has (have) attempted to bully you in the past. If you are the victim of bullying, and you feel uncomfortable reportIng this fact to adult personnel at school, contact another appropriate adult.

Expand Research

Much of the abundant information available about bullying is repetitious. There is a tremendous need for research beyond assessing the nature and extent of the problem. While studies are beginning to identify solutions, there are a host of issues that desperately need further analysis, such as the correlation between bullying and learning deficits. With the demand for better test scores all over the country, the bullying element should be factored into the strategy equation.

Although we talk about bullying as one large category, we recognize that there are many subgroups of individuals and behaviors within that large category. Provocative targets are distinct from passive targets. Reactive bullies are different from proactive bullies, and elitist bullies are in a separate category. These distinctions deserve unique responses and instruments to measure effective interventions.

Why are some children devastated by the cruelty they face and others more resilient? Are certain kinds of bullying more demoralizing, or is it the nature of the child that determines the reaction? We need instruments to assess verbal and emotional bullying abuse, which are not as easily identified as physical abuse and sexual harassment.

There are other issues worthy of research—evaluation of interventions, usefulness of literature, and materials for different age groups; bullying research that addresses the developmental needs of preschool, primary, and elementary school children, middle school and high school students; and decisions about collecting and disseminating bullying data in a systematic way that can be available to all interested persons.

We need very specific information about the shift from target to bully and the percentage of students who experience aggression who become aggressors, and we need to know how we can create a culture in schools, in families, and in society that does not tolerate abusive behavior.

We need a body of research examining ways to overcome the barriers that currently exist in education, legal, and family systems that prevent us from protecting children from each other. We are in need of legal research to pull together current and past cases of bullying and peer harassment in various jurisdictions for reference and citation.

Above all, we have to ask the right questions. Answers will follow, and some will deserve further questioning. Our thinking keeps changing, and we have to stay open to new ideas even if they contradict previously held beliefs. It is research, after all, that pushes our accepted wisdom in new directions. An example of this is the current theory that babies should be put to sleep on their backs, contrary to past professional advice, followed by several generations of parents, to put infants to sleep on their stomachs. A more personal case in point occurred when Paula attended a Girl Scout camp and burned her hands on a cooker that the campers had devised. One counselor insisted that she rub grease on the burn and cover it with tin foil, while another counselor was equally firm that the burn should be treated with ice water. Over the course of the day, each counselor persisted in applying their treatment of choice.

Bless the researchers who will be steadfast in their quest.

Ensure Accountability

Who will take up the seven priorities identified by the Commission for the Prevention of Youth Violence, listed in chapter 11? Who will fund such a worthy task? There is a host of agencies, organizations, and individuals who are paying attention to peer abuse and school safety, but who can pull all those efforts together? Priority seven of the commission is: "Ensure national support and advocacy for solutions to violence through research, public policy, legislation, and funding." In 1987, a distinguished group of clinicians, researchers, and educators gathered at the Schoolyard Bullying Practicum, convened at Harvard University by the National School Safety Center. They identified five central ideas that need to be addressed to prevent bullying. The fifth idea was: "The United States should follow the lead of Japan and Scandinavia, whose governments have addressed bullying problems with national intervention and prevention programs." Imagine if we had acted on that recommendation more than fifteen years ago! Fifteen years from now, will we still be referring to recommendations, priorities, etc.? We do not want for good ideas, what we do want for is systemic action!

Should bullying be addressed as part of the larger issue of school safety, youth violence, gangs, and drug and alcohol abuse prevention, or should it have its very own niche? Can bullying be included in the larger context but at the same time be defined as peer abuse, a form of child abuse deserving all of the attention, resources, and services that child abuse and neglect generates?

In 1972, Donna Stone, president of the Stone Foundation, decided to donate $500,000 to an organization that was dedicated to preventing child abuse. When she discovered that no such organization existed, she used the money to found the National Committee to Prevent Child Abuse. That agency has since changed its name to Prevent Child Abuse America, and today it has thirty-eight chapters in thirty-seven states working on advocacy, education, and services to parents and families.

Peer abuse is an issue whose time has come! Our schoolchildren are in desperate need of a Donna Stone, a single-minded agency, or a visionary foundation to lead the way.

Focus on Language

It would be very helpful if all of the committed organizations and individuals were using the same language to describe bullying behavior. To be specific, we use the terms *bullies, targets,* and *witnesses.* Formerly we used the terms *bullies, victims,* and *witnesses.* We changed our terminology when we heard the word *target* being used because it seemed more hopeful than *victim.* The word *bystander* is being used by some advocates, rather than *witness.* We prefer *witness* because it implies an active role. When we ask students for a definition of *witness,* they say it is someone who sees something and has to tell the truth about what they've seen. The term *bystander* seems to imply a more passive role.

Even if we can't agree to use the same words, could we agree on the concepts? Most people, adults and children alike, still equate bullying with physical fighting. The damage that is caused by verbal abuse and emotional/psychological abuse deserves much greater attention and concern. At present, there is too much acceptance of bullying that doesn't qualify as physical or life-threatening. Sexual bullying is rampant, not only in our middle schools but in our elementary schools, much to the surprise of the educators and administrators who are present when students are given an opportunity to talk about this facet of peer abuse. Sexual bullying includes physical, verbal, and emotional elements. If we are going to use the word *bullying* inclusively, we must commit to educating others about the range of hurtful behaviors encompassed by the term.

Those of us working on our BullySafeUSA program have discovered that children don't believe that all teasing is bullying. When children of equal power give and take with each other, it is not considered to be abusive. Once again, language is significant to help children sort out the differences between joking, teasing, and bullying. It will require a concerted effort to spell out the continuum, but will be well worth the time to eliminate the confusion in children's minds. Adults need to be very clear about what is acceptable and unacceptable behavior.

Peerhaps it would be helpful to use some sound bite language to get our messages across: e.g., "Sticks and stones can break your bones, but words can break your heart;" "It's not cool to be cruel."

Collaboration between a large number of groups and individuals could begin with language. Children could be encouraged to get involved by developing slogans for schools, having poster contests, and maybe even creating videotapes with antibullying messages. Working through our semantic challenges will prepare us for more difficult assignments.

On the subject of language, there is something that each of us can do: make our grammar gentler! Our everyday conversation is sprinkled with violent metaphors such as "The thought struck me," "That play was a knockout," "I'll take a shot at that question," "Let's hit them with another approach." If we became more sensitive to our language, perhaps we could remind ourselves on a daily basis to soften our speech and reduce the rudeness. I've shared this with a number of people, who find themselves erasing words in mid-sentence and enjoying their reach for a substitute word or phrase.

The city council in Zapopan, Mexico, has banned swearing in

public, imposing fines of up to $400 or jail terms of thirty-six hours on those who utter "bad words." The law doesn't define "bad words," leaving it up to police to decide which utterances are against "morals and good customs."

Will such a law change behavior? It will certainly make people more aware of what they are saying—and where they say it!

Reduce Access to Weapons and Monitor Media Violence

Students carry an estimated 270,000 guns to school every day, and guns are involved in 75 percent of adolescent killings, making some school grounds dangerous places for children. Twelve American children are killed each day by guns. Statistically, if a gun is kept in the home, the risk of homicide in the home is three times greater and the risk of suicide is five times greater. Limiting children's access to firearms has to be a major preventive tactic.

Tied in with weapons accessibility is marksmanship accuracy that students acquire at video arcades. Lt. Colonel David Grossman, author of *On Killing,* spent twenty-five years in the military studying how to enable soldiers to kill. A major challenge was to desensitize young men who had grown up with a strong message that "Thou shalt not kill." When recruits were taught to shoot by aiming their guns at bulls-eye targets, they often had difficulty killing the enemy when assigned to the battlefield. When the shooting targets were replaced with silhouettes of people, it made it easier for them to overcome their psychological resistance to killing. This same technique is used today in violent electronic games. When violent video games were first introduced, game players scored points for destroying aliens from outer space, monsters, and robots, but current games reward players who kill people. The combination of practiced accuracy and desensitization places children in danger when weapons are easily available to students under stress.

Some video games, TV shows, movies, and certain kinds of music are part of the mass-media influence identified as a high risk factor. Since the 1950s over a thousand studies have linked media violence with aggression in children and adults. There are those who disagree with those conclusions and say that it's possible that people who are prone to violence just tend to watch more violent programs. A study released in the March 29, 2002, issue of *Science* followed 707 children for seventeen years. Teens who watched three or moe hours of TV a day were five times more likely to commit agressive acts in the next several years than those who watched less than one hour a day, researchers found. The research was distinct from other studies because it linked TV viewing in general—not just viewing of violent programs—to later agression. LeeAnn Smith, a founder and the first executive director of MediaWise, believes that every thinking adult must ask the following question: "If media does not have the power to affect our thinking and behavior, why are companies spending billions of dollars each year to influence our buying preferences?"

Controlling the quality and quantity of television viewing is a major parental responsibility. A Stanford University study compared second- and third-grade students at two public schools in San Jose, California. The students in one school were encouraged to limit their television use to seven hours a week. At the end of the study, the children had reduced television watching by a third and their "aggression rating" was put at about 25 percent lower than those students at the other school. The American Academy of Pediatrics has released a policy urging parents to avoid television for children under two years old. The news release stated, "While certain television programs may be promoted to this age group, research on early brain development shows that babies and toddlers have a critical need for direct interactions with parents and other significant care givers for healthy brain growth and the development of appropriate social, emotional, and cognitive skills."

Web filtering systems are not the solution some had hoped for.

The software does not completely block all sites with X-rated and violent content on the one hand, and blocks many sites that young teens should be able to access on the other.

There are some hopeful signs. Retail stores such as Sears and Toys 'R' Us have pulled violent video games from their shelves, and Wal-Mart and Kmart use a bar code scanner system to block children under age seventeen from buying titles branded "mature" by a game industry ratings board. Both the American Academy of Pediatrics and the American Medical Association Alliance have produced some excellent brochures on the subject of electronic violence.

Taking on opposition groups organized around parental rights, gun issues, and first amendment free-speech concerns is not for timid souls. All the more reason for coordinated collaboration. Other countries have tackled these obstacles successfully. Canada, Great Britain, Australia, and some Latin American countries incorporated media education into school curricula. No developed country on our planet supports the proliferation of handguns that is tolerated in the United States.

Improve Teacher Training

Teachers who are entering the teaching field need better preparation for the classroom realities they face. Women and men who invest their time and money to become qualified educators can be quickly disillusioned when they first come in contact with disrespectful students and adversarial parents. The attrition rate for new teachers is the strongest statement on this subject. Education programs at the university level should include more information and background on the issues of bullying and classroom management. Standard textbooks used at the university level do not give enough depth to the topic of bullying and its disruptive effects.

These observations come from a valuable connection with Dr. Blanche Sosland, professor emerita, Park University, Parkville, Missouri. Several years ago, Dr. Sosland invited me to speak to her undergraduate class about our previous book, *Bullies & Victims*. On the Monday night before the shootings at Columbine, she had assigned her students to read our book, never anticipating the horror that was to come. One of her students wrote a twelve-page journal entry about how chilling it was to read our book in the context of Columbine.

Twenty-five of Dr. Sosland's students observed me working with a fifth grade class in an actual public school setting, and then I went to the campus to process the experience with Dr. Sosland's student teachers. The student teachers were amazed at how oblivious the fifth graders were to the presence of such a large number of guests and how much the children were willing to reveal about their hurts, their fears and their shame.

Dr. Sosland believes that teachers are eager for skills to deal with their classroom management issues, and while much is now being written about the dimensions of the problems of bullying, there is not enough material being disseminated about practical solutions and application. With the deepest humility, at Dr. Sosland's request I am including the following quote: "There is no textbook in twenty years of teaching that has been so appreciated by my students as *Bullies & Victims*."

Our plea is for more intensive preparation and skill training for the student teachers we need so desperately in the twenty-first century.

Emphasize Parent Involvement

The challenge is to make a connection with parents who are currently detached from the bullying problem. If they do not know that their child is in distress or are unaware of the root cause of their child's apparent misery, bullying is probably not a priority concern. Parents of bullies might be pleased with their children's popularity, not realizing the fear factor that is maintaining their son's or daughter's magnetism. These parents and parents of witnesses may see no reason to attend a meeting about bullying. Our task is to help parents understand that the dynamics of peer abuse affect everyone in the system, whether their child is directly or indirectly involved.

It is crucial for everyone connected to the school community to be on the same page as we press for solutions, and the most difficult group to harness is the parents. The Illinois legislature, in its wisdom, called for a Parent Teacher Advisory committee with specific tasks required. A committee that is mandated by the state should grab parents' attention. Short of such dramatic mandated involvement, schools and their parent associations need to be vigilant in their drive to engage parents. One private elementary school in the Midwest conducted a bullying survey of its students and distributed the survey results to all of the parents. The students' comments and observations were riveting, and a meeting to discuss the survey was well attended. Our hope is that once parents become aware of the depth and breadth of pain for children affected by bullying, they will want to be partners in the solution.

Empowering Children

Bullying prevention and intervention is not something you can do *to* students or *for* students as much as you can *with* students—all students. From skill training to surveys to activities to classroom discussions to books to community service to assemblies to role-playing to "buddy" systems to pledges to restorative justice to peer mediators to mentoring to empathy training to mobilizing witnesses—the possibilities for student empowerment are tremendous. Witnesses, especially, are key to changing the school culture because of their knowledge about the preponderance and the specific acts of abuse as well as their power to make a difference.

Time is the greatest obstacle. The current demands on schools consume every single teaching hour. But disentangling painful situations, dealing with anguished parents, and calming crises is time consuming, too.

Young children believe in fairness and they yearn for justice. They count on adults to keep those beliefs and yearnings intact. When they are treated with respect, when they are taught to be kind and compassionate, when they are surrounded by people of integrity, when they live with honesty, when they earn the pride of responsibility, they will build a world that will be safe for our grandchildren—and theirs.

Address Homophobia

Attitudes about homosexuality are linked to both youth suicides and youth homicides. That is a shameful fact and must be addressed. We cannot expect to change the belief systems of those who believe that homosexuality is a sinful choice. But we can expect that schools will not tolerate denigrating sexual language that causes untold shame, anxiety, and rage. We can expect that children will be protected from the physical and psychological assaults related to their sexuality. The consequence of allowing such abuse to flourish is too treacherous to consider.

As Franklin McCallie, former principal of Kirkwood High School, a suburban school in Kirkwood, Missouri, puts it: "100 percent of parents want their children to be safe at our school." He made this statement in response to criticism about the formation of a Gay Straight Alliance club at the high school.

McCallie had been asked to serve as principal in 1979 when the school was in the throes of interracial problems. Kirkwood High School was under an Office of Civil Rights investigation for alleged "discrimination against black students for unequal disciplinary consequences." By involving parents, faculty, students, and the Kirkwood Ministerial Alliance, the tension was alleviated, though not eliminated. For over twenty years, KHS has continued to conduct programs to reduce racism and bring black and white students together.

When sexual harassment of female students by males came to his attention, he again took steps to defuse a problem that made some students feel vulnerable and fearful for their safety at school. Then in 1998, the student newspaper conducted a survey about school bullying and name-calling; 61 percent of the students admitted that they insulted people daily with such words as *gay* and *faggot*. McCallie drew upon his past experiences of cultural intolerance between students and brought in speakers, former students, films, discussions, and workshops for faculty, parents, and children about homosexuality. This activity soon led to public scrutiny and set off a series of Letters to the Editor in the local newspaper, some of them quite critical of the Gay Straight Alliance club and making accusations of proselytizing.

One recent graduate, upon hearing about the controversy, wrote, "As I look back, I realize that it was only a handful of people who made my days at school hell. But others seemed hesitant to befriend me for fear of what others would think. I was spit on, tripped, punched, had my books knocked out of my hands, and things hidden from me. I was called 'fag,' 'fudgepacker,' 'homo,' and 'queer.' I couldn't even sit in classes or take tests without being called names. I barely graduated. I would pray every night that the Good Lord would take my life so I wouldn't have to go to school; I tried to commit suicide on four or five occasions, but I never had the courage to go through with it."

McCallie believes that the fight to preserve the safety and protect the rights of gay and lesbian students and teachers in American schools is just beginning. Opposition should not be allowed to interfere with the rights of every student to accomplish goals in both the cognitive and affective domains. McCallie feels that every student needs to be challenged by the educational process and to experience that excitement in an atmosphere of safety, security, and acceptance. It is unthinkable that a principal should be disputed for taking that position.

Massachusetts is the only state in the country to regularly fund violence prevention programs for gay and lesbian teens. Jason Beaubien, with National Public Radio, cited a 1999 survey conducted by the Massachusetts Department of Education showing that lesbian, gay, and bisexual students were more likely than their peers to report attempted suicides, to be truant, and to be assaulted. The state has been developing programs to make schools more comfortable for homosexual youth and to keep them in school. A Gay/Straight Youth Pride celebration attracted two thousand students in its third year. Creating a sense of community for students who have been harassed, taunted, and disaffected has brought about a significant improvement, but there is more that can be done. Though the program is not without criticism from a parent coalition that objects to the use of state funds to affirm homosexuality, the state should be a model for the nation. Unfortunately, it takes courage and conscience for a state department of education to assertively meet the needs of all of its students, including those who are gay and lesbian. Massachusetts can be proud of its concern.

For some school districts, legal action may be necessary to bring about change. According to an Associated Press report, August 29, 2002, the Washoe County School District agreed to a $451,000 settlement and to new policies to protect gay and lesbian students, formally recognizing that students have a constitutional right to be open about their sexual orientation and requiring regular student and staff education about sexual harassment. District trustees signed the settlement without admitting wrongdoing. Derek Henkle, a former student, sued the district after claiming that he had been beaten up by his classmates, insulted by a principal, and once was lassoed around the neck. According to court documents, the harassment was so pervasive that Henkle, following the advice of principals, went to three different high schools in the school district from 1995 to 1997.

Confront Sexualization of Children

When elementary school children are citing "sexual" bullying as the form of bullying that causes the most distress, there is a message we must heed. Children are repeatedly exposed to sexual language and images from a very early age. These messages are everywhere—television, movies, music, billboards, magazines, advertisements for clothing, the Internet, etc. It is almost impossible to shield young children from this sexual exposure. Do you know that if you look up White House.gov you will find current information about news, appointments, speeches, photos, and the history of the White House, but if you punch in White House.com you will find an X-rated pornographic Web site?

In our culture you can hear first graders talking about French kissing, and three-year-olds with older siblings sing songs about "getting hot" and taking their clothes off. They may not even understand what they are talking about, but they know that it is grown-up and off-limits, which makes it even more appealing. Even fashions encourage small children to imitate the sexy midriff-baring styles of music entertainers. A major retailer removed thong underwear for girls, sizes 7 to 14, when enough parents protested.

Schools are a hotbed of sexual rumors. Any and all sources of sexual data find a welcome repository in school boundaries. Healthy messages coming from families, neighbors, religious institutions, youth organizations, and health education classes in schools are desperately needed to counter the constant onslaught of sexual material coming at our children.

Assess the Impact of Budget Cuts

At least fifteen states grappled with budget shortages in 2002. Many of the state legislative initiatives directed at bullying prevention have no budgets attached. When there is no money, there is no priority. When there is no priority, there is no service. The deficits play serious havoc with education needs. Cuts are being considered at the same time that administrators are under considerable pressure to show improvement in subject competency and test scores.

A supportive school administrator in Florida cautioned that education priorities are established by politics rather than philosophy. Unfortunately, he said, it is tourism, taxes, and trade-offs that will determine what happens for children.

Some schools are eliminating counselors, some are contracting for fewer hours for school nurses. Some schools are saving money by cutting visual arts, music, drama, and dance programs. There are child advocates who believe that counselors, nurses, and arts programs are as important as math, history, and science.

"Short $240,000 in $1.4 million budget, the first thing the leaders of the Edgemont School District did was to combine the middle school and high school, eliminating three teachers and a principal. Next they dropped the gifted program, chopped the guidance counselor's hours in half, ended full-time kindergarten and recruited volunteers to coach track and wrestling. Now, they are cutting Fridays," wrote Jodi Wilgoren in the *New York Times,* June 9, 2002.

More and more rural schools around the country are shortening the school week to four days and extending the hours as a partial solution to the budget deficits. Reduced bus costs are the main savings factor. Wilgoren reports that four-day school weeks are in operation in some districts in Colorado, Wyoming, Arizona, Louisiana, Utah, and South Dakota. The states of California, Arizona, and Arkansas have adopted legislation to allow for the shorter week.

Some early studies indicate that students are doing quite well on the shortened week, but it is too soon to predict. While there is positive conjecture about the students' response, the four-day schedule is hard on working parents. A more serious threat to the welfare of the classroom is the cutbacks in school counselors and school nurses. Parents are so concerned that in at least one Kansas community, a foundation was set up to receive checks from families who are determined to retain their school counselors and nurses who play a crucial role in bullying education and prevention.

The crunch between reduced time and resources along with enormous pressure to raise test scores is destined to cause stress, and its inherent consequences, for our faculties and students.

Promote Prevention

Several years ago at a child abuse prevention conference in Iowa, someone remarked that the real S & L crisis in this country was not "Savings and Loan," but "Sooner or Later." Prevent Child Abuse America estimates that the United States spends approximately $94 billion every year as a direct or indirect result of child abuse and neglect. That equals $258 million every day. These costs are associated with the identification and treatment of abused and neglected children, the involvement of our judicial and law enforcement systems, medical and mental health treatment, and more. The costs of prisons are not included in this figure. Our current prison/parole population is 6.6 million. We are spending an absolute fortune on the Later instead of investing in the Sooner.

The most obvious primary prevention path begins with the family system. Families that protect their children from being hurt at home and prepare them not to hurt others will prevent myriad problems. We have put forward two exemplary programs that offer individualized, in-home support for new parents and high-risk families to direct them on a positive parenting track—Parents As Teachers and Healthy Families America. Whether it be Parents As Teachers, Healthy Families America, Head Start, or another quality home-visiting model, it is unquestionably cost effective to prevent child abuse and peer abuse from occurring in the first place, than it is to treat it later.

We must care about other family systems as well as our own. I feel compelled to share some words of wisdom from Terry McClain. "If you brutalize your children, don't ask any questions or wonder where you went wrong when they grow up into killers. If you allow your neighbor to brutalize his children, don't wail and gnash your teeth when those children grow up and kill yours."

The American Psychological Association public policy office reports that access to firearms, alcohol and drug use, involvement with antisocial groups, and exposure to violence through mass media are primary risk factors that contribute to violent behavior. These four areas are obvious issues for prevention strategies, as well.

There are two social models that bear mentioning: smoking and seat belts. The behavior change around tobacco usage and the use of seat belts offers two of the most hopeful prospects for societal transformation. In our family, it was our children who were shown films at school about people with pink lungs who didn't smoke, and people with black lungs who did. Consequently, they pleaded and persuaded my husband and me to give up cigarettes. It was our grandchildren who changed our habits regarding seat belts.

Frankly, I didn't see the necessity for such an inconvenience. I had transported three children for years by driving with my left hand and protecting them in the front seat with my outstretched right arm. When our grandchildren refused to ride with us until we fastened our safety belts, we succumbed.

Isn't it interesting to note that these two significant changes in our health habits were transmitted from children and grandchildren to us as parents and grandparents rather than vice versa? Here's to intergenerational learning and hope for the future, which brings us back to Donna Stone: "Anything is possible, the impossible just takes a little longer." Let us begin!

Maintain Passion

Our society has a reputation for craving instant gratification. We are not known for our willingness to wait for long-term solutions.

Many years ago, when Paula was about ten years old, she came home from Sunday school and announced that they had spent the morning discussing Moses. When I asked her what she had learned, she replied that the teacher told the class that Moses led his people through the desert for forty years, but he was not allowed to enter the Promised Land because God punished him for losing his temper. I thought that was a rather harsh interpretation, so I consulted with Rabbi Gershon Hadas, a dear friend and mentor, to seek his interpretation. Rabbi Hadas believed that the lesson we are to learn from the story of Moses is that if a person takes on an enormous challenge, he or she is not meant to see the completion of that dream within his or her lifetime. Some of us will be involved in the beginning of dreams, some of us will be involved in the middle of the dream, and some of us will witness the fulfillment. If a dream is important enough, it must be handed down to the next generation.

Beginnings of dreams are inspiring, creative, and energizing. Culminations of dreams are fulfilling, rewarding, and exhilarating. Keeping the dream alive during the middle period is demanding. It requires a person with the passion to maintain the fire for an indeterminate amount of time—passion that cannot be extinguished even though the end is not in sight.

Peter Yarrow is a person of passion. He created a video with the wonderful song, "Don't Laugh At Me," as is dedicating himself to bullying prevention. When the school shootings happened, the media was energized. Talk shows, newspapers, magazines, television shows kept us vigilant. Officials mobilized safety plans. Teachers and parents were inspired to be more attentive to students' needs. Students reported warning signs to adults.

Hopefully, there will never be another shooting to keep our outrage on full alert. In the absence of a crisis, the children once visible in handcuffs and prison jumpsuits will become invisible again. And what about the children who suffer in quiet silence, day after day? Who will sustain the fervor for their longings? It is up to us to keep the passion alive.

CHAPTER THIRTEEN

LETTERS FROM CHILDREN

*"The greatest revenge is not to defeat the enemy
but to change his heart."*
—Author Unknown

Our final plea is for children's pain to be listened to with respect and a sense of urgency. In this chapter we are including a small sample of the thousands of letters that we have received. These letters were selected from hundreds of classroom assignments. *Every* student in the class sent a letter. Some wrote as bullies, some wrote as targets, some wrote from the perspective of being a witness, some wrote from multiple roles. No student ever invoked a disclaimer that no bullying took place in their school. The pain that is taking place is staggering. I see it in the eyes of the children, their teachers, their principals, their counselors, and their parents. I share their frustration, their heartache, and their tears. We must find a way to break the pain chain!

These first two letters were written by Ruth Ann Supica and Teegan Fifield, young women who attended different middle schools where I conducted student empowerment sessions.

Courage

by Ruth Ann Supica

The excited sound of seventh-grade laughter and voices tumbled down the hallway as the students filed into the gym. I scanned the room, searching for my friends, and soon spotted them near the door to the restroom. I weaved my way through the mass of people and sat down next to my best friend, Lauren.

"So, what exactly are we doing here?" she questioned.

"Well, according to Mrs. Marks, we're supposed to be listening to a speaker about bullying, peer pressure and put-downs." I said this somewhat sarcastically, because the entire year our grade had been lectured over and over again on these topics. We were earning the reputation as the worst class in the school, which was not a reputation that my friends nor I were particularly proud of. As our science teacher stood in front of the entire eighth-grade level, attempting to get our attention, my friends and I sat back, prepared to sit through another monotonous speech full of harsh remarks about "Kids these days . . . " and "Your maturity level when you put someone down is not greater than that of an eight-year old."

But as soon as she started talking, I snapped to attention. She had this way about her, as if she knew how to reach into our minds and souls and make us think. And for once, I actually began to think about what it was she was preaching about. I thought about all the kids who came to school every day, despite knowing that they would have to face cruel comments and sneering faces all day long.

One boy, in particular, came to mind. Every day, this boy came to our first hour late, and I suspected it was because he needed to get medicine from the nurse. But this didn't stop the kids in the class from making fun of him. They punched him in the shoulder and said, "Hey, man! Where have you been?" And another would add, "How's that girlfriend of yours? Oh sorry, we forgot. You don't have a girlfriend. You only have boyfriends." This harassment would continue until the teacher cut in, forcing the boys to stop. But it was too late—it always was. The boy would put his head down on his desk in shame. The worst, though, was when he tried to retaliate. His attackers only laughed and continued the cruelty until the entire room was laughing at his expense.

As I sat in the auditorium, absorbing everything the speaker had to say, thoughts of this poor boy crept into my head. I sighed, thinking how sorry I felt for him, not that there was anything I could do. I tuned back into the speaker and listened intently to her words of wisdom.

"Now, before I leave today, I would like to give everyone here an opportunity to say anything he or she wants to on the subject of bullying or peer pressure. You may apologize to a friend, thank someone for his or her kindness, anything. And this is the one time I can promise that no one, but no one, will laugh at you."

The stillness in the room made me believe her. Slowly, I saw a few hands raise tentatively in the air behind me. One girl wanted to apologize to a friend she had been ignoring recently. Another thanked a boy for his kindness when she slipped on the steps the other day. It was then that my moment of courage happened. The speaker called on me, and with shaking hands and clammy palms, I began to talk.

"What you said today really made sense. I know that it's true, because I see it every day in class. There is one person who is always made fun of. It doesn't matter why—it could be the way he looks, talks or even takes notes." My voice shook. "I think that everyone here has made fun of him at one time or another. I know I have. And now I really regret it. To us, it may be just a game, but to him, it must hurt. And I think . . . well, we need to stop."

Scared of my classmates' reaction, I felt like the silence that followed lasted forever. But then, soft clapping started in the front of the room, quickly spreading through the entire crowd. By the time I looked up, the soft pitter-patter had turned into a thunderous roar of applause. I had voiced something that everyone was feeling.

Later on that day, the boy whom I had been talking about came up to me privately and said thank you.

I noticed that from that day on, people began to treat him a little better. The teasing stopped, and people greeted him in the halls with a friendly, "Hi!" It was those little, everyday things that I noticed, and I'm sure he noticed them, too.

This story was published in *Chicken Soup for the Teenage Soul III*. I am the "speaker" referred to in the story, and it is reprinted here with the permission of Ruth Ann Supica and the publishers of *Chicken Soup for the Soul*.

Bullies

by Teegan Fifield

What is a bully? A person who picks on someone? Well, yeah, that's true, but a bully is also so much more.

I was in kindergarten, eating glue, and yelling at my teacher and classmates. That's why I got sent to the principal's office for the first time. I'll never forget the fear that soon turned to pride, as I walked into the principal's office. I was proud, proud to have people fear me.

Through the years the principal's office became my second home. I got in many fights with the boys my age. I soon got used to teachers yelling at me and filling out plans and detentions. Right after seventh grade started I realized that being a bully wasn't what I wanted for my life. I wanted to have friends, no enemies. So I began to change. It was a slow process, changing the way I acted, the only way I knew.

Starting eighth grade I promised myself that this year would be different. This was the year I'd make a difference. This was the year, my year to free myself and become a new person.

Well, I'm sad to say that right off I began picking on people. This continued on and on until one day something changed my life. The author, SuEllen Fried, came to talk to the eighth grade. She talked to us about why people are bullies. During the assembly I sat back and really took a look at my life and the lives of those around me. I realized that I really was a bully. I've never felt more shame than I felt that day. I decided that I had to change before I really messed up.

So I started to change right then, with an apology to a friend whom I had hurt so deeply. I never knew such little words as "I'm sorry" could change so many things and help so much. I'm on a search to find the real me, someone I'm not sure I'll ever find. I never knew what an impact each one of us has on life until I really looked. I wasted so many years being a bully instead of being nice. I've definitely learned my lesson. And although I'm trying, I will never be the "perfect angel" by far. I admit that I have a bad temper, but I'm working on it.

To all the bullies out there, it's not worth it. You can't judge people by their differences because that's what makes them who they are.

The following letters are printed as they were received, without the students' names.

Letter #1

My belief is that everyone is bullied at some point in their life. I also believe that this same person will be a bully, witness, and a target as well. I know I have been all three at different times, but it doesn't have to be that way. My story is told from a witness's point of view.

During a typical day at my school, as I walk though the halls before homeroom, bullying can be all around. Mainly, it's someone whispering, "Oh my God! Did you see what she's wearing today!" or "I can't believe he thinks his hair looks cool like that!" Usually, it's just little things you think won't hurt someone. But that's not how it works.

There is this girl in my grade who is a target for verbal bullying. People say things behind her back, but act caring and concerned when she's around. I have tried to be respectful to her, but sometimes that's hard to do. I feel like I'll become a target if I be her friend. She is really quiet, and usually doesn't catch on to what people are saying about her. Because I'm a witness, I feel trapped in the middle of things. The angel on one shoulder is telling me to do what is right and just. The devil on the other says "Just go with the flow, or you might be next."

Normally, I listen to neither of the two and do nothing. I

pretend I don't know what's going on and tell myself, "What could I do about it anyway?" This is just as wrong. As I grow older and learn more, hopefully the angel will become more persuasive and start winning. Until then, I'll probably continue to be a witness and carry on as I have before.

Letter #2

I guess that everyone can say that there is at least one bully in their grade. I guarantee that most adults can recall exactly who bullied them when they were in school. See, in many schools, the bullies are mostly guys that think that making someone's life miserable is probably funny. That is mostly how it was here. At least that is what I thought.

Sure, I usually picked on a few people. You know, just for fun. Who hasn't? But when SuEllen Fried came to our school for an assembly on bullying, my whole perspective changed. I realized that what I was doing wasn't just harmless fun anymore, it seriously hurt people's feelings. I was a bully! Before the assembly, I had always pictured a bully as being a boy who was a little bigger than everyone else. Also, I thought of someone with a bad home life. But after this assembly, I realized that a bully can be anyone. At first I was like "Me? A bully? No way! It's just a little fun!" But I went on to notice all of the people I was hurting. Even my best friends.

There was one girl in particular that everyone (especially me) loved to pick on. I don't think that it was just because she was different, or because she was lousy at sports, or because she was dressed funny and her hair was cut like a boy's. I think that it was because she just stood and took all of our crap.

I am pretty sure that it all started in fourth grade. That was when she first got her hair cut really short and it looked pretty bad. She was always left out of everything, like kickball at recess. But when she was allowed to play (which usually was only because she told on us and we were forced to play with her), she would make a complete fool of herself. She would try to make people feel sorry for her by falling.

One time in fifth grade, I remember that we were arguing about something and I went up to her and pushed her down. Then after that, I began to bully her more and more. Even to this day I still do and it is three or four years later. Of course, I am not the only one who still does, practically everyone does. And if anyone is ever nice to her, it's only because they want something from her.

Everyone says that the reason bullies pick on others is because they are self-conscious about themselves, which I think is basically true. I believe that the reason I picked on others is to make myself feel better because that person has more faults. But I think that I am the only one with faults because in order to bring myself up I need to tear others down.

Letter #3

Last year my handicapped brother and I went to the pool and people would talk about my brother. They weren't comments—they were bad things like "retard" and "idiot."

This wasn't funny. It was verbal bullying on him and emotional bullying on both of us. I am 100 percent sure he didn't like it. I know I hated it. I told them to shut up, he's not a retard, he's my brother. Then they would stop. I'm sure they would make fun of him when I'm not around.

I was embarrassed. I thought people would be nice to him. There are a lot, but some people would be jerks. He had people stick up to him. Then they got to know him and they stopped.

I was happy!

So my brother told the lifeguards and if they saw anyone bully him they made them stop and sit out. So it isn't nice to make fun of the special needs. It is very, very mean.

Letter #4

It's hard enough being a middle school student, but to be a middle school student and have only 1 true friend and never go to anyone's house is hard. Most kids don't experience that but my friend Rick did. Every day he came to school hoping he would have a better day than the last, hardly ever did he have a normal day because of all the names and things the so-called "popular" people say and do to him. Once a kid even slugged him and said he was a fag. That was when I realized I wasn't the only one who felt so horrible about what was going on to him when he came to school.

There were two other girls, Lisa and Tina, we all decided to finally do something about it, so the next day when the boys were talking about him, me and the other girls told them that that wasn't cool and for them to stop, but when we did the other boys said, "Oh, and you think you're cool hanging out with that loser." I couldn't believe it. As soon as they said that, Lisa and Tina completely changed their mind about standing up for him. I was alone again and amazingly started losing some of my friends who became bullies!

I never knew people could be so cruel to others. This whole thing started out small and became very sad and horrible for Rick. I continued to stand up for him and they did it less and less to the point they just ignored him and a couple of people apologized to him and me. With this I learned, always treat others the way you want to be treated.

Letter #5

When I was in 4th grade I would walk into class late. I was called names, they laughed as they pointed at me. When we went outside for recess the best thing to do was play kickball. When I would ask if I could play they either looked away or said "No."

There was not just one person that would pick on me it was all of the kids. They made fun of me because of my hair, clothing, and shoes, my whole life.

I was in 7th grade, I was tired of everyone picking on me. I sometimes told my mom that I was sick and that I could not go to school. I was never sick. I just said that so that I would not have to go to school.

There was no sexual or physical bullying. They would point at me and laugh and they would yell untrue things about me during class. I felt that none of my classmates liked me too much.

In 6th grade it didn't happen as much as it did in 4th and 5th grade. In 4th and 5th grade it was a thing that happened to me every day. In 6th grade the same thing happened but not as much.

I never got F's on my report card but sometimes I got D's. Then in front of the whole class they would yell out what I got. The thing that really burned me was that the teacher never did anything.

In the beginning of 7th grade there was a girl by the name of Shannon. She was popular, and that surprised me that she reached out to me. She would let me eat with them at lunch and at recess she would let me play kickball with them. Since that day I will never forget what she did for me. I still hang out with her and a lot of other people, too. I still know that people talk about me behind my back, but now it doesn't bother me as much as it used to. Shannon has helped me out with a lot of things in my life.

Letter #6

I think the main type of bullying at our school is verbal. Once the rumors start, they don't stop. No matter what, people won't forget it. When one rumor starts, people just add on to it what they think is funny and interesting. I've never understood why people enjoy seeing others suffer.

I have this best friend, Ashley that has been through a lot of bullying but Ashley never listened to the rumors. She knew what was true and that's all that mattered to her. A horrible rumor was started by her ex-best friends, who heard something and just had to spread it around. They mostly spread it because they didn't like Ashley.

When Deb and Rona started the rumor, they knew that the other kids would believe it, because they barely knew Ashley. They just kept adding more and more until it was to their liking. They had no reason to do what they did. There is no excuse for how Ashley felt and how much pain she was going through.

The rumor ended. Ashley never backed down. She confronted Deb and Rona and asked why they did what they did. They wouldn't give her an answer. They probably never will. I guess they think that they don't owe an explanation for what they've done.

I admire Ashley's courage and strength because I know that I could never endure the pain she had to. I wish everyone could be like Ashley. If everyone could be like her, eventually bullying will stop, because the bullies will get sick of no one listening. I don't think that will ever happen, but I can wish, can't I?

Letter #7

When I was about 10½ in 5th grade I was very short for my age and all of my friends thought that I was so cute and small. There was also this kid who was the most popular boy in the whole 5th grade, he only had friends cause he made fun of people. One day he started making fun of me, (of course I had to be the target). He said things like "fat butt" and "whale." I ignored him for as long as I could. One day I got so mad that I yelled out to him "hey short stuff" (he was short too). I felt a huge lump in my throat when he came over to me and called me those names that had haunted me for that long while. After the war of this big shot boy and I, I felt really bad so I apologized. He accepted my apology but he still does continue making fun of me but over the years I have come to be so secure with myself that I don't care what he says.

This kind of disgusting harassment was verbal, cause he was saying those awful things to me. There were swearing words too. When he said "whale" and "fat butt" I started thinking "am I really fat?" Then I stopped eating my after school snacks. All of my friends told me that I was too skinny. I finally starved myself so I stopped my fast and started eating again. My feelings were terrible when I heard him say that to me.

To stop him, I started apologizing and just say sorry really quick but he still called me names. Well that backfired. Then I sat down by him in science and explained everything. He stopped for the rest of the year but this year he still does a little bit.

I learned to love yourself and be completely secure with yourself. Also to never make fun of somebody to get back at them and to help the bully understand that too.

Letter #8

In our school, many kids get bullied everyday little kids and even big. But there is one girl that I want to tell you about. She want to go school and she was in a good mood, but in her classes she would get made fun of because she dressed like a boy and even styled her hair like a boy so her fellow peers would make fun of her. They would find some lame reason to make fun of her because it was so easy. Like make fun of her because she stinks etc.

A lot of the times the only way she had friends was if she bought them thing like jelly pens and CDs and Post-It notes and the list goes on. She threatened to turn people in who called her names such as B.O., say things like "hey the boys room is that way" and on and on. Boys would go up to her and say stupid things like "hey will you go out with me?" Then they would walk toward their friends and be comforted by their laughs.

But there was one person who was really and completely nice to her. The most popular guy in the whole school. He had a smile that could charm any girl's heart. He would say nice things like "hey how is it going?" He would give up high fives when they passed each other walking in the hallway. Last week he died in a terrible tragedy. Everyone, and I mean everyone cried. This girl was very sad of his horrid death. Some of the girls that were mean to her realized how nice he was to B.O. so they tried being nice. The day of his wake one of the girls ran up to B.O. and they gave one another a hug and cried on each others shoulders. Til this day she is nice to B.O.

Letter #9

I used to bully people. I used to bully people in almost every kind of way. I did it because that was what lots of my friends did. When I would bully people, I thought about how the other person may have felt, but I didn't care. I only cared about what my friends thought.

Me bullying others would occasionally get me in trouble. That didn't stop me though. I mainly bullied during school. I don't remember lots of the things I did, but one sticks out in my memory.

My friends and I were walking home from school one day and I saw a kid. I thought I would be cool and get cocky with him. The person I was cocky with ended up being four years older than me. The person walked up to me and tackled me into the ground. I felt like he had broke my spine. Then he punched me repeatedly.

After he had left, my friends helped me up. I was mad my friends didn't help me. They told me I deserved it. Him tackling me left an imprint in the ground.

The next day we walked by that spot and the imprint was still there. It stayed there for almost a week.

That didn't stop me from being a bully. I learned not to mess with everyone bigger than me. I didn't stop being a bully until I figured out I didn't care what others thought. Also when everyone got bigger than me. I have never bullied anyone since.

Letter #10

The town that I used to live in was a pretty bad community. Not close-knit the way my new town is. So the people there on welfare or people that take church donations weren't treated too kindly. I never realized until now that I used to treat people like that pretty bad. Here's one example of how people were treated.

Karla was the type of girl everyone loved to pick on. Her dad left her mom when she was little. Her mom works hard, and refuses to go on welfare. She always dressed in clothes that were either too small or too big, because she couldn't afford better. She was picked on every day at school. And I don't mean just once a day, I mean all day every day. If you were looking for someone to dis, Karla was always the one. I guess she must have told her mom, because they went on welfare. I guess her mom gave up. I don't really know how everyone found out, but they did. Then they started to make fun of her even more, because her mom didn't work. She did start to look and dress a little better, but that didn't matter. Still as far as everyone else was concerned, she was a "dirty."

After a month or so after that they moved. During that month, her mom came to school to talk to the staff about it. It didn't help. She even got snickers and dirty comments in the hall. I felt so bad. After Karla moved, I was feeling really horrible about what I'd done. I tried to imagine how she could have felt, that I couldn't. I was the most sorry that she moved without warning. No good byes, no announcements. They just picked up and left. Now that I look back on it the thing I regret most is not saying that I was sorry. So Karla, if you're out there. I'm so sorry. And I mean that from the bottom of my heart.

Letter #11

Sometimes I make fun of this kid because he has big teeth. I sometimes tell people things about him that make him feel bad. I suppose this is verbal bullying.

I also make fun of this other kid that is really annoying to everyone. I sometimes call him names and sometimes push or punch him. I guess this would be physical.

The reason that I do it is because sometimes people do things to me and make me mad. Once they do that I start getting mad and either calling them names or punching. I am probably not right to do this but I can't really help it.

I know this other kid that thinks he can beat everyone in our whole school up. He just does anything that he wants to. He hardly ever gets in trouble for any of the things that he does. He is just mean to kids and says that if they tell on him he will beat them up. He doesn't care what others feel like and he doesn't care if he hurts them. I think he does it because he wants everybody in school to think that he can hurt them so nobody will ever pick on him. I don't think he is as big and tough as everybody thinks. It is just that he hurts everybody so it makes him look a lot better to people.

I also think he does it because he wants to get attention from people he likes and wants to look good in front of them. I think that if he didn't get so much attention for what he does he might stop. I think his bullying is physical, verbal, and emotional.

I don't think there is much difference between him and me I guess. He does it to look good but I do it to get back at people when they make me mad. That's about the only difference between him and me. I think if everyone stopped bullying it would be a lot funner place to be.

Letter #12

A few years ago, maybe five or six, there was a boy that was always being made fun of. He was really smart. But he was always doing weird stuff, like for example, acting like a cat.

Some, well most of the boys in our grade made fun of him. Some of the girls did, too. (He still had a couple of friends.) If you went up to him and just said, "hi" or something he would meow or hiss at you.

He would bring cold lunch to school all the time. Not just some of the days, every day. Sometimes people would call him a "nerd" or "geek" because he was so good at science and math. When we did this, he would get so upset his face would turn beet red. It looked like he was going to explode.

His mom would walk him to school, too. One time he was getting made fun of on the playground. It looked like he was about ready to cry. I sort of felt bad for him, but I didn't say anything because, well, I thought maybe I'm not sure that people would start to make fun of me, too.

Then about four or five years after he moved away I thought I never said, "sorry" or anything. Now me and my friends feel bad because we will never see him again.

Letter #13

I know this kid in my grade that gets picked on all the time. People call him names and call him gay, faggot, and homo. I feel sorry for him because it happens every day.

Last year, people started making fun of him when he was taking a shower for basketball. They started nasty rumors and he felt terrible. One time he colored his hair and people said he was trying to be Justin from N'SYNC. He did kind of look like him but he didn't need to be made fun of.

Sometimes, people make him so mad that he starts fights with them. When he first moved here, no one liked him. He got beat up all the time. I see people just go up and punch him for no reason and just laugh. He would come to school the next day with bruises all over his arm. Just a couple of nights ago, people held him down and punched him in the chest and kicked him in the balls. I didn't get to see it but I heard about it and felt terrible. His chest was all red when he came to school the next day.

I hope people stop picking on him soon. It isn't funny and I don't think they would like it if he did it to them.

Letter #14

People used to call me names and if I did something they didn't like they would slap me across the face. They would push me down.

If I would be talking to someone they would tell them not to talk to me. They would make them leave. If they were sitting at a table and I walked by and sat down they would leave. And then I would sit by myself and wait until my friends would come and sit with me. Most people would say that I didn't have any friends or that I wasn't good at anything.

They wouldn't pick me in any gym events if we picked teams. When I got stuck on their team they would say oh no. They wouldn't throw me the ball. It was like I was invisible.

They would pick on me for the littlest things like if I didn't dress a certain way. Or if my shoes weren't cool enough. Or if I wasn't good at something they would call me names or talk about me behind my back.

When I would walk into a room they would make noises. They would throw stuff at me. They wouldn't stop when I asked them to stop. It stopped after a while but then it started up again. But since we got into a higher grade it has stopped. It doesn't really bother me that much anymore.

Letter #15

Most people picture the perfect bully as a male, oversized person picking on or hurting people that are different or smaller than themselves. They have a high self-esteem when it comes to anything kids say or do to them. It seems that everything they do is right and everybody is scared of them so nobody mouths off or does anything back to them. This theory is not always true, at least not the part about being male and oversized. Come to think of it most of what I just wrote is not true.

There is a girl in my grade who most of the time is getting made fun of or embarrassing herself because she is trying too hard to impress everybody. It's either she's not smart enough, or she's not skinny enough or she's not athletic and for several other reasons. Nothing she does is ever enough for anyone.

Almost everybody makes fun of this girl. It is not just certain people. Even I have made fun of her before. I really regret it now though. Nobody should have to put up with what she puts up with every day.

One time when I was in 7th grade our principal had a meeting in the auditorium to talk to us about the disrespect and bullying we all have towards other students. She told us that she had parents calling her practically crying on the phone because their children were getting bullied in school. She told us that we need to start respecting each other a little bit more. After that a little bit of it stopped, but not much. It just didn't sink in to most of us that we were hurting people's feelings and that it wasn't just harmless fun. I knew she was mostly talking about this girl, but she never said any actual names.

This girl is not the only one that gets bullied in our school.

Tons of kids' self-esteem gets lowered every day because some jerk who decides to make fun of them or pick on them. I think maybe kids should start sticking up for each other more. That is the problem with our schools, not enough kids have the courage to stick up for others. They all just follow and laugh with everybody else.

There has been so many school shootings because of kids who decide to make fun of or neglect other kids. I definitely don't want to be the one that pushes another kid to bring a gun to school.

Letter #16

I know this girl who got up every morning at 5:45 A.M., showered, got dressed, dried her hair, put makeup on, and was on the school bus by 7:05 A.M., not having any time for breakfast. She always had a hard time trying to find something to wear because she would always try to find something that made her look thin.

When she got on the bus she got teased for being fat, ugly, and stupid even though she usually got a 3.5 for a grade point average. They called her cow, pig, fatty, made cow noises, and pretended that every time that they looked at her they would go blind. Every time this happened she would tell them that they are immature because they are in the seventh grade, but acting as if they are still in the second grade, kind of like some of them haven't grown up since they were in second grade.

By the time she got to school she was pretty upset, but changed her mood as if nothing had happened, however, it didn't work. From when she got to school at about 8:05 A.M. until 3:22 P.M. when school got out it was a long day. Almost every class went the same way as the bus ride did on the way to school. Then it was time for the bus time home on either the activity bus if she was in a sport or on the regular bus. It goes the same as the bus ride there. Sometimes it was so hard to hold her tears in that she just had to let it all out. If she were strong enough to hold her tears in on the bus, she would cry a lot at home.

I know this girl very well. She is now in the eighth grade and life is going just a little bit better. She was in volleyball in both seventh and eighth grade along with cheerleading. She is now in track on the eighth grade team. She always has a smile on her face, or at least tries to anyway and is usually in a good mood now.

I don't know of anyone who would want to be treated like this because it isn't any fun. I don't think anybody would want to live his or her life like this. That girl was me. I was the one who always got called names and teased and I just wish that it would stop. I know that I am not the only one, but I have a bit of advice to get through these tough things. Just think highly of yourself, don't even listen to the rude things people have to say about you when it probably isn't true, and just be strong.

Letter #17

The day began in first hour in 6th grade. A girl was always sitting there brushing her hair, doing her makeup, painting her nails. She was always doing something. The girl wasn't very smart and was happy at times and sad at times. She was mostly sad though.

Why she was always sad was because people would make fun of her constantly. Why she got made fun of was because of the way she dressed, acted, and caused people to think she wasn't pretty. Deep down inside I knew she was beautiful, like a blossom ready to bloom. Other people didn't look at her that way.

When I saw those people make fun of her I wanted to switch places with her. I didn't want her to suffer from constant teasing and humiliation. Why I wanted to do this was because she had been getting so much teasing all her life and I haven't, so I wanted her to experience what it would be like not to be teased for a moment in her life.

But I knew in reality I couldn't. I was just sitting there frozen in agony. Wishing someone would stop it. But no one did. I had to do it myself. So I did. I walked over there and YELLED STOP! Then it was silence. I couldn't believe I just did that.

Ever since I did that I have always stuck up for people. I think since I did that, that one girl had such a big effect on her life. She has always stood tall and never gave up. That girl is one big blessing from God.

Letter #18

When I was in vocal music, the teacher was busy in her office, and a kid was making fun of another person's hair cut. She had just gotten the haircut and it was the first time she had come to school. The bully would call her rag doll and all sorts of names.

While I was sitting here I heard him call her a name. I don't think that he knew he was pretty much lowering and lowering her self-esteem. When I saw this I remembered you coming down to talk about bullying. I realized that I was witnessing a verbal bullying situation.

I didn't do anything for a while. I just waited until I got angry enough to tell him to stop. By this time two people were on her case about her new hair cut. When the other person joined, they were laughing really hard. I couldn't believe how someone could make fun of another person and not feel bad about it!

When I finally got the courage, I told them to stop, but they didn't. They just said, "Stop what?" I said, "Stop making fun of her!" They go "Oh, you mean Rag Doll?" I looked them straight in the eye and asked them what would you do if someone was making fun of your hair and calling you a rag doll. They both just turned around and stopped making fun of her.

From this experience, I have learned that sticking up for other people isn't that hard. At least it wasn't in this case. I learned that making fun of people is a horrible, nasty thing to do. Not just one person can stop bullying, but if people work as a team you can prevent bullying.

Letter #19

I think it all started in the second grade. Our teacher was Mr. Waltney, the funnest and funniest teacher ever. Back then everyone had fun. Whenever we went to recess, there was always someone else to jump with, or hopscotch with, or play kickball with. Everybody had someone else. Except Mickey. It was as if Mickey didn't have a last name. Nobody knew it. Nobody used it. To the students, Mickey's full name was just Mickey. One time his pants fell down in kickball. People poked him and called him names every day, including me. We'd do it enough until he'd cry and then we'd keep doing it and calling him a crybaby. But Mickey never told anyone, a teacher or counselor or principal. That's why we kept doing it. It was like a new game.

Whenever we teased Mickey, we used physical abuse, like poking or pinching.

Back in second grade, it never occurred to me or anyone that this could be really hurtful to Mickey or that it could leave a scar on his self-confidence. Nobody cared what happened to Mickey.

One day, he moved. Nobody knew where or even cared. If anybody missed him it was because they couldn't tease him anymore.

Thoughts we'd like to leave with you . . .

Bullying is a form of child abuse. It is not child's play or a rite of passage. It is stinging, heartbreaking, damaging behavior that has led to suicides and homicides, and it is rampant. We must not deny it or attempt to diminish its impact in any way. Nothing we do is more important than protecting our children—even from themselves.

Peer abuse comes in the form of physical, verbal, emotional (nonverbal and psychological), and sexual interactions, and each form carries its own brand of hurt. Our concern must be for every child—children who bully, children who are targets, children who witness. Children often shift from one role to another. We must embrace them with sensitivity to their changing needs.

While we focus on particular children, we must have a vision to shape the overall climate in our schools. This will require the commitment of every adult member of the school community, especially the principal. The teaching profession deserves more honor and respect than it presently receives. The current shortage should be a solemn warning. Why must the problem reach crisis proportions before we become energized about it? And why are we directing so much attention to test scores without connecting the impact of bullying on learning?

Schools, alone, cannot be expected to assume responsibility for eliminating peer abuse. Parents and family systems have the earliest and most continuous influence on children's behavior. When schools and families are in synchrony, promoting the same character traits and values, the benefits will multiply.

Our best strategy is prevention! From birth, children need to be cherished and disciplined. Our greatest gift to the next generation is to ensure that all new parents have the support and information they need to be the best parents possible. Bullying prevention programs and processes should begin in preschools and day care centers and most certainly should be instituted in elementary schools. By middle school, our efforts will be on intervention, and since this is the time when bullying peaks, we must bring intense energy to this age group. High school students will require a more sophisticated approach—enabling them to act as mediators, peer counselors, and mentors to younger students.

Bullying must be viewed in a larger context. Community and cultural forces and exposure to violent imprints from movies, television shows, video games, music, the Internet, cyber chats, access to weapons, drugs and alcohol, and gang influences play a significant part in the lives of kids. It would be naïve to discount the power of these influences.

Homophobia, the sexualization of children, and the socialization of boys and girls are issues that have risen to the top of the pile. These are major topics to address and are made more difficult by the social forces that impinge on their solution.

The bullying dynamic of pain, rage, and revenge begins with children and gets acted out on the global scene when adults take it to its highest order. Current international conflicts are riveting examples of this cycle of a situation that begins with pain, turns to rage, and becomes an act of revenge. If we can be successful in teaching children how to manage their anger, to resolve their conflicts without violence, to use their empathy, to treat one another with kindness and dignity, and to stop the pain, our future looks brighter.

Finally, and most important of all, is the need for advocates at all levels, people of passion to carve out this cause as their *raison d'etre*—reason for being. There are thousands who have taken this theme to heart, and they are making an incredible difference. We need a sponsor to make it possible for us to use our synergy in a purposeful way. It is exciting to contemplate what could be accomplished if we joined forces to meet our mutually compatible goals. It is no sin to attempt and fail. The only sin is to fail to make the attempt.

Gary Adams and I have written a song to spread the message of kindness. Music has such a wonderful way of keeping words in your head. We offer it to our readers with the request to share it as often as possible. The phrase, "Kindness is contagious, catch it!" was created by the artist Rita Blitt. We are grateful for her special words that became our title.

Kindness Is Contagious

Words: SuEllen Fried
Music: SuEllen Fried and
Gary Adams

Sticks and stones can break your bones but words can break your heart. If you lis-ten to these words then you can play a part. To

make this world a bet-ter place each and ev-'ry day You can be a spec-ial friend by

BULLIES, TARGETS, & WITNESSES

NOTES

1. National Academies National Research Council.
2. American Psychological Association, press release 8/17/2001.
3. Nickelodeon and the Kaiser Family Fund. Talking with Kids National Survey of Parents and Kids, telephone survey conducted between 12/9/2000 and 1/18/2001.
4. Vossekuil, B., Fein, R., Reddy, M., Borum, R. and Modzeleski, W. "The Final Report and Findings of the Safe School Initiative: Implications for the Prevention of School Attacks in the United States." Washington, D.C.: United States Secret Service and United States Department of Education, 2002.
5. "Deaths from 282 Selected Causes by 5 Year Age Groups, Race and Sex: Each State and the District of Columbia 1995–1998." National Center for Health Statistics, 2000.
6. Centers for Disease Control and Prevention. "Youth risk behavior surveillance-United States. 1997," *Morbidity & Mortality Weekly Report.* 1998: 47(SS-3): 1–89.
7. Ibid.
8. Ibid.
9. Kahiala-Heino, R., Rimpela, M., Marttunen, M., Rimpela, A., and Rantanen, P. "Bullying, depression and suicidal ideation in Finnish adolescents, school survey," *British Medical Journal,* 919 (1999): 948–951.
10. Husemann, L. R., Eron, L., Lefkowitz, M. M., and Walder, L. O. "Stability of aggression over time and generations," *Developmental Psychology.* 20 (6) 1984: 1120–1134.
11. Olweus, D., *Bullying at School, What We Know and What We Can Do.* New York: Blackwell.
12. Vossekuil, B., Fein, R., Reddy, M., Borum, R. and Modzeleski, W. "The Final

Report and Findings of the Safe School Initiative: Implications for the Prevention of School Attacks in the United States." Washington, D.C.: United States Secret Service and United States Department of Education, 2002, 12–13.

13. Viadero, D., "Research skewers explanations behind teacher shortage," *Education Week,* April 10, 2002.

14. Asidao. C., Vion, C. and Espelage, D. "Interviews with middle school students: bullying, victimization and contextual factors," Presentation to the American Psychological Association, August 21, 2000.

15. Floyd, Nathaniel. "Pick on Somebody Your Own Size: Controlling victimization," *Pointer.* 29 (2) 1985. 9–17.

16. Anderson, C. and Dill, K. "Video Games and Aggressive Thoughts. Feelings and behavior in the laboratory and in life," *Journal of Personality and Social Psychology.* 78 (4) 2000. 772–790.

17. Dodge, K. and Coie, J. "Social information processing factors in reactive and proactive aggression in children's peer groups," *Journal of Personality and Social Psychology.* 53 (1987), 1146–1158.

18. Selman, R. and Demorest, A. "Observing troubled children's interpersonal negotiation strategies: implications of and for a developmental model," *Child Development.* 55 (1) 1984, 288–304.

19. Adler, Patricia and Peter, quoted in an article by Karen Peterson, "Cliques Make Fitting In a Tought Task for Teens in High School," *Detroit News.* January 24, 2001.

20. Olweus, D. "Bullying at school: Long-term outcomes for the victims and an effective school-based intervention," In R. Huseman (ed.). *Aggressive Behaviors: Current Perspectives.* New York: Plenum Press, 1994.

21. Coie, J. and Dodge, K. "Aggression and antisocial behavior," In N. Eisenberg (ed.) *Handbook of Child Psychology,* (5th ed., Vol. 3). New York: Wiley and Sons, 1998.

22. Seligman, M. "The American Way of Blame," *American Psychological Association Monitor.* Vol 29, July 1998.

23. Rodkin, P., Farmer, T., Pearl, R. and VanAcker, R. "Heterogeneity of Popular Boys: Anti-social and prosocial configurations," *Developmental Psychology.* 36 (1) 2000.

24. Staub, E. "Aggression and Self-Esteem," *American Psychological Association Monitor.* Vol. 30, January 1999.

25. Slater, L. (2002) "The Trouble With Self-Esteem," *New York Times Sunday Magazine.* February 3, 2002.

26. Nansel, T., Overpeck, M., Pilla, R., Ruan, J., Simons-Morton, B. and Scheidt, P. "Bullying Behaviors Among U.S. Youth: Prevalence and association with psy-

chosocial adjustment." *Journal of the American Medical Association.* 285 (16) 2001. 2094–2101.

27. Dodge, K. and Coie, J. "Social information processing factors in reactive and proactive aggression in children's peer groups," *Journal of Personality and Social Psychology.* 53 (1987), 1146–1158

28. Husemann, L.R., Eron, L., Lefkowitz, M.M., and Walder, L.O. "Stability of aggression over time and generations," *Developmental Psychology.* 20 (6) 1984, 1120-1134.

29. Ladd, Gary, quoted in Marano, H.E . "Big Bad Bully," *Psychology Today.* 50 (1995), 50–68.

30. Perry, D. G., Kusel, S. J. and Perry, L. C. "Victims of peer aggression," *Developmental Psychology.* 24 (1988), 807–814.

31. Craig, W. and Pepler, D. "Peer processes in bullying and victimization: an observational study," *Exceptionality Education Canada.* 5 (1995), 81–95.

32. Vossekuil, B., Fein, R., Reddy, M., Borum, R. and Modzeleski, W. "The Final Report and Findings of the Safe School Initiative: Implications for the Prevention of School Attacks in the United States." Washington, D.C.: United States Secret Service and United States Department of Education, 2002.

33. Cortina, L., Magley, V., Williams, J. and Langhout, R. "Incivility in the workplace: incidence and impact," *Journal of Occupational Health Psychology.* 6 (1) 2001, 64–80.

34. *Linking Neuroscience to the Care and Education of Young Children.* St. Louis: Parents As Teachers National Center, 2001.

35. Perry, Bruce. Keynote presentation at the Kansas Governor's Conference on Child Abuse, October 19, 2000.

36. Johnson, J., Cohen, P., Smailes, F., Kasen, S. and Brook, J. "Television viewing and aggressive behavior during adolescence and adulthood," *Science.* 295 (5564) 2002, 2468–2471.

37. Buchanan, A., Gentile, D., Nelson, D., Walsh, D. and Hensel, J. Paper presented at the International Society for the Study of Behavior Development, Ottawa, Canada. August 6, 2002.

38. Slavin, P. "Children's Voice," *Child Welfare League of America.* Vol. 9, no. 2, March 2000, 4.

39. Gilligan, C. *In A Different Voice.* Cambridge: Harvard University Press, 1982.

40. Simmons, R. *Odd Girl Out: The Hidden Culture of Aggression in Girls.* New York: Harcourt, 2002.

41. Lescheid, A., Cummings, A., VanBrunschot, M., Cunningham, A. and Saunders, A. *Female Adolescent Aggression: A Review of the Literature and the Correlates of Aggression* (User Report No. 2000-2004). Ottawa: Solicitor General, Canada, 2002.

42. Kindlon, D. and Thompson, M. *Raising Cain: Protecting the Emotional Life of Boys.* New York: Ballantine, 1999.

43. Levant, R. "Desperately Seeking Language:understanding, assessing and treating normative male alexithymia," In Pollack, W. and Levant, R. (eds.) *New Psychotherapy for Men.* New York: John Wiley and Sons, 1998, 43.

44. DeAngelis, T. "Are Men Emotional Mummies?" *American Psychological Association Monitor.* Vol. 32, 2001.

45. Ibid.

46. Murray, B. "Boys to Men: Emotional miseducation," *American Psychological Association Monitor.* Vol. 30, 1999.

47. Crick, N. and Bigbee, M. "Relational and Overt Forms of Peer Victimization: A Multi-informant Approach," *Journal of Consulting and Clinical Psychology.* 66 (2) 1998.

48. Goode, Erica. "High Self-Esteem Debunked," *San Francisco Chronicle.* November 3, 2002.

49. Craig, W. and Pepler, D. "Observations of bullying and victimization in the school yard," *Canadian Journal of School Psychology.* 13 (2) 1997, 41–59.

50. Twemlow, S., Fonagy, P. and Sacco, F. In Shafii, M. and Shafii, S. (eds.), *School Violence: Assessment, Management, Prevention.* Washington, D.C.: American Psychiatric Press, 2001.

RESOURCES

ORGANIZATIONS

American Medical Association
Dr. Michael D. Maves, Executive Director
515 State Street
Chicago, IL 60610
Tel: (312) 464-5000 FAX: (312) 464-4184
Web site: www.ama-assn.org

American Medical Association Alliance, Inc.
Hazel Williams, Executive Director
515 N. State Street 9th Floor
Chicago, IL 60610
Tel: (312) 464-4470 FAX: (312) 464-5020
E-mail: amaa@ama-assn.org

American Psychological Association
Phil Lombardo, PhD, Executive Director
750 First Street NE
Washington, DC 20002
Tel: (202) 336-5500,FAX: (202) 336-6069 (800) 374-2721
E-mail: publicinterest@apa.org
Web site: www.apa.org

Aspen Center for Integrative Health
Laura Dizon, Project Director
P.O. Box 285
Aspen, CO 81611
Tel: (970) 920-2957 FAX: (970) 920-3015
Web site: www.aspennewmed.org

Character Education Partnership
Esther Schaeffer, Executive Director
1025 Connecticut Avenue NW, Suite 1011
Washington, DC 20036
Tel: (202) 296-7743 FAX: (202) 296-7779
Web site: www.geninfo@character.org

CHARACTER Plus
Cooperating School Districts
Linda McKay, Director
8225 Florissant Road
St. Louis, MO 63121
Tel: (800) 835-8282 FAX: (314) 692-9700
E-mail: lmckay@csd.org

Chicken Soup for the Soul
P.O. Box 30880
Santa Barbara, CA 93130
E-mail: webmaster@chickensoupforthesoul.com

nternational Youth Foundation
Rick Little, Founder and CEO
32 South Street #500
Baltimore, MD 21202
Tel: (410) 347-1500 FAX: (410) 347-1188
E-mail: youth@lyfnet.org
Web site: www.lyfnet.org

Junior Judges—helping kids make smart choices
Mediators Achieving Peace
Texas Young Lawyers Association
P.O. Box 12487
Austin, TX 78711-2487
800-204-2222 Ext.6429

RESOURCES

Family Literacy Foundations
Cathy Kazanjy, Coordinator
Washington Elementary School
910 West Anahurst Place
Santa Ana, CA 92707
Tel: (714) 445-5100
E-mail: ckazanjy@sausd.k-12.ca.us
Web site: www.sausd.k-12.ca.us

Linking the Interests of Families and Teachers (LIFT)
Michael Toolmiller, Ph.D.
Oregon Social Learning Center
160 E. 4th Avenue
Eugene, OR 97401
Tel: (541) 485-2711 FAX: (541) 485-7087
Web site: www.oslc.org

The National School Safety Center
Ronald Stephens, Executive Director
141 Duesenberg Drive, Suite 11
Westlake Village, CA 91362,
Tel: (805) 373-9977 FAX: (805) 373-9277
E-mail: orders@nssc1.org

Parents As Teachers National Center
Sue Stepleton, Executive Director
2228 Ball Drive
St. Louis, MO 63146
Tel: (314) 432-4330 FAX: (314) 432-8963
Web site: www.patnc.org

Prevent Child Abuse America
Sid Johnson, President
200 South Michigan, Suite 1700
Chicago, IL 60604
Tel: (312) 663-3520 FAX: (312) 939-8962
Web site: www.preventchildabuse.org

Safe And Drug Free Schools
Bill Modzeleski, Director
U.S. Department of Education
400 Maryland Avenue, SW
Washington, DC 20202
Tel: (202) 260-3954FAX: (202) 260-7767
Web site: www.ed.gov

CommonWealth Consulting
LeeAnn Smith
915 Valentine Road
Kansas City, MO 64111
Tel: (816) 931-6933 FAX: (913) 831-0262
E-mail: lsmith@togetherkc.org

SOCCSS
Jan B. Roosa, Ph.D.
9229 Ward Parkway, Suite 370
Kansas City, MO 64114
Tel: (816) 444-3366 FAX: (816) 237-1942
E-mail: jbroosa@planetkc.com

Youth Court
Alameda County Administration Building
221 Oak Street
Oakland, CA 94612
Tel: (510) 832-585
E-mail: info@youthcourt.org

CURRICULA AND PROGRAMS

Anti-Bullying Centre at Trinity College in Dublin, Ireland
Dr. Mona O'Moore, Director
The Centre was set up initially as an independent research body targeting the area of bullying. In response to requests and needs, the Centre now offers a resource reference library open to the general public; advice and guidance by phone or in person for researchers, parents, teachers, schools, and organizations; research advice and survey assistance for individuals, schools, and organizations; counseling serv-

ices for both the victim and the bully; in-service and staff development for schools and organizations; conferences and workshops for pupils, parents, and teachers.

Tel: (01) 608 3488 / 608 2573

E-mail: Imcguire@tcd.ie

Web site: www.abc.tcd.ie/school.htm

BeCool

A program developed specifically to nourish the key elements of emotional intelligence—impulse control, empathy and self-awareness. Within the context of teaching how to be assertive, BeCool teaches kids specific reflective thinking techniques to promote self-control and interrupt the tendency to impulsively act out. Video scenarios model three different ways to respond to conflict:

1. Blowing up (HOT)
2. Giving up (COLD) and
3. In control (COOL)

Four age ranges are addressed in the six-part series—Lower Elementary, Upper Elementary, Middle School, and High School. Each level series comes with individual modules, complete with a minimum of three video tapes and a comprehensive teacher's guide, to teach coping skills in different problem areas. The four modules are:

Module 1: Coping with Criticism—2 Live-action videotapes, Chester cartoon, Teacher/Parent videotape, and Teacher's guide $149 order #1043.1

Module 2: Coping with Teasing—3 Live-action videotapes, Chester cartoon, Teacher/Parent videotape, and Teacher's guide $149 order #1043.2

Module 3: Coping with Bullying—2 Live-action videotapes, Chester cartoon, Teacher/Parent videotape, and Teacher's guide $149 order #1043.3

Module 4: Coping with Anger—Anger/Other and Anger/Self each include 2 Live-action videotapes, Chester cartoon, Teacher/Parent videotape, and Teacher's guide $149 eachorder #1043.4 and #1043.5

James Stanfield Co., Inc

P.O. Box 41058

Santa Barbara, CA 93140

Tel: (800) 421-6534 FAX: (805) 897-1187

E-mail: maindesk@stanfield.com

Blueprints for Violence Prevention: The Bullying Prevention Program

Dan Olweus and Susan Limber.

Outlines in detail the elements of a bullying prevention program. The bullying prevention program has as its major goal the reduction of victim/bully problems among primary and secondary school children. It aims to increase awareness of the problem, to achieve active involvement on the part of teachers and parents, and to develop clear rules against bullying behavior, and to provide support and protection for the victims of bullying.

Center for the Study of Prevention of Violence (303) 492-1032

Institute of Behavioral Science

University of Colorado at Boulder

439 UCB

Boulder CO 80309

Tel: (303) 492-8465 FAX: (303) 443-3297

E-mail: cspv@colorado.edu

Bullies Are A Pain In The Brain

Trevor Romain

This book blends humor with practical suggestions that empower kids to stop bullies from hurting others, and get help in dangerous situations while preserving their self-esteem. 112 pp. Ages 8–13

Free Spirit Publishing Inc.

217 Fifth Avenue North, Suite 200

Minneapolis, MN 55401-1299

Item #FS222-466 $9.95

Tel: (800) 735-7323 FAX: (612) 337-5050

Bully Free Classroom: Over 100 Tips and Strategies for Teachers K-8

Allan L. Beane, Ph.D.

More than 100 prevention and intervention strategies you can start using immediately. All are easy to understand and simple to implement. Includes 45 pages of reproducible handout masters. 176 pp.

Free Spirit Publishing Inc.

217 Fifth Avenue North, Suite 200

Minneapolis, MN 55401-1299

Item #FS222-572 $21.95

Tel: (800) 735-7323 FAX: (612) 337-5050

The Bullying Prevention Handbook

Dr. John Hoover and Dr. Ronald Oliver

This is a comprehensive guide for "bully-proofing" your school—understanding, preventing, and reducing the day-to-day teasing and harassment referred to as bullying. 159 pp.

National Educational Service

ISBN 1-879639-44-0 $29.95

RESOURCES

BULLYPROOF: A Teacher's Guide on Teasing and Bullying for Use with Fourth and Fifth Grade Students
Nan Stein and Lisa Sjostrom
Contains eleven sequential lessons. Class discussions, role-plays, case studies, writing exercises, reading assignments, art activities, and nightly homework combine to give students the opportunity to explore and determine the fine distinctions between teasing and bullying. Children gain a conceptual framework and a common vocabulary that allow them to find their own links between teasing amd bullying and, eventually, sexual harassment. 60 pp. $19.95

BullySafeUSA
SuEllen Fried
BullySafeUSA, a program developed by SuEllen Fried and offered by Fried, Sue Farrar, Su Randall, Vicki Price, and Mary Fischer, offers a range of services, including student empowerment sessions with students grades three through eight, teacher in-service workshops, parent seminars, and three-day Training Institutes for counselors, administrators, educators and community advocates.
4003 Homestead Drive
Shawnee Mission, KS 66208
Tel: (913) 362-2226 FAX: (913) 362-2886
E-mail: harvfried@ hotmail.com
Web site: www.bulliesandvictims.com

Community Matters
Rick Phillips, Executive Director
The Safe School Ambassador program is designed for middle, junior, and senior high school students. Twenty-five to forty students are recruited from all parts of the student population and trained to: Notice, Act, and Support. They are equipped with eight strategies to intervene and are supervised by qualified, trained adults.
P.O. Box 14816
Santa Rosa, CA 95402
Tel: (707) 823-6159 FAX: (707) 823-3373
E-mail: team@community-matters.org
Web site: www.community-matters.org

Conflict Resolution in the Middle School: A Curriculum and Teaching Guide
William Kreidler, $38.00
Educators for Social Responsibility
23 Garden Street

Cambridge, MA 02138
Tel: (800) 370-2515 / (617) 492-764 FAX (617)-864-5164
E-mail: educators@esrnational.org

Connecting the Dots to Prevent Violence: A Training and Outreach Guide for Physicians and Other Health Professionals
This manual was developed to help physicians and others discuss youth violence with professional and community groups. The manual contains the following prepared material to help deliver presentations and workshops on youth violence prevention.
- Key resources and databases with search tips
- Instructions for preparing presentations
- Speeches on youth violence prevention
- PowerPoint presentations
- Case studies
- Issue briefs
- Audience handouts

The entire training package and the report are available online at: www.ama-assn.org/violence. Hard copies are available at no charge while supplies last.
American Medical Association
515 North State Street
Chicago, IL 60610
Tel: (312) 464-4520 FAX (312) 464-5842

Disarming the Playground: Violence Prevention through Movement
Rena Kornblum, MCAT, ADTR
A movement-based curriculum for teaching impulse control and anger management, as well as protective behaviors. Movement activities that can be used by teachers, parents, social workers, dance/movement therapists, and other professionals. Detailed lesson plans include step-by-step directions for all movement activities. Cross-referenced for skill level, age appropriateness, length of lesson, etc. 180 pp. Activity book, 150 pp. $39.95
Wood 'N' Barnes Publishing & Distribution
Tel: (405) 942-6812 FAX: (405) 946-4074
Web site: www.woodnbarnes.com

"Don't Laugh At Me" (DLAM)
The DLAM Project, founded by Peter Yarrow of Peter, Paul & Mary, disseminates educational resources. There are three curricula, one for grades 2 to 5, another for grades 6 to 8, and a third for summer camps and after-school programs—all uti-

lize inspiring music and video as well as materials based on well-tested conflict resolution curricula. It is designed to provide teachers, school counselors, social workers, administrators, and other professionals with an entry point for year-round social and emotional learning and character education programs, as well as to interface with and energize efforts of this kind.

Operation Respect
2 Penn Plaza, 23rd Floor
New York, NY 10121
E-mail: info@dontlaugh.org

The Essential Curriculum
Dr. Leslie Teel Dunn, Executive Director

The Essential Curriculum is available to teachers in kindergarten through grade 8. This program seeks to develop responsible citizens whose behaviors, attitude, and values are reflective of four essential principles of effective human interaction: the positive use of errors, the appropriate roles of reason and emotion, the fulfillment of one's unique personal responsibilities, and the application of universal human rights. A controlled study involving over 3,000 students found that students in classes using the Essential Curriculum had an enhanced ability and willingness to admit and correct mistakes, the ability to work without disrupting others, improved self-control, persistence in efforts to succeed at a task, and were better able to empathize with the needs and situations of others. In addition to the curriculum, curricula-related products and supplies, a teacher's curriculum manual for individual grade levels, and a teacher training video kit are available.

The Teel Institute
101 East Armour Boulevard
Kansas City, MO 64111
Tel: (816) 753-2733 FAX: (816) 753-3193
E-mail: infor@teelinstitute.org
Web site: www.teelinstitute.org

Get Connected

Get Connected is a program to reduce bullying and increase kindness among elementary and middle school students. Get Connected classroom kits are available for three grade levels: K-2nd, 3rd-5th, and 6th-8th. All Get Connected classroom kits include: A teacher's activity guide with more than 20 activities that teach empathy, compassion and respect; a "Kindness is Contagious . . . Catch It!" classroom poster; four "Kindness is Contagious . . . Catch It!" buttons. The K–2nd and 3rd–5th will also include: "What Kindness Means to Me" video where students

express the importance of kindness, thirty "Kindness is Contagious . . . Catch It!" stickers. The 6th–8th will also include thirty Kindness is Contagious folders. A limited time offer: *On Target To Stop Bullying,* a teachers guide with 8 activities to raise the awareness of bullying and offer strategies to reduce bullying behavior.
STOP Violence!
301 E. Armour Blvd
Kansas City,MO 64111
Tel: (816) 753-8002, FAX (816) 753-8056
www.stop-violence.org

"I Can Problem Solve"

Myrna B. Shure, Ph.D.

This award-winning, research based prevention program can be incorporated into the classroom or adapted for use by school mental health staff. ICPS is a cognitive approach that teaches children how, not what, to think. The curriculum is divided into two main sections:

- Pre-Problem Solving Skills—learning a problem solving vocabulary, identifying one's own and other's feelings, understanding other people's point of view
- Problem Solving Skills—thinking of more than one solution, considering consequences, deciding which to choose, and sequential planning

The ICPS curriculum involves:

- Formal Lessons—children learn problem solving skills through games, stories, puppets, illustrations and role plays
- Interaction in the Classroom—children learn to use ICPS concepts during every day classroom interactions
- Integration into the Curriculum—children learn to use ICPS concepts as they work on marh, reading, social studies, science, and other subjects

ICPS for Preschool (59 lessons): $39.95
ICPS for Kindergarten and Primary Grades (83 lessons): $39.95
ICPS for Intermediate Elementary Grades (77 lessons) $39.95
Raising A Thinking Child Workbook (ICPS for Families) $29.95

Research Press	Department of Psychology
Dept. 249	Drexel University
PO Box 9177	245 N. 15th Street MS 626
Champaign, IL 61826	Philadelphia, PA 19102
Tel: (800) 519 2707	(215) 762-7205

E-mail: mshure@drexel.edu
Web sites: www.thinkingchild.com, www.researchpress.com

RESOURCES

Quit It! A Teacher's Guide on Teasing and Bullying for Use with Students in Grades K–3
Merle Froschi, Barbara Sprung and Nancy Mullin-Rindler, with Nan Stein and Nancy Gropper
Contains ten lessons focused around three sequential themes. Each lesson is divided into activities geared to the developmental needs of students in kindergarten through grade three. Class discussions, role plays, creative drawing and writing activities, physical games and exercises, and connections to children's literature give children a vocabulary and a conceptual framework that allow them to understand the distinction between teasing and bullying.
A joint publication of the Wellesley College Center for research on Women, Educational Equity Concepts, and the NEA Professional Library

Selected Bibliography of Children's Books About Teasing and Bullying for Grades K–5
Nancy Mullin-Rindler
This annotated bibliography contains hundreds of listings of children's book and classroom resource materials, as well as references for teachers and parents. 53 pp.
$10.00
Center for Research on Women
Wellesley College
106 Central Street
Wellesley, MA 02481-8203

Second Step
Second Step is a violence prevention curriculum that teaches skills to reduce impulsive and aggressive behavior in children. The materials, which are targeted for preschool through junior high, focus on empathy training, impulse control, and anger management. The curriculum is divided into kits for each grade level. The kits include lesson plans, a teacher's guide, video lessons, laminated classroom posters, reproducible homework sheets, and a family overview video that introduces parents and caregivers to the very same skills their children are learning. Student achievement tests showed that perspective-taking and social problem-solving skills improved significantly after children participated in the Second Step program.

Steps to Respect is built on definitive research on recognizing, reporting, responding to, and reducing bullying. The self-contained, easy-to-use program is designed for systematic schoolwide implementation. The program includes training for staff and parents, with student lessons for the upper elementary grades (3 to 5 or 4 to 6).

313

Committee for Children
568 First Avenue South #600,
Seattle, WA 98104
Tel: (800) 634-4449 ext. 200 FAX: (206) 343-1445
Web site: www.cfchildren.org

The Sexual Respect Curriculum: Dealing with Sexism and Sexual Harassment with Intermediate School Students
Peter Miner
Peter Miner is an eighth grade teacher at a public school in New York. The curriculum deals with sexism and sexual harassment for middle school students and is divided into eleven lessons. Each lesson includes a survey, cartoon characters with captions, a discussion guide, and a log-writing assignment. The results of an attitude survey showed that both males and females who experienced this curriculum significantly altered their attitudes on the sexual harassment scale in a positive direction. 25 pp. $12.00
Peter Miner
247 Wadsworth Avenue #5W
New York, NY 10033
Tel: (212) 795-4003

Stick Up For Yourself! Every Kid's Guide to Personal Power and Positive Self-Esteem
A 10-Part Course in Self-Esteem and Assertiveness for Kids
Gershen Kaufman, Ph.S., Lev Raphael, Ph.D., and Pamela Espeland
In simple words and real-life examples, it shows children how to stick up for themselves with other kids (including bullies), big brothers and sisters, even parents and teachers. It tells things you can say without putting people down, and things to do without getting into trouble. 110 pp. $11.95; Teacher's Guide 128 pp. $19.95
Tel: (800) 735-7323 FAX: (612) 337-5050
E-mail: help4kids@freespirit.com
Web site: www.freespirit.com

Teaching Tolerance Educational Program
Southern Poverty Law Center
Classroom resources include a magazine, curriculum kits, films, and books. Many of the materials are free, and there are discounts for bulk orders. The magazine *Teaching Tolerance* is published twice a year. The magazine profiles K–12 educators, schools, and programs that are promoting diversity and equity in inspirational and replicable ways. A two-year subscription is free. Bulk orders are available for $1.00/ea.

RESOURCES

400 Washington Avenue
Montgomery, AL 35104
Tel: (334) 956-8200 FAX: (334) 956-8488
Web site: www.Tolerance.org

What to Do When Kids Say "NO"
What to Do When Kids Say "NO" is a teacher handbook that was developed by the Behavior Intervention Support Team (BIST) of Ozanam Home for Boys in Kansas City, Missouri. It was created originally for students who were acting out, having problems in regular classrooms, and were assigned to an alternative school environment, but the material is now being requested by public schools for use with traditional students. The BIST believes that kids get in trouble because:
  • They don't know any better—Need: Information
  • They test limits—Need: Consistency
  • Can't manage feeling due to
        —Abuse/Neglect
        —Organic/Neurological problems
        —Unattached/Unbonded relationships
The philosophy behind this program is geared to helping children change their behavior. The emphasis is on protection rather than punishment. Punishment can work in the short run in that it can force cooperation, but it can also provoke passive-aggressive behavior and rage which later may be acted out destructively. 64 pp.
Ozanam Home for Boys
421 E.137th Street
Kansas City, MO 64145
Tel: (816) 508-3652 FAX: (816) 508-3652
E-mail: me3652@ozanam.org

Youth Service America
YSA is a national resource center and alliance of more than 300 organizations committed to increasing the quantity and quality of volunteer opportunities for young Americans. Founded in 1986, YSA's mission is to strengthen the effectiveness, sustainability, and scale of the youth service and service-learning fields to create healthy communities and foster citizenship, knowledge, and the personal development of young people. SERVEnet is a program of YSA. Through www.servenet.org, users can enter their zip code, city, state, skills, interests, and availability and be matched with organizations that need volunteers. SERVEnet is also a place to search for calendar events, job opening, service news, recommended books, and best practices.

Youth Service America
Department P, Suite 200
1101 15th St. N.W.
Washington, D.C. 20005

MEDIA VIOLENCE RESOURCES

American Academy of Pediatrics
"Understanding the Impact of Media on Children and Teens"
"The Internet and Your Family"
Both of these brochures are available for purchase in packs of 100
American Academy of Pediatrics
Division of Publications
141 Northwest Point Boulevard
PO Box 747
Elk Grove Village, IL 60009-0747
Web site: www.aap.org

Media Education Foundation
MEF is a nonprofit educational organization devoted to media research and production of resources to aid educators and others in fostering analytical media literacy.
Web site: www.mediaed.org

The Lion and Lamb
The mission of the Lion & Lamb Project is to stop the marketing of violence to children. They do this by helping parents, industry and government officials recognize that violence is not child's play—and by galvanizing concerned adults to take action
Web site: www.lionlamb.org

CATALOGUES

Channing Bete Company
Tel: (800) 628-7733 FAX: (800) 499-6464
Web site: www.channing-bete.com

Free Spirit Publishing Inc.
Tel: (800) 735-7323 FAX: (612) 337-5050
Web site: www.freespirit.com

RESOURCES

Jalmar Press and Innerchoice Publishing
Tel: (800) 662-9662
Web site: www.jalmarpress.com

Sunburst
Tel: (800)431-1934 FAX: (888) 872-8380
Web site: www.sunburst.com

PLAYS

A Town Called Civility
Claudia Friddell
Gilman School
5407 Roland
Baltimore, MD 21210
FAX: (410) 532-6672

Bang Bang You're Dead
William Mastrosimone
The play requires a minimum of eleven actors, little in the way of production values, and runs forty minutes. You can download the play and perform it for free
by following the license agreement and instructions on the DOWNLOADS page.
The play is a free gift for students to perform in schools, garages, street corners,
parks, houses of worship—any place there can be communication and discovery
about how we've made the world's violence our own. And how we can change it.
Web site: www.bangbangyouredead.com

The Wrestling Season
Royalty: $60.00 per performance
Cost: $5.95
Dramatic Publishing
311 Washington Street
Woodstock, IL 60098
Tel: (815) 338-7170 FAX: (815) 338-8981
E-mail: plays@dramaticpublishing.com
Website: www.dramaticpublishing.com

INDEX

INDEX

INDEX

INDEX